P9-CFA-974

Marty Lu.

all of the best

L. F. Walker

What Others Have Said About
An Olympic Journey...

If you knew nothing at all about Dr. LeRoy Walker, you would be impressed with him at first meeting. Some people exude dignity, others warmth. Dr. Walker is that rare individual who combines the two in great measure. When you first learn that this man, more handsome, vibrant and nimble-minded than most of those half his age, is now approaching eighty without the slightest sign of slowing down, you are left to shake your head in admiration and wonder. Dr. Walker is quite simply one of the most extraordinary men I have encountered in any walk of life.

The story of his life, told here in vivid and engaging detail, is the story of a large and remarkable family. It's a story of times and places in this country now long gone—but whose echoes can still be heard. It's a story of a kid who refused to accept limitations or boundaries imposed by size, race, class, age or any other circumstance; who instead became a jack-of-all-trades and a master of many—athlete, coach, scholar, administrator, ambassador.

Along the way, LeRoy Walker never succumbed to narrowmindedness, either as victim or practitioner. He somehow transcended all the barriers, both those society imposed and those which, more insidiously, a lesser man's own thinking might impose. Instead, Dr. Walker embodies universal virtues of honesty, decency, intellect, toughness and kindness, which command the admiration and respect of all who are privileged to know him.

Consider yourself lucky to have picked up this book. Just as generations of American athletes and the present-day Olympic movement are lucky to have had LeRoy Walker. Just as I am lucky to call him a friend.

—Bob Costas, NBC Sports

§

When LeRoy Walker led the U.S. Olympic Team into the arena for the Opening Ceremonies of the Centennial Olympic Games, the moment was rich in symbolism. Atlanta, the Olympic Host City, was the city of his birth. No one had done so much, during half-a-century, to help young American athletes pursue excellence in Olympic sport. The U.S. Team would prove to be the most successful in Olympic history. LeRoy's personal story of courage and determination made him a mentor for many of our greatest athletes and prepared him for leadership of the world's strongest Olympic organization.

—John Krimsky, Deputy Secretary General, USOC

§

Dr. LeRoy T. Walker has been a beacon for decades in the Olympic movement. He has been both a witness and an influence in many of the more significant decisions that have determined the movement's future. His stories provide an insider's view of some of the most watched events in history and, as his humility has hidden many of his accomplishments, I am grateful for this written record of how one man can make a real difference. It is clear that LeRoy loves the Olympic movement, and from where I sit, the feeling is mutual.

—John Naber, Four-Time Olympic Gold Medal Swimming Champion, President, US Olympians

§

I have been very fortunate in my lifetime to cross paths with many of the legends of sport, entertainment and business. Surprisingly, there are few people who make a lasting impression on you in regard to their ability, success, character and genuine passion for what they do. Dr. LeRoy Walker is such an individual. I have watched him from a distance and have dealt with him up close and, on all occasions, he was the same: thoughtful, considerate of the opposite opinions, and tireless in his attempts to bring about the success of all concerned. Without question, he stands tall in my view as one of the truly great men of sports in American history. I certainly hope everyone gets a chance to read his story, especially those who are young enough to emulate his great character.

—Billy Packer, CBS Sports Broadcaster

§

An Olympic Journey

The Saga Of An American Hero:
LeRoy T. Walker

by Charles Gaddy

Griffin Publishing Group
Glendale, California

Editorial Statement

In the interest of brevity and unencumbered prose, the editor has chosen to use the standard English form of address. This usage is not meant to suggest that the content of this book, both in its references and to whom it is addressed, is intended as restrictive or exclusive regarding any individual or group of individuals, whether by gender, race, age, or any other means that might be considered discriminatory.

Chairman: Daniel R. Wilson
President: Robert Howland
Director of Operations: Robin Howland
Managing Editor: Marjorie L. Marks
Book Design: Mark M. Dodge

10 9 8 7 6 5 4 3 2 1

Cataloging-in-Publication

Gaddy, Charles.
   An Olympic journey : the saga of an American hero : LeRoy T. Walker / by Charles Gaddy. -- 1st ed.
   p. cm.
   Includes bibliographical references.
   ISBN: 1-882180-92-5

   1. Walker, LeRoy T. 2. Olympics--Biography. 3. Coaches (Athletics)--United States--Biography. 4. Afro-American executives--United States--Biography. I. Title.

GV721.2.W35G33 1998   796.4'8'092
                                        QBI98-689

Griffin Publishing Group
544 Colorado Street
Glendale, California 91204
Telephone: (818) 244-1470   Fax: (818) 244-7408

Manufactured in the United States of America

Dedication

To Shawn, Melodie,
Wanda and Desmond.

To "Cush" and Carolyn.

To my wife, Nancy,
for her
enduring enthusiasm
for this project.

And in loving memory of
Katherine and Mary Walker.

CONTENTS

❖

Acknowledgments

My heartfelt thanks to the many people who helped me gather the material for this publication. Among them, I am especially grateful to those interviewees who generously gave of their time during the hectic period preceding the Atlanta Games, particularly LeRoy Walker and his assistant, Tony Britt, and those on the United States Olympic Committee. I am grateful to Billy Payne, Andrew Young, Gail Jones and a number of staff and volunteers of the Atlanta Committee For The Olympic Games.

A special thank you is reserved for Marjorie Lewellyn Marks, Managing Editor of Griffin Publishing Group.

When interviewees are quoting others from times and events long past, they are doing so from their best recollections; even so, it is possible that such recollections are imperfect.

❖

INTRODUCTION

When the roll is called of the great Americans of the Twentieth Century, the name of LeRoy Tashreau Walker, Sr. surely must be counted among them. His story reaches far beyond mere achievements and honors and into that rare realm of those visionaries who become inspirations for the ages.

The story is not one of a victimized African-American. He would be repulsed by such a theme. His is the story of a remarkable and courageous American who only asked that he be allowed to compete. His is the story of an undiscovered hero that speaks to the youth of the world and brings hope to a nation that still gropes through the dark valleys of racism.

The grandson of slaves, LeRoy Walker's name can be heard today on every continent of the world. But he, who has coaxed warring factions in Africa to sit at the table of reason, held counsel with presidents, emperors and tribal chieftains, had spent half his adult life relegated to separate public drinking fountains marked "colored," felt the sting of the back of the bus and the humiliation of exclusion from public dining and lodging.

The youngest son of thirteen children born to Willie and Mary Walker in Atlanta, Georgia in 1918, LeRoy was nine when his father died. Willie Walker had put bread on the table by shoveling coal in the steam locomotives that rolled out of Atlanta at the time. When his father died, LeRoy was sent to Harlem to live with his older brother Joe.

Without complaint or excuse, LeRoy Walker triumphed. With much of his professional life juxtaposed against some of the worst decades of segregation, racial bigotry and Jim Crowism in America's history, he prevailed.

A gifted college track coach, he was fielding Olympic champions, while often finding it necessary to drive as much as 100 miles out of the way to find a place to eat and sleep for himself and his team during track meets.

Walker was a star athlete of such versatility that in college he was selected to an All-American team at the quarterback position, having never gone out for football in high school.

An honors scholar, Walker's teaching skills and leadership qualities propelled him to the chancellorship of a major university.

His story is a rich tapestry into which is woven the accounts of boyhood on the streets of Harlem at a time when that city-within-a-city was experiencing a period now referred to as the Harlem Renaissance, a time when the greatest of black artists, writers, performers and musicians gathered to share their luster with each other and with the world—just before the Great Depression dimmed the brightness of Harlem and the rest of America.

The big-band music of his teen years in Harlem captured his heart and nearly his soul. On any given night one might hear the music of Duke Ellington, Cab Calloway or Jimmie Lunceford at the nightclubs near Walker's neighborhood. Working one Summer as the valet for the Lunceford Band, Walker was convinced that this job would surely be his only opportunity to travel "somewhere past South Ferry."

Following scholastic and sports honors in high school, Walker continued to excel in the classroom and on the field at Benedict College in Columbia, South Carolina. It was at Benedict that he first saw the love of his life. Katherine of Washington, D.C. became his wife, best friend, and life companion.

Walker went directly from Benedict to earn his Master's Degree at Columbia University in New York, then had to face one of the greatest disappointments of his life when he was discouraged by a faculty department head from entering a doctoral program there because "a Negro has never done that before." He was accepted at New York University where he earned his doctorate degree in 1957.

His success as a track coach took flight when Lee Calhoun, his star hurdler at North Carolina College, took the gold medal at the Olympic Games in Melbourne, Australia in 1956. For the next twenty years there would be athletes who had been coached by Walker competing in each of the Olympic Summer Games.

His selection as head track and field coach for the U.S. Olympic Team would come in 1976 in Montreal following years of success coaching the Olympic track teams of the nations of Israel, Jamaica, Trinidad-Tobago, Kenya and Ethiopia. His coaching career produced more than 100 All-Americans, forty national champions and winners of a dozen Olympic medals.

These former athletes made their successes and contributions in their communities and in the nations of the world.

Walker suffered the personal loss of friends when many of the athletes and coaches on the Israeli Olympic Team were horribly slaughtered in a terrorist incident in Munich, Germany during the 1972 Games. He had coached the Israeli track team in 1960.

This is the story of a unique man, his contribution to youth, his rise to the presidency of the United States Olympic Committee—the most powerful organization in the history of amateur athletics—and the crowning moment when he led the parade on July 19, 1996 into Olympic Stadium in Atlanta, Georgia, only city blocks from his humble origins.

His old friends say that Walker has not changed; that he is still the common man they knew in his youth and that he has accepted his earned honors and accolades with grace. They still call him "Po Belly," a nickname he has been unable to shake since a teenaged buddy tagged him with it during a basketball game.

This is the story of Po Belly's journey past South Ferry.

On the day of opening ceremonies, there are two things we can't control, the world's political climate and the weather.

—Billy Payne, President
Atlanta Committee for the Olympic Games

Olympic Stadium, Atlanta, Georgia USA—July 1996

Forty-eight hours before the opening ceremonies of the Olympic Games in Atlanta, Georgia and against a backdrop of a number of political struggles around the world, the host country suffered one of its most horrendous domestic tragedies.

On Wednesday, July 17, a TWA jetliner, just before 9 p.m. and a few minutes into its flight from John F. Kennedy International Airport to Paris, vanished from the radar scopes over the Atlantic. Two-hundred–thirty souls perished when the plane, according to witnesses, blew apart in a fiery explosion.

At this writing, the cause is thought to have been a spark igniting fuel vapors.

Sharing headlines with the story of the air tragedy, the Games' opening ceremonies began in Atlanta with all the hopes and ideals associated with the spirit of the international Olympic movement, a time when it is hoped that conflicts can be set aside for peaceful athletic competition among the youth of the world.

An orange-colored Southern sky at dusk on Friday, July 19, would set the stage for a stunning opening ceremony of the Twenty-Sixth Games of the Olympiad.

Following a typical sweltering July day in Georgia, the evening was perfect with a slight cooling breeze bathing spectators.

Two blimps hovered over the stadium—one for television, the other marked POLICE. President Clinton was there with his family, as were leaders from around the world. It was rumored in the stands that the police helicopter was filled with sharpshooters with high-powered rifles with scopes. Whether or not that was accurate, it would be hard to imagine that in history there has ever been tighter security for a public gathering.

For 100 years, beginning with Athens, each host city had left its imprint on the colorful history of the Modern Games.

It was Atlanta's turn.

The delegations from 197 countries would pass in review around the track before the 85,000 people in the stands. An estimated three-and-one-half billion people around the globe had gathered before their television sets to witness what was called "the largest peace-time gathering in the history of the world."

By tradition, nations enter the stadium in alphabetical order, with two exceptions: Greece, birthplace of the ancient Games is first, the host nation is last. The general din of spectators was punctuated by selective bursts of applause and cheers when a nation's athletes passed by their countrymen in the stadium.

After almost two hours of parade ceremony and following the announcement of Zimbabwe, the spectators took a collective breath. The host country followed.

As the American flag was carried into the light at the top of the long ramp that reached to the rim of the stadium, there was an explosion of cheers, screams and applause—the kind of human thunder that has been duplicated few times in recorded history.

Before the American delegation had cleared the ramp to make its counterclockwise trip around the oval, the Atlanta Symphony Orchestra quickly launched into a march that still stirs the blood of even the most hard-bitten among us, John Philip Sousa's "Stars and Stripes Forever."

The Americans rose as one, bringing everyone else to their feet to join in clapping out the cadence of the rousing, patriotic march.

Alone out front, the flag bearer, Olympic medalist wrestler Bruce Baumgartner ignored the flag-carrier pouch slung around his neck and proudly held the staff at arm's length above his head while leading the parade of his life.

Just behind Baumgartner and in front of the largest delegation in the International Olympic Movement marched a handsome

African-American with graying temples. He was resplendent in the official United States parade uniform: blue-blazer, white slacks, red tie and white Panama hat.

LeRoy Walker, President of the U.S. Olympic Committee, had come home.

His expression spoke to the dignity that has marked his life. Not somber, but holding in control the powerful emotions that coursed through him.

Recalling this moment, he said:

When I started down the ramp, looked up at the flag and heard the noise, I thought about my mother and how proud she would have been of her son. I thought about my family who was there, and how they were reflecting on seeing their father and grandfather coming in leading the delegation and I thought about all of the people who had helped me get to this point. I doffed my hat a number of times as I walked around that stadium, and there was a purpose for that. I was acknowledging people in the stands who had helped me get here. And I thought as I watched Baumgartner holding that flag, what a great country this is, where a boy who was born on the other side of the tracks could lead our delegation into the stadium.

While the great majority of Americans who were witnessing the spectacle did not know his name, the five-foot, nine-inch figure on the track was known to the President of the United States, the heads of state in the stands and many around the world watching the televised event, and to countless athletes and coaches on every continent.

Earlier in the week, Juan Samaranch of Spain, the president of the International Olympic Committee, had draped the golden garland of the Olympic Order, his organization's highest award, around this man's neck.

The crescendo of sound ricocheted from the stadium out into the canyons of the city, the echoes rolled across the tiny rooftops of the modest houses on Parsons Street, where Walker's life had begun 78 years earlier.

Sweeping away from the stadium after a fly-over salute, the fighter jets of the United States Air Force Thunderbirds screamed over the streets of his early childhood, where on Summer nights, seven decades earlier, he had been required to remember his mother's rule that he could play outside only until the streetlights came on.

Then, when Mary Walker would appear on the front porch, she expected her son to be within her sight. It was time to study.

It was there on Parsons Street, at his mother's knee, that she had instilled in him a piece of wisdom around which he would mold a philosophy of life.

She exhorted him to do the very best he could at whatever task was before him and she made him an unconditional promise that, for its time and place was truly remarkable. "There are enough fair-minded people in the world who will finally recognize what you have done." The little boy believed her.

How did this child who, so long ago, played stickball in the streets near the site of Olympic Stadium get to march in this parade of the world?

The distance from Walker's boyhood home on Parsons Street to that stadium in Atlanta is two miles.

On the way there, his story covered six continents, seventy-eight years, and millions of dreams.

❖

CHAPTER ONE

THE TWENTIES & THIRTIES

Mary and Willie

Atlanta Georgia....June 14, 1918

The war news from the Western Front in France was not good. The Germans, in a surprise attack, had pushed the Allied Armies of World War I back to within thirty miles of Paris. It would be a month before the tide turned.

On this day in Atlanta, Georgia, Mary Walker dealt with a struggle of her own. She was giving birth to her twelfth child, and last son, at her small home at 875 Parsons Street.

Mary and Willie Walker would name the boy LeRoy.

Willie, the son of freed slaves, had migrated to Atlanta from the little town of Milledgeville, Georgia, hoping that steady work on the railroad would feed his burgeoning family.

Atlanta could already boast a population of nearly 200,000, which was impressive for a Southern city that had raised itself from the ashes of the torch of the Civil War Union General William Tecumseh Sherman. From the fires of war were forged a fierce determination and pride held by the people of that city.

When LeRoy Walker was born, blacks lived in the southwest quadrant of the city and were limited to labor-intensive jobs that were mainly in service to prosperous—and even not-so-prosperous—whites.

LeRoy's older brothers and sisters worked as maids, housekeepers, cleaners and cooks. LeRoy's father, Willie, worked as a fireman on one of the many giant steam locomotives that rolled out of Atlanta. The enormous demand for passenger and freight service had already transformed Atlanta into a major rail and transportation center. By 1925, Southern Railway had begun a deluxe run from New Orleans to New York with a stop in Atlanta.

There was wealth in Atlanta and at or near the top of the list was the Candler family. Asa G. Candler owned the Coca-Cola Company, which he would later sell to Ernest Woodruff for $25 million. In 1918, the Candlers lived in a $210,000 mansion on Ponce de Leon Avenue in Druid Hills. Asa was mayor of this proud Southern city that was now beginning to see a respectable skyline etched against the sunset.

Whatever the city was becoming, its glories were not to be shared with African-Americans. Segregation was enforced with the backing of the law. It was pervasive and unchallenged. Blacks who didn't "stay in their place" literally risked their lives.

LeRoy's father was barely etched into his memory. Willie Walker's work kept him away from home much of the time. When he was there, he needed rest.

Willie was one of the legions of black men who fed the insatiable appetites of America's coal-fired steam engines. The term "back-breaking work" could well have been coined from a fireman's toil. A shovel full of fuel weighed from thirty-five to forty pounds, depending on the type of coal. The repetition contributed to the numbing drudgery of a single, never-ending motion: scoop up the coal, hit the pedal that would swing open the door to the firebox, and fling it in.

There is no record of Willie Walker's hours nor his runs but when he was "firing" there were no regulations, no union protection. A ten-hour "run" was almost routine. Some men worked sixteen hours or more in one stint.

It can be assumed that Willie had it no better or worse than the thousands of other black men who did the same thing. There was no chance for advancement, all of the engineers were white.

Once the train pulled out of the station there was little or no relief for the fireman. An example comes from Lawrence Scales of Raleigh, North Carolina. Scales is the son of a fireman who worked during the same period:

"My daddy had to shovel eighteen tons of coal into the engine in four hours on the run from Raleigh to Columbia, South Carolina," said Scales, "In those days, men were men; good men. You had to be. The firemen were black. The whites couldn't stand that hard work."

A fireman could only hope that he would be assigned to a "good" engineer and an engine that didn't leak steam. A "good" engineer would occasionally back off on the throttle on the downhill instead of leaving it open, helping the fireman conserve the head of steam. That would allow the fireman a rare chance to stand and catch his breath.

When Willie Walker came home from work he attempted to shore up his position as patriarch. Disciplining the older children was at the top of the list.

But he was blessed in his marriage with a strong, intelligent and capable wife who had to deal with a houseful of lively children.

The Walker children were expected to perform their assigned chores and to behave themselves, at home and at school. That was their contribution to the family unit. Good behavior and attention to assigned tasks would always keep a Walker child out of trouble. Backsliders were held accountable.

When he was old enough to notice such nuances, LeRoy observed that the older children were always models of comportment the day before their father returned from work. It was hoped, of course, that any grievance their mother might be intending to report would be forgotten or at least softened by continuous exemplary conduct for a twenty-four hour period.

Willie conducted a version of a family council, at which time he would ask Mary for a full report. The saints were praised and dismissed, the sinners held for questioning and punishment, the harshest reserved for the older boys.

When the leather belt was applied, LeRoy remembered, "There was not a lot of hollering and screaming." His father was fair and before administering the corporal punishment would go over in great detail what the issue was all about.

When LeRoy was two-years-old, Elsa Mae, the thirteenth Walker was born.

She was a blessing for him and as they grew up. The two youngest siblings formed a loving and protective bond.

The Neighborhood

LeRoy and the neighborhood kids had fun playing games on the sidewalks of the city streets, especially on Summer nights after the streetlights came on.

The child's determination to excel in athletic competition began with his drive to compensate for a physique smaller than many of the other neighborhood boys.

They staged sprints from one streetlight to the other. Long after the competitions of the day had been settled, a lone child remained on the street.

LeRoy was training for the next day's races and, in solitude, ran himself to exhaustion in order to gain a fraction of a second's advantage in the next day's race.

He batted the stickball for hours against the cinder block retaining wall across the street. With each whack, he sharpened his quickness and his hand-eye coordination.

The youngster was becoming a confident, if not driven competitor, and he was developing a champion's thirst for victory. The boyhood games on Parsons Street became more than games to LeRoy. They were dream fields where the fantasies of future athletic glories were played out.

§

LeRoy remembered his siblings this way:

Joe owned a restaurant in Harlem, but came home for special occasions. He would later become the most important male figure in LeRoy's formative boyhood years.

His sister Laura, nicknamed "Lump," worked as a maid in an expensive Atlanta neighborhood. She often brought home expensive hand-me-down items, given to her by the white people, and lavished them on the children, particularly LeRoy.

Eddie and Robert worked the lawns and gardens of the affluent white Atlantans.

Andrew was a cook in one of the downtown Atlanta hotels.

Willie Jr., "the best cook in the bunch," became a chef at a Chicago Hotel. He taught his brother, Joe, to cook barbecue of such succulence that Joe took it to Harlem as the specialty dish of his popular eatery.

"There was a grown brother named John, and I would hear them talk about some of the others: Mac, Mathew, and Lawrence. Many of them passed away when I was young. Some of them I knew less because they had grown up and left Atlanta. I would only see them at reunions and on rare occasions," said Walker.

Even as a boy, Walker admired his mother's skill in dealing with the "big boys." "Most of the time she was strong enough to do all the chastising over the minor issues," recalled LeRoy. "She could speak volumes by just clearing her throat. We would act up at the table and she would just clear her throat, and that got our attention. But if there was a major problem, like a fight, she would wait until she could tell my daddy."

Soon after LeRoy entered first grade at Ashby Street Elementary, his teachers saw unmistakable signs of an intellectually gifted child. He was also encouraged by his family and members of the community to expand his mind.

Miss Harvey who lived across the street would have LeRoy recite poems at church. He was so skilled at recitation that he was sent to other churches on special occasions, such as Easter, to astound the congregations with his ability to memorize lengthy religious poems and passages.

It was during this time that the boy acquired his middle name, Tashreau, after a poet.

The teachers were beginning to use LeRoy as an example of a "good reader." While he was getting a lot of attention for his intellectual prowess, his response to it was telling.

"While I thought of my abilities as perhaps being different from those of some of the other kids, I didn't think of it as a separation from them," he said.

Mary Walker made sure her brood was exposed to the teachings of the Bible and took them to Berean Seventh Day Adventist Church for the many programs and studies during the week.

She insisted that her children read and she made up for a lack of reading materials in their home by promoting her book of choice, the Bible.

"I read and studied the Bible from cover to cover," he remembered. He came to consider himself an expert on "the good book."

It was Mary's dream that her son would become a concert pianist. One of her most prized possessions was the family piano and for a time she paid for lessons for LeRoy and Elsa Mae. Miss

Bullock, a teacher of recognized ability, came to the Walker home to instruct the children and she would assign an exercise to be completed after she left. When LeRoy could determine that his mother was in another part of the house, he was on the street for a stickball game with the neighborhood kids. If Mary happened to inquire, Elsa Mae would cover for her brother by assuring that before he went to play, he had completed Miss Bullock's assignment.

LeRoy and his friends were more than curious about the college down the street and most particularly about the athletes they could see on the campus of Morehouse, the prestigious institution for higher education for young blacks.

"I think that is one of the things that inspired me to love sports," he said. Instead of running the neighborhood youngsters off the campus, some of the coaches and athletes saw an opportunity to influence them.

"There was a fellow named Frank Forbes, long-time coach, who became a sort of mentor to so many of us," Walker said. "There was also Charlie Clark, who had been an outstanding Morehouse athlete and Coach B.T. Harvey."

Clark established a community club to keep the children involved in programs. Walker never forgot the unselfish outreach of those three men and the impact they had on him, especially the assurances from Clark that "LeRoy, you are little, but you can do it."

"Watching and listening to them as a kid made a big difference in my life, they had tremendous influence over the youngsters because of what they asked us to do in terms of athletic standards as well as moral standards," he said.

In 1926, Willie Walker died suddenly. Details were not recorded but it was thought to have been a heart attack. He was probably younger than 50.

Nine-year-old LeRoy was left with the vaguest memories of his father, but his death would precipitate one of the most profound changes of his life.

LeRoy Goes To Harlem

(Friend) Jose (Mendez) and I turned one way at the corner of 123rd and
7th Avenue and our other two buddies went the other way. It just shows
you what a razor-thin edge your life can hinge on.

—LeRoy T. Walker

While some of her children had left home, Mary Walker still had nearly half of her brood depending on her. She faced rearing them alone. Even before the Great Depression, the outlook was bleak for a poor African-American widow in Atlanta, Georgia with a houseful of kids to feed. There were no welfare checks, no entitlements. There would be no man coming home with a paycheck or to help discipline the boys.

LeRoy's brother Joe was a huge, genial man who had to depend on his keen intellect and forceful personality to offset his lack of education. In a few years in Harlem, Joe established the very popular and successful "Joe's Bar-B-Que" restaurant. Among the celebrities who were regular customers was the boxing champion Sugar Ray Robinson, who owned a bar next door. Joe would later establish other eateries as well as a contracting business that specialized in cutting and installing glass. Eventually his firm was awarded large and lucrative government contracts that included Camp Butner, a military base near Durham, North Carolina.

A year-and-a-half after his father's death, Joe made a trip to Atlanta to persuade his mother to allow LeRoy to live with him and his wife, Millie in Harlem. The couple was childless at that time. Later the marriage produced two sons, Joseph and Eddie.

Mary Walker reluctantly agreed to Joe's argument that the child would at least be exposed to better schools and a different atmosphere. She was somewhat comforted that LeRoy would return to Atlanta during holidays and the Summer months. Walker holds vivid memories of the day Joe came to pick him up. "He came down driving a Pierce-Arrow, the biggest car I had ever seen."

When LeRoy moved into brother Joe's duplex apartment at 361 121st Street, he was moving into a black city within a city.

The area was just passing the peak years of what is now referred to as the Harlem Renaissance, a time of intellectual and cultural discovery led by, among others, W.E.B. DuBois, Langston Hughes, and Countee Cullen. This decade of early black activism, soul searching, and discovery, changed America.

Langston Hughes wrote:

Little dark baby, little Jew baby, little outcast
America is seeking the stars, America is seeking tomorrow
You are America, I am America

Harlem was two square miles and as far as the eye could see LeRoy Walker could behold a quarter of a million people of his own race. It was safe, it was exciting and, in the words of poet Arna Bontemps:

It was like a foretaste of paradise. A blue haze descended at night and with it, strings of fairy lights on the broad avenues.

Harlem's beginnings can be traced to a complex set of economic, political, and racial factors that allowed African-Americans to establish a toehold in an accessible section of New York City with a good transportation system, wide avenues, and housing that was better than that offered blacks in many other cities.

It became a center for commerce, trade and entertainment.

Harlem could boast the greatest jazz musicians in the world: Duke Ellington, Billie Holiday, Dizzie Gillespie and the great dance and show bands of Cab Calloway and Jimmy Lunceford. In the Savoy ballroom, dance steps were being invented so often that black dancers could make a good living teaching private lessons in the homes of downtown whites who wanted to learn them.

A new excitement swept over the city because of Harlem's night life.

Whites wanted to experience the music, dancing and bootleg booze. With that craving came the realization that there was money to be made.

While many blacks resented the influx of whites into the bastions of business in what they considered their part of town, some of the fanciest night clubs were owned and managed by whites for an all-white clientele. The most famous was the Cotton Club.

Owney Madden, a mobster who had spent years of hard time in prison, opened the Cotton Club in 1923. He was not the only organized crime figure who saw entrepreneurial opportunities in the Harlem haze. For the socially elite white patrons, the idea that one might rub elbows with a gangster made an evening at the clubs even more exciting.

The house band at the Cotton Club featured a young pianist and composer named Duke Ellington. His orchestra played during the extravagant nightly floor shows.

The requirements for the members of the female chorus lines were rigid and not negotiable. The candidates had to be young, beautiful, tall, "leggy and not too black." A smooth, light brown-colored skin was perfect. Cab Calloway even performed a song in those days titled "She's Tall, She's Tan, and She's Terrific!" The high-toned temptresses were selected based on an acceptability quotient determined by white males.

Chorus girl Lena Horne was the epitome of tanned elegance. She was destined to move past the Cotton Club chorus line into the movies, and later earn super-star status on Broadway, in nightclubs, and in the recording field.

The Harlem clubs were expensive and the profit margins excellent. Whites from downtown swarmed in after their evenings at the Broadway theaters.

Not all of the clubs were segregated and there were some for blacks only. It was into this vibrant and colorful era that a Southern child would begin to broaden his experience and make a home with his loving and formidable brother who enrolled him in Public School 129.

"It was my brother Joe who gave me real focus, just by his own example," said LeRoy, "I learned discipline from Joe."

Joe and his wife, Millie, enjoyed having the boy in their home. He was cooperative, of good humor and easy to manage. LeRoy was eager to bring home good grades from school. He followed Joe around as much as possible and enjoyed Millie's excellent meals.

Under Joe's protective eye, LeRoy easily found his way into a boy's life in Harlem. His school work was balanced with a love for sports and competition that has endured.

The Met

Without access to playgrounds in his neighborhood, LeRoy and his city friends invented different versions of games that could be played on the sidewalks or in church basements. There were games of handball, tag, stickball and stoopball.

There was a basketball goal in the basement of a neighborhood church, where LeRoy learned the finer points of the game by using the posts of the basement "as my pick."

When LeRoy's love for basketball had deepened to the obsession level, Joe intervened.

While Joe made it a point to avoid profanity in front of his brother, he was, on this occasion, particularly frustrated. "You can't go through life just bouncing a damned basketball, LeRoy!" he said.

It would be Joe's first attempt to expose the youngster to something other than sports. That opportunity came when George F. Driscoll, a wealthy white contractor who had done business with Joe's glass cutting enterprise, made the generous offer to take LeRoy to the Metropolitan Opera along with his own family. Driscoll had met and liked LeRoy and told Joe he would send a limousine on the evening of the performance.

LeRoy remembers: "I came in one day to find a suit box on the bed in my room, and when I saw it was black with silk on it, I put it back, thinking there must have been some mistake."

When Joe explained that the suit was a tuxedo and that arrangements had been made for the opera, LeRoy protested that the date was the same night the Rangers were playing and, furthermore, he didn't want to go to the opera under any circumstances.

"Joe weighed 280 pounds and few people argued with him," said Walker. "Joe explained that while he had been successful in business there were many cultural aspects of life that he had missed. He reminded me that Mr. Driscoll had been kind enough to include me for an evening at the opera, was sending a limo for me, therefore I was to put on the tuxedo that he had bought for me and go the opera 'even if it kills you.'"

The opera was Aida. While LeRoy didn't understand a word, he followed the story line in the program and found that he liked the music and was fascinated by the sound of another language. "That interest in other languages grew," he said, "and surely helped me get my doctorate because I had to learn French and German."

It would not be the last time that LeRoy would attend the Opera. However, he recalled that on that first night he had the one overriding fear with which every boy in the world could relate:

"I didn't know how I was going to get out of my house, dash to that limousine in that tuxedo, without my neighborhood buddies seeing me!"

The young man soon realized that he could rely on his intelligence and his small strong body to survive the many challenges a boy living in Harlem might encounter.

The invisible lines that divided Harlem from the rest of Manhattan and that divided Spanish Harlem from Black Harlem were just as significant a point of departure as the 38th Parallel in Korea or the Berlin Wall. Black kids were safe in Harlem and they knew where the boundaries were.

Sanctuary was often determined by how quickly one could traverse a few blocks. LeRoy could count on his speed in sports to extricate himself from tight spots. His speed was put to the test many times. One evening he walked Delores Rodrigues, a Latina schoolmate, to her home following a study session. They had become friends and kindred spirits in the classroom; both were good students.

As they reached her door, the girl noticed a gang of neighborhood boys watching them from the shadows. Fearing for his safety, she urged LeRoy to come inside and wait them out. He declined and formulated his strategy.

"I would casually walk to the corner as if I hadn't spotted them," he said, "and once I got to the corner I knew I could count on two things. They would never catch me if I got the jump on them, and I knew the chase would end at 116th Street. They would never cross it."

It worked.

The issue of fighting; that is, under what circumstances he should not raise an incident or dispute to that level of violence, had been settled before LeRoy moved from Atlanta. The rules of engagement had been clearly established by his older brothers following an incident during a stickball game. "I hit another fellow with a broomstick and he chased me all the way to my house," LeRoy said.

Two of his older brothers, observing the chase, stopped the two children to hear the story. It was then that they established LeRoy's guidelines for fighting. He was never to start a fight because then the intent was to hurt the other person, but defending himself was sometimes necessary.

"I never forgot that. I was very aggressive, however, if I thought someone was trying to take advantage of my size," LeRoy said.

The only time LeRoy's brother Joe was ever summoned to Haaren High School for a discipline problem involving LeRoy was following an incident in which LeRoy came to the defense of Delores Rodrigues.

The two were talking in the hall when another boy pulled her hair. As they tried to walk away he pulled it again.

"That set it off. I whipped him down three flights of stairs, beat him up good, and they still had to pull me off of him. It was one of the few times I ever got mad—even in football when I was abused I seldom got mad about it," he said.

The Defining Street Corner

Walker recalled that the very worst behavior by the boys in his neighborhood involved the vendors, the men who pushed big two-wheeled carts loaded with fresh fruits and vegetables through the streets. They did a lively business in those days but were sometimes the hapless objects of a "game" devised by Walker and his friends. As the other boys studied the approaching vendor from the stoops of the brownstones, it was LeRoy's job to set the plan in motion.

"Since I was the fastest runner, I would take just one piece of fruit right in front of the fellow and, of course, he would begin chasing me." Walker backed off his top speed just to keep the chaser engaged. As LeRoy's friends began helping themselves to the now-abandoned cart, "I began to run right back toward them so the fellow chasing me could see my three buddies picking up a piece of fruit. Then he would start charging toward them and stop chasing me. That's the worst thing we ever did."

LeRoy and his three buddies were inseparable until a decision at a street corner one night changed the course of their lives.

A defining moment in LeRoy's life occurred at the corner of 123rd Street and Seventh Avenue one night during his junior year in high school.

The boys played basketball nearly every night in a church basement (the 135th Street YMCA had yet to be constructed).

"We hung out together, played together and enjoyed a close friendship. I was no better or worse than the other three," he said.

At the corner there was a discussion about the night's activity. Even though they had nothing specific in mind, two of the boys wanted to do something other than play basketball.

LeRoy and Jose Mendez decided to go on to the church basement and shoot baskets.

"We turned down one street at that corner and they turned down the other," recalled Walker.

"Later that evening, the other boys were arrested for breaking into one of the small shops that were often set up in the basement levels of the brownstones," he recalled.

"In those days, black delinquents were sent directly to reform school.

"Those two boys just got worse and worse in there. Eventually, one of them wound up in Sing Sing, the other with a cement 'collar' around his neck at the bottom of the Hudson River."

Jose Mendez became a noted surgeon, but later died piloting his own plane.

"That just goes to show you what a razor-thin edge your life can hinge on," LeRoy said. "Had Jose and I turned the other way at that street corner, it probably would have ruined our lives."

§

By the time LeRoy entered Harlem's Haaren High School, elements of his talents and character had been well-established.

He was a gifted athlete—small, fast, coordinated and graceful.

He possessed a mental quickness that coaches dream about.

The accumulations of his marks in the classroom were now beginning to establish his potential in the realm of academics, bringing the notice of his teachers, family and friends.

As a personality, he was publicly reserved, without swagger or bluster and maintained a dignity that was sometimes interpreted as aloofness.

His passion was reserved for those closest to him and not for public display.

In later years his friend Ted Wheeler, former head track coach at Iowa would say:

"He has grace and, like slow-growing crabgrass, he is a forceful innovator. He opened doors that were sealed and walked on."

Growing Up With Joe

Many African-American celebrities of the time were seen sampling Joe Walker's succulent, Southern-style chicken and rib dishes. Among them were athletes, coaches and the big-band leaders who were playing the Harlem clubs.

As LeRoy entered his teen years, his relationship with his brother began to take on a more mature phase and, while LeRoy was picking up Joe's skills, the older man was learning from the youngster.

An astute businessman, Joe was highly skilled in dealing with people. He knew what his customers enjoyed in the way of food preparation and how they liked to be treated. He was demanding of his staff but received from them a degree of loyalty and respect that was essential to the successful operation of the business. Part of Joe's people skills may be attributed to his ability to listen to others. He paid particular attention to the ideas of his young brother.

As LeRoy began to get old enough to help out in the restaurant, Joe realized that the teenager had an uncanny eye for detail and analysis. LeRoy's ideas for ways to raise the profit margin were never lost on Joe. The youth's assessment of how the barbequed ribs were being cut and served is an example: LeRoy saw profits walking out the door in the stomachs of customers who ordered the rib sandwich. Joe's standard sandwich consisted of three ribs. Some customers were being served four. LeRoy traced the discrepancy to the dividing of the ribs after the meat came off the rotisserie. The wait staff was allowed to cut the meat and in their haste to keep the operation moving at top speed, they often hacked off four ribs instead of three. For every three times the mistake was made, the makings of another sandwich were lost.

LeRoy's solution was simple. He suggested that the chef alone be responsible for cutting and stacking the portions of the ribs for serving.

Joe agreed and presented the problem and new policy to his staff.

"I liked his approach," LeRoy recalled. "He didn't rant and rave at the help but simply persuaded the chef it would be much more orderly and the customers would get more consistent servings if he would cut and stack the meat."

The profit margin went up.

At the height of Joe Walker's success in the glass-cutting business he had thirty to forty union men working for him. During his teen Summers, LeRoy often worked with the crew. The young man earned the admiration of the men who watched him prove himself willing to work hard and to take the same risks hanging from a belt outside a window forty stories up. As he gained more experience, LeRoy sought and was given more responsibility. He was allowed to handle payday that fell on Fridays. LeRoy saw it as an opportunity to make a little extra cash by turning the occasion into a ceremony for the laborers to enjoy.

The "pay table" was placed in the large basement of Joe's restaurant. A keg of beer was set up and there were plenty of pretzels. "I didn't want them to start drinking hard booze," Walker said, "and I knew if they started on beer they would stay with that."

He also innovated a procedure that would put some extra money in his pocket.

"It was to my advantage to not put the money in regular pay envelopes," said Walker. Instead, the cash was stacked on the table and as each man came up, LeRoy counted the cash into the worker's hand.

"As often as not, the men would toss a dollar or two back on the table as a sort of tip for me."

Instead of writing home to Atlanta for spending money, LeRoy was sending money to his mother and sisters.

"I would later tell these stories to my athletes in an effort to encourage them to become less financially dependent on the folks back home, many of whom were already making enormous sacrifices to keep their kids in college."

Walker's formidable gift for analysis would sustain him through the decades of his life as a coach, teacher and administrator.

It would be difficult to overstate Walker's love for sport. From his childhood until today the thrill of competition has never dimmed, whether participant, coach or spectator.

At Haaren, basketball was his forte. Years of shooting baskets in church basements had honed a keen eye and a quickness that allowed him to become a star athlete.

In the classroom, he was especially adept at math and the sciences. His study habits were good but short, as he learned that he was able to quickly grasp a problem.

Walker was, as he is today, able to handle a multitude of activities, assignments and chores and simultaneously excel at them.

It was not too much for the teenager to achieve good grades while playing sports, helping Joe in the restaurant and having fun with his friends.

He missed "Mama" and Atlanta, and went back often for special occasions and in the Summers.

New York was a Mecca for a child with a consuming love for sport. The city had developed youth leagues. The police precinct determined on which team a youngster played.

LeRoy drew inspiration from the sports events he was able to attend, often with Joe. There was no greater thrill for him than witnessing the superb black "show" teams of the time, decades before African-Americans would be considered for professional sport.

The Renaissance Players, called the "Rens," were not into the clowning that later became the draw for the Harlem Globetrotters. They were a group of superb athletes who played a breathtaking style and game of speed with lightning passes and awesome ball handling. "At the time they could have beaten the Celtics," said Walker.

The Harlem kids got to know gifted players like Eric Saitch, "Pappy" Ricks, and "Tarzan" Cooper. Saitch and some of his teammates encouraged the kids and lectured them on some of the finer points of the game.

Madison Square Garden was the venue of a young athlete's dreams and Walker watched premiere sports events there.

Columbia University was a few blocks from Joe's home and LeRoy spent hours watching the great collegiate athletes at practice there.

LeRoy lettered in basketball and soccer during his freshman, sophomore and junior years at Haaren. The school had no track.

But football was not in the cards for LeRoy in high school. Fearing injury, his mother, Mary, would not permit him to play and her obedient son obliged.

The Summer following his junior year was destined to become one of the most exciting of his life, another "defining" period for a teenager now awash in the sometimes conflicting currents that coursed through his heart and soul.

It was Harlem's seductive musical scene that would provide an intense Summer romance.

LeRoy Meets Lunceford

In the late-Thirties and early-Forties, there were the "sweet" or commercial orchestras and at the other end of the musical spectrum, the hot jazz bands. Louis Armstrong's hot and improvisational horn was lighting a musical fire. American jazz would become one of the lasting musical gifts to the world.

The top hotels, ballrooms, nightclubs and concert halls became elegant venues for the bands of Tommy Dorsey, Woody Herman, Glenn Miller, Benny Goodman and Harry James. They played engagements at the Roosevelt Hotel in New York, the Arragon Ballroom in Chicago, Hotel Pennsylvania, Glen Island Casino and the Hollywood Palladium.

A booking in any of these famous watering holes meant national exposure on network radio. The National Broadcasting Company's live band remote broadcasts reached millions. Listeners from coast to coast, in cities and small towns, stared at their radios in homes, bars, hotel rooms, and barracks, as some golden-throated announcer introduced the great bands to explosive applause and cheers.

It was an unforgettable sound that fed the fantasies of the millions who couldn't be there. For the band leaders, the millions of young people were potential customers for a three-minute disc of recorded music that spun at 78 rpm. In a word, radio exposure meant money.

The scene was different for the equally great black bands. They were not allowed in the venues where broadcasts originated. White America dictated precisely where and how black entertainment would be served up.

Black vaudeville performers were still required to put on black face makeup with exaggerated painted lips over their already black faces, another reminder to blacks of their "place" and who set the rules.

In New York, the black bands played Harlem. The brilliant Duke Ellington was denied exposure in the grand hotels and clubs. Later in his career he was asked if that situation made him angry. He replied that it did but "instead of pouting about it, I put that energy into composing."

Ellington's genius would not be denied. He and other excellent black bands played to packed nightclubs in Harlem.

In his teen years, LeRoy Walker was captivated by those bands. Besides Ellington there were Cab Calloway, Chick Webb and Jimmy Lunceford.

Jimmy Lunceford's band came out of Fisk University in Tennessee in the late Twenties. By the mid-Thirties, the band's swinging style and showmanship were so compelling that white band leaders would break away to catch their performances. George T. Simon who reviewed all the bands of the era for Metronome magazine wrote: "Jimmy Lunceford's was, without a doubt, the most exciting big band of all time."

The band came to play the Cotton Club and other bookings around the New York area.

"Blacks stayed at the Theresa Hotel," said Walker. "They were supposed to be able to stay at any hotel, but (were) not allowed. So, it was either the Theresa or a private home."

Lunceford loved the food at Joe Walker's restaurant and in conversation with him worked out an arrangement for some of the members of the band to stay at the Walker home. LeRoy was thrilled. "We had a duplex at the time and they lived in the upstairs quarters," said Walker.

An incident involving a member of the band's staff simply added to LeRoy's good fortune.

The young band valet—whose job it was to take care of the instruments, lay out the costumes and run errands—was a compulsive poker player.

To pay off a gambling debt, at a time when it was ever so wise to do that, the valet pawned the saxophone of one of the orchestra's star players and was fired.

When Joe Walker was made aware of the situation, he suggested that Lunceford hire LeRoy for the Summer. He did.

LeRoy loved his work and the excitement of being backstage when the band performed. "I got to be very proficient at the job," he said, "I learned which costumes to lay out for which night without having to be told."

He was also meeting other famous performers and soon many of them knew him by name.

When bookings took the Lunceford Band farther away from New York, big brother Joe began to worry. First there was Hershey, Pennsylvania, then Philadelphia, then Cleveland.

Near the end of the Summer, the band was booked for a European tour. "I went to Jimmy and begged him to let me go" Walker recalled. "In my pleadings I reminded him of how good I was at the job."

Lunceford agreed that his work had been exemplary but shook his head.

He wanted LeRoy to finish school. "I don't want to be the cause of you dropping out."

The teenager was crestfallen. "I was so hurt," he said. "Jimmy's decision meant that I had just lost (what I thought was) the only chance I would ever have to get to Europe."

To Joe Walker's great relief, Lunceford made his decision in the boy's best interests. Joe had always held to the dream that it would be LeRoy who had the best chance of the thirteen siblings to advance scholastically. There was already talk in the family that he would be the first of the Walker family to go to college.

The New York schools had already begun the school year by the time LeRoy, lingering as long as possible, finished up the Summer band job.

Fearing the youngster would backslide, Joe sent him back to Atlanta for his senior year. He was enrolled in Atlanta's large Booker T. Washington High School where he would meet the next adult male who would have significant impact on the direction of his life.

Thelman Hope Giles Crawford, named for several of his uncles, answered to the nickname, "Dad," an appropriate moniker for a coach who had become a father figure for so many young men.

"Crawford and head coach Leslie Baker were the kingpins of basketball in those days," said Walker, "They really sharpened my basketball skills."

Crawford was also an excellent classroom teacher with a special gift for languages. Walker flourished under his influence.

The basketball team won the League's state championship. Walker was one of the stars.

The vitality of youth has a way of healing old disappointments and Walker very much enjoyed his last high school year in Atlanta.

His enterprising spirit had not been diminished. When he and some other boys were assigned to study period in the home economics room, supervised by the home economics teacher, he persuaded her to teach them how to prepare good food. They learned to put together scrumptious sandwiches. The items were not elaborate. Walker's specialty was Southern banana pudding, for which he still claims a reputation.

Lena Horne

With a limited menu, they set about marketing their food to members of the faculty. The faculty and staff either had to bring their lunches to school or stand in long lines at lunch hour to get into the few cafes nearby.

The boys had the good sense to send the prettiest girl in the school to take the faculty's orders for sandwiches. Her name was Lena Horne.

"We had no idea at the time she would become a superstar in movies, recordings and on the Broadway stage," said Walker. "We were all just kids starting out."

Even in high school Horne's stunning beauty generated some not-always-welcome attention from the opposite sex.

"We loved her and felt very protective of her," Walker remembered.

§

Not long after graduation, LeRoy headed back to Joe's house in New York. The year was 1935.

For the next year he worked with his older brother.

It was during that year that his former high school basketball coach, "Dad" Crawford, showed up at Joe's home in Harlem to visit his former player.

Crawford was on his way to a meeting in Europe where he would serve as a translator to Dr. J. J. Starks, President of Benedict College in Columbia, South Carolina.

Starks had lured the talented Crawford away from Booker T. Washington High School and had installed him as head basketball coach and a teacher of languages.

Crawford had stopped in Harlem to persuade Walker to come to Benedict. Walker agreed.

"The good mentoring he had been providing me had not been long interrupted," said Walker.

He began his freshman year in the Fall of 1936.

LeRoy Goes To Benedict

It was the Fall of my freshman year. I walked into my French class the first day. There stood Walker and the language professor, T.H.G. Crawford. After greeting us in English, Crawford turned to Walker, who was a junior then, and to Yancey, one of his classmates, and began to carry on a conversation with them in French and other languages. They did this for nearly an hour. We were shocked and dumbfounded.

—Charles T. Brooks, Sr., former Benedict student

Following Emancipation, black leaders had realized that it would be necessary for them to provide for the education of their own. They found themselves in the euphoric state of freedom, and at the same time, unwanted by either the North or South. It would be 100 years before white Americans would even begin to consider an integrated system of education for all citizens.

In 1870, Mrs. Bathsheba A. Benedict, a strong-willed champion for education, decided to buy an old plantation, then on the outskirts of Columbia, South Carolina, and establish Benedict Institute for the higher education of young blacks.

Its stated purpose was "to be a power for good in society." Chartered as a college in 1894, the institution has been a beacon for black youth ever since.

Coaches at black institutions were required to carry a full schedule of classes. Meager budgets would not allow coaches the luxury of foregoing classroom duties. Many of the coaches of that day were among the most skilled educators on campus. That was especially true of Crawford, who was superbly gifted in languages. He passed along his own excitement about the beauty of foreign languages to Walker and many other of his students.

In the firmament of world-class alumni that Benedict has produced, there is no brighter star than LeRoy Walker.

His entry at Benedict marked the first time a member of his large family had reached that educational level. He was driven to succeed.

With financial aid as an athlete and the good grades he had earned in high school, Walker approached this new phase of his life with confident expectations.

Katherine

LeRoy had hardly learned his way around the campus when he met the love of his life.

She had her back to him, posting papers on the student bulletin board that had been strategically placed at a campus junction most likely to be passed by every student at some time during the day.

LeRoy asked directions to a campus building and without turning to look at him, Katherine McDowell answered his question. She was a sophomore at the time and a student library assistant.

She asked his name and when the pretty coed turned to look at him for the first time, LeRoy asked if she would accompany him to the "get-acquainted" dance that was being held that evening on campus. She accepted—and for the remainder of her life, Katherine would be at his side.

An only child, Katherine grew up on Irving Street in Washington, D.C.

Following her mother's death, Katherine's father, who worked at a downtown hotel, remarried. She was much beloved by a number of aunts and uncles who tried to make up for the loss of her mother by being particularly attentive to her.

LeRoy and Katherine fell deeply in love and became an inseparable fixture on the campus. They were voted "most popular couple" by the student body for three successive years.

Katherine would look on with pride as LeRoy became an honors student, a sports star, and a campus leader. Each year he was elected class president and so began the honing of his skills in presiding and making presentations.

Long before he entered college, LeRoy had left a trail of high achievement. His mother had instilled in him the belief that he could accomplish great things if "you don't let this environment dictate what you do."

It was obvious to all from the very beginning that Benedict had been blessed with a youth of unlimited dimension.

"He was brilliant," said Charlie Brooks, a football and basketball teammate of Walker's. "What turned us all to him was his great and magnetic mind. I considered myself fortunate to know such a gifted person."

Throughout his college years, Walker lettered in basketball.

"Benedict didn't have a track," Walker recalled, "but through a special arrangement with the University of South Carolina, I was able to work out there and became a sprinter of national ranking."

The most unusual story of his collegiate sports career is that involving football.

Because of his mother's fear that he would be injured, Walker never played football in high school.

He reported for football practice at Benedict he said, "almost on a dare."

Several of his friends had teased other players, saying that Walker was coming out to "set them down."

When he showed up for the first week's practice, coaches Lesley Stallworth and Walter Dean were impressed with what they saw as Walker's potential for development.

His greatest assets were speed and intelligence.

Least threatening was his size. "In shorts, I weighed in at 155," he said, "but I sort of facetiously told the coach that I could be as good as he could make me because I had no bad habits to break."

At Morehouse—and later in New York—watching the great athletes at Columbia, "I had seen good football," he said, "therefore I could think good football."

On the day the heavy equipment was passed out, Walker didn't show up.

He told the coach that he had misgivings about entering a sport at the college level in which he had had no previous experience and he didn't want to embarrass himself.

Coach Stallworth assured Walker that there was a place for him on the team as backup quarterback.

LeRoy was so small the trainers had to alter his shoulder pads.

A natural play maker, LeRoy had the complete confidence of his squad. They saw that he could pass, kick and, if ever allowed to get outside a defender, no one could catch him.

When an injury sidelined the starting quarterback, LeRoy was called on and never looked back, leading the Benedict team to a conference championship during his junior year.

He was named All-America by the Pittsburgh Courier.

The Wedding

Two days before Christmas 1938, Katherine and LeRoy were secretly married.

Katherine visited friends in Chester, South Carolina. LeRoy drove from Columbia to join her before a friendly Justice of the Peace, Mr. Yarborough. The license fee was $2.

Many years later, while recounting the economy and simplicity of the ceremony to his daughter, Carolyn, Walker jokingly suggested it would be nice if she would consider the same format when she decided to get married.

The only witness to the wedding was a friend of Katherine's. With no time for a honeymoon, LeRoy quickly returned to Benedict for the holiday basketball schedule.

There was no announcement of the marriage because campus policy did not include provisions for married students. With their carefully guarded secret, they returned to their respective dorms; college life for them was, as far as others could observe, unchanged.

The couple especially enjoyed the invitations to LeRoy's coach's home on Sunday afternoons. It was a relief to get out of the dorms and spend time in the company of another married couple with whom they now had more in common.

Walker's original career goal was medicine. A boyhood friend was already in pre-med and his coach's wife was a nurse supervisor at a local hospital. They spent many hours discussing the medical field. He was positive he wanted to settle into a field that would allow him to "work with people."

Walker always had a keen ear for languages and, inspired by "Dad" Crawford's teaching, attained such fluency as an upperclassmen that Crawford used him to impress the freshmen on the first day of class.

After introducing himself, Crawford would turn to Walker and converse in French, then German.

Former student Charlie Brooks recalled that he was "absolutely dumbfounded to hear a foreign language spilling from the lips of a student not much older than I was."

Walker's years at Benedict were filled with all the fun, gratification and accomplishment that could possibly surround a dedicated collegian. He had been an honor student, a campus leader, president of each of his classes and a star athlete.

His years in undergraduate school, however, would reveal a challenging nature and a formidable measure of stubbornness.

By now it was clear to observers that one of the characteristics that would stamp Walker's personality was that of an independent thinker.

Decades later his friend William C. Friday, President Emeritus of the University of North Carolina, would say that "LeRoy was not a 'run of mind' sort of person."

Not an habitual "wave-maker," Walker would, seemingly out of the blue, balk and challenge, as he did when faced with a Bible course.

Benedict College required for graduation a course in Bible study taught by Professor Redfern, a New Englander, former missionary, and one of the most respected teachers on campus. During his senior year, Walker signed up for the course. Due to his early and constant study of the Bible during his intensive religious training at home and at church, Walker found that his own depth of knowledge on the subject was sufficient.

After two classes he filled out a "drop" slip and asked Katherine to turn it in for him. When she forgot, LeRoy was faced with the prospect of an 'F,' a delay in his three-and-a-half-year graduation date, and his honor student status.

He went to Redfern to plead his case.

Walker proposed that the professor give him a test "on anything about the Bible and if I can write an 'A' paper, will you give me a 'B'? If you don't, sir, I can't graduate and it will affect my whole life."

Redfern, aware that Walker was one of the best students enrolled at the college, agreed, and gave him a series of tough essay questions.

Walker filled two exam books with detailed answers that included companion stories from the Old and New Testaments. The professor thought it an "excellent paper" and said, "I'm going to give you a 'B.'"

While it may have seemed out of character for such a meticulously thorough and careful man to have put his degree in jeopardy, he had simply decided it was a waste of his time, given his religious training, to take a Bible course.

It would not be the last of his risk-taking.

The ranks of those who knew Walker personally during his collegiate days have now been thinned by death and disability. Yet among those who remember are Charlie Brooks, Class of '42; Leola Caison, Class of '38; and Dr. Edmund McDonald, Class of '38.

Each has vivid and loving memories of Walker and his impact on Benedict College, then and now.

Brooks believes Walker to be "among the most beloved students in the history of the institution" and that it was Walker who inspired him to pass on a legacy of helping others. During his years of high school coaching in Columbia, South Carolina, Brooks taught his athletes the lessons of unselfishness that he had learned from Walker. "Even today," said Brooks, "I pray that if I have not been able to help someone this day, it has then not been a good day for me." Brooks credited his contact with Walker as his inspiration.

McDonald, a retired dentist from Sumpter, South Carolina, believes that some people are born to excel and Walker is one of them. McDonald recalled that Walker loved watching athletic events of any kind. In the undergraduate days, Coach Crawford would take some of his athletes to the auditorium in downtown Columbia to watch wrestling matches "when the wrestling was real." Crawford would also arrange trips for them to attend athletic events in Atlanta.

Leola Caison remembers Walker as "a very pleasant person and a good student." She believes that he came to Benedict to "give his best and he represented the college so beautifully throughout the years." Caison remembers Walker's mother as a beautiful woman who was "a religious person."

Because of his ability to handle heavy course loads, Walker was able to finish his requirements in three-and-one-half years, at the end of the Fall semester of 1939.

He returned to receive his diploma in the Spring of 1940 with his classmates.

Katherine had graduated the year before and had gone to New York to work as Joe's office secretary.

LeRoy decided to continue his academic momentum and headed for New York to help Joe and to enroll in a Master's Degree program.

Joe and Katherine were most supportive.

❖

CHAPTER TWO

THE FORTIES

By the time Walker had graduated from college, he had basically become the man that we know today. Physically, he was handsome by any measure. An intelligent face, brimming with energy, he was perpetually photogenic. Age has not faded the impact of the features. He was blessed with a rich, baritone speaking voice that served him well in his leadership and speaking roles.

Over the years, his body remained hard and fit, a testimonial to the positive affects of the precepts of physical education: exercise, diet, and play. Walker moved with a dancer's grace and spoke with perfect diction. His ear for languages and his travel have left him with a subtle sophistication that never overshadowed his common touch. He remains a compelling, powerful, yet compassionate force. The years would only burnish the aura.

Walker at Columbia

Walker's attachment to Columbia University goes back to the days of his boyhood in Harlem. Only a few blocks away from Joe's house, the school was practically a part of his neighborhood. He had only to walk through a park to approach the perimeter of the campus. It was there the youngster watched the great athletes practice and play. He would later learn of the venerable school's academic reputation. Columbia had come to symbolize the gateway to his dreams.

Given his interest in science and his now-proven classroom abilities in those studies, LeRoy again considered becoming a medical doctor. However, that course of study had a built-in delay. Having graduated mid-year, he had a six month wait for a Fall semester. Added to that was a year's waiting list at the few pre-eminent black medical schools. Facing eighteen months of waiting, Walker began to change his mind.

He now focused on two areas in which he had excelled and which had given him great satisfaction: sports and science. He set his sights on a Master's degree in physical education and health sciences. He was accepted at Columbia, and enrolled for the Spring semester of 1940.

The family arrangement worked well. Joe and Millie were delighted to have LeRoy and his new wife stay with them. Joe grew to love Katherine and to appreciate her bookkeeping skills as she made herself useful to him and his business enterprises while Millie enjoyed her role as surrogate mother to LeRoy.

Walker was now challenged by a respected graduate school that boasted a faculty that included some of the top people in their disciplines. Chairman of the Department of Physical Education and Health Sciences was a man named Jesse Fiering Williams. He was the author of "Personal Hygiene Applied," a respected tome used widely as a textbook, which held as its premise that if you understood your body, in all its glorious physical possibilities and limitations, you would be better able to take care of it. After exhaustive studies Williams had gathered a body of work that was formidable. Students clambered to be enrolled in his classes.

Williams, while impressed with Walker's transcript from Benedict, challenged him to defend his choice of the degree he was pursuing. He was concerned about LeRoy's lack of "activity background" in gymnastics and other sports. William's philosophy dictated that one could not fully understand or teach the elements of sport without personal exposure to them. Walker's problem was that Benedict had no Department of Physical Education and therefore no official record-keeping of his physical education activity. The ultimate frustration was that Walker had more than the experience in sports that Williams was requiring, except for gymnastics.

Walker pleaded, "I have excelled in sports all my life, but at my school we didn't have a major in physical education."

Williams, nevertheless, entered eighteen "activity deficiency" points that would have to be made up. It meant Walker would be required to enroll in preliminary courses in the sports "activities " outlined by Williams, which added significant class time and lab fees. Even though he had been a star player in high school and college, LeRoy was now being put through a lab on the basics of the game.

F. W. Marooney, one of Walker's science professors at Columbia, taught preliminary basketball. The graduate students had put together a basketball team worthy of scrimmage with the area varsity squads and on one of those occasions professor Marooney happened to witness Walker's skill on the court. Later Marooney chided Walker for enrolling in a beginner's class just to make a good grade. Walker replied that it was Williams who had made that decision. Marooney conferred with Williams who then removed the deficiency points, except in gymnastics. From that dubious start grew a teacher-student relationship that later resulted in Walker's serving as Williams' first student classroom assistant.

The student began to study and appreciate the professor's teaching techniques, and in the years that followed, took many of them for his own. Walker described Williams as a "master teacher," primarily because of the knowledge of his subject and "he lectured as if he were talking to each person individually." Never behind the lectern, Williams was in constant motion around the classroom, with a voice described by Walker as "like music." "Often, some of the assistant professors would monitor his classes," said Walker. Williams' impact on Walker's teaching philosophy was profound. LeRoy would later realize that while courses in teaching methods were useful, in the final analysis "you teach as you have been taught."

Walker, the overachiever, now had proof that he could meet the challenges of graduate study. A year later, he received his master's degree with grades in the honors category. An unexpected visitor showed up at the graduation exercises.

Back to Benedict

"We want you back at Benedict," said the college's president J.J. Starks, who appeared at LeRoy's graduation at Columbia to watch him receive his master's degree. Walker was surprised to see him.

Starks wanted to establish a Physical Education Department at Benedict and was convinced that Walker was the person to do it. He would also coach football, basketball, track, as well as teach a full schedule of classes. Walker accepted, while making himself a promise that he ultimately would seek a doctorate degree at Columbia. Starks was convincing, and while the salary was low, LeRoy and Katherine would have an apartment in one of the dorms at no expense. Walker agreed and jumped into his new position with energy and enthusiasm.

Walker's return to the campus as a professor and department head had its unique dynamics. The brief interlude since he had been a student there with great visibility meant that many of the upperclassmen had as much of an adjustment as he. He was, however, accepted by those students because he earned their respect.

Walker's typical day began with an early morning workout with some of the athletes who wanted to run. The athletes soon learned that the coach was not about to let them miss a class. He made sure the physical training was completed in plenty of time for showers and 8 a.m. classes.

It was the first time the students at Benedict had been introduced to the academic elements of physical education. Walker set up class schedules in anatomy, physiology, kinesiology and exercise physiology. Some of the students joked that they now didn't know whether they were in physical education or pre-med. Influenced by the precepts ingrained in him by Jesse Fiering Williams, he explained that to be accomplished in the finer points of physical education it was necessary to know the human body and to know the impact of exercise and sport on it.

"There is a lot more to it than throwing and catching a ball, and knocking each other down," he said to them. Walker's last class was from 2 p.m. to 3 p.m. Football practice began at 3.

At the outset of his coaching career, Walker established his distaste for long practice sessions. Two hours for football, maximum. Later, in his Olympic coaching, a ninety-minute session was all he required. While demanding total effort during football practice sessions, Walker's players enjoyed the relief from the intensity. There were no night "skull" sessions.

"What made it enjoyable for them is that we did not go through the machinations of coming back at night to go over films and tapes," he said. "My athletes had fun because they knew that when it was over they could go to the dining hall or meet their girlfriends." Walker insisted that his "second practice" be held in the library. After dinner he wanted them to study.

It was usually after sundown before Walker was able to get back to his campus apartment and Katherine. It was a pleasant time for them. "Katherine was pregnant with LeRoy, Jr. and we would often go for walks together or to a movie," he recalled.

Pearl Harbor

Katherine heard it first on the radio in their dormitory apartment. It was Sunday, December 7, 1941. The Japanese had bombed an American naval base in Hawaii and many Americans were dead. On hearing the broadcast, the same questions flashed through Katherine's mind that millions of American wives, mothers, brothers, sisters, friends, and loved ones dealt with: Does this mean war? Will he be called? Will he be killed?

The next day President Franklin D. Roosevelt declared war, and for the next four years America and the world would be traumatized. FDR and America worked day and night to put the country on an all-out war footing. The key element would be to meet the manpower requirements for a global conflict with Japan and Germany. The Selective Service Act would allow the United States to call to arms the youth of the country through quotas given local draft boards.

When the Spring semester of 1942 ended, LeRoy joined his brother Joe for the Summer to work at a major government construction job near Durham, North Carolina. The country needed military bases now as quickly as they could be built and the army's Camp Butner was to be one of them. Joe landed the glass-cutting contract for his company and was happy to have his brother on board for the project that would take most of the Summer. Six months into her pregnancy, Katherine was content to remain in her campus apartment at Benedict.

When Joe and LeRoy came to Durham in the Summer of '42, it was to seek out lodging for the glass-cutting crew. Durham had only one hotel where African-Americans were allowed to stay and the quality of those accommodations often drove visitors to seek quarters in private homes. The Walkers roomed in a home across the street from the NC College for Negroes.

Joe's arrival with his crew on the construction site at Butner caused a local stir. The fact that a black man's company had procured a lucrative contract on a major project in the South was, to say the least, unusual.

When word got around, a sociologist from North Carolina College for Negroes in Durham appeared at Butner to meet and interview Joe and LeRoy. From this came an invitation for LeRoy to visit the campus. It was during this time that Walker met college President James Shepard, "whom we later learned was a local Democrat but national Republican."

"I thought the college campus there was the most beautiful I had ever seen," remembers Walker. "The grass trimmed to perfection, against all those shrubs, trees and flowers." The work went well at Butner. It was hard and challenging, but LeRoy and the crew made good wages.

He stayed in close telephone contact with Katherine in Columbia and as the Summer progressed the couple contemplated two looming and life-altering events: the joyful prospect of the birth of their first child and their anxiety over LeRoy's eligibility for the draft.

On August 7, Katherine gave birth to a son, LeRoy T. Walker, Jr. LeRoy was still at Butner when he got the news. He soon returned home and "was elated to find Katherine and our son in good health and doing fine. Katherine was so happy and looked even more beautiful."

That Summer Dr. Starks suggested that Walker take a leave to Bishop College, a small school in Marshall, Texas.

"It was an effort to save me from the draft," said Walker. The college's head coach had been drafted and Bishop was glad to get the young man.

In the Fall of 1942, LeRoy, Katherine, and their son moved into a campus apartment at Bishop, where LeRoy would serve as head basketball coach, track and field coach, dean of men, in addition to teaching a full schedule of classes.

When teachers at small black colleges were offered campus housing, there were more benefits than might appear obvious. In communities in the South and Southwest, housing that would be available to black educators would often be unacceptable to them. Beyond the obvious economic advantages of free rent and utilities, campus housing meant an environment secure from the racism encountered everywhere outside the college perimeter. The college benefited by having faculty families living next to students, thereby elevating the level of behavior of the student body.

At Bishop, the Walkers occupied an apartment in a men's dormitory. The strict dorm rules he had set down included no loud or raucous activity, and no moving about the halls after 11 p.m.

One incident placed the dean in violation of his own rules.

Walker and a small group of staff people enjoyed playing poker. Returning well past the dorm "quiet hour" one evening, LeRoy found that he had forgotten his apartment key. Katherine had locked the door and was fast asleep.

"I was trying to knock on the door and muffle the sound at the same time," he recalled. When Katherine didn't respond, he had to knock with increasing force until he heard a male voice yell out from the darkened building "Whoever that is better be quiet—it'll be too bad if Dean Walker wakes up and comes after you!"

Just before he was spotted by the students, a sleepy-eyed Katherine opened the door, with her own admonishment that he was causing enough commotion to awaken the baby.

Walker continued to hone his coaching skills. He led his basketball team to the finals of the Southwest Championship only to be beaten by a desperation shot by a player on the opposing team named Marques Haynes, who was destined for stardom with the famous Harlem Globetrotters.

LeRoy fielded a track team with some success, but by now many of the best athletes were being drafted into military service.

Selective Service had not forgotten Walker. Before the school year at Bishop was up, he received notice to report for a physical. As he was sitting in a room with other young men, waiting to be called for his physical examination, Walker was suddenly surprised to see Wes Hamilton, an Omega fraternity brother. Hamilton, now with the rank of Colonel, served the Special Services Command, a support branch that conducted training programs for personnel in many diverse categories the military lumped under "specialties." Special Services was also the military's way of shielding many of the country's top athletes.

After hearing Walker's story, Hamilton made a decision that would spare LeRoy combat duty and inadvertently put the young coach on a path that would, in a number of ways, enhance his professional expertise. Walker was put in charge of physical training in the Army Specialized Training Program at Prairie View College, "the Texas A. & M. for black students," in Prairie View, Texas, a small college town not far from Houston. He also coached football and when coach Sam Taylor left to serve the Red Cross, Walker became head coach for basketball and track. As always, he taught a full class schedule.

ASTP cadets at Prairie View were being trained for officer ranks in the U.S. black outfits. Walker drew a Captain's pay and remained there until the war ended in the Summer of 1945. Later, when he applied for GI benefits, he learned that his duty was not considered "active" military service.

Prairie View

The job at Prairie View was in some ways remarkable in retrospect. Walker was able to coach the undergraduate teams as well as the more sophisticated ASTP athletes, many of whom had come from the prestigious sports programs at some of the larger universities. They were thrown together at the little college in Texas to the great delight of the coaching staff. Before a rule was passed to prevent it, the ASTP teams would scrimmage the college varsity, and, according to Walker, "would really beat up on them, but it made them better." The superior ASTP athletes helped coach the college varsity. Consequently, "we almost had a coach for each position."

Life at Prairie View was pleasant. The campus housing was comfortable. While her husband dealt with a hectic schedule, Katherine settled into a domestic routine that she created for their infant son. His birth marked the beginning of Katherine Walker's lifelong devotion to the training and welfare of her children. Her skills were considerable and instinctive. Establishing a parenting philosophy that was loving, motivational, and highly disciplined, Walker said she was the family's rock and refuge. She did not work outside the home.

"I told her that I would be the breadwinner and take care of her, if she would train the children and take care of the home," said LeRoy. Decades later, LeRoy's lifelong friend and mentor John

McLendon would pay tribute to Katherine and her contribution to LeRoy's success.

"She was a dear person and just a model coach's wife," he said. "She was what we all hoped our wives would be." In a revealing and sensitive summation on the sacrifices of coach's wives and families McLendon continued:

"Coaches are not only away a lot, they, like doctors, are always on call. Players are constantly needing their coaches. If they have an accident, you go to the hospital. If they need help, you go to their dorms. College athletes need to feel that you care more about them than anyone else. You just seem to have another family to whom you have to give all your time, while you try to fit in your own family.

"It takes a marriage partner who doesn't worry about that, carries on with the home and family during the absences and makes sure it doesn't change any feelings for each other.

"In one of my methods classes, I went over this with my students. If you are going into athletics, you are going to have to choose a person who can still feel as if she is No. 1, even if it seems like you love those athletes and those programs more than anything else in the world. Katherine Walker was truly a great person."

Walker and Jim Crow

Those things hurt me...they really hurt...

—LeRoy T. Walker, speaking about the effect of bigotry and racism

Racial violence in America in the Thirties, Forties, and Fifties was overt, routine, and very often life-threatening. A black person could be subjected to any form of threats, violence, or harassment at any place or time.

African-American men, particularly, were targeted and they never knew when or under what circumstances they might to be singled out and victimized.

Even the most accomplished, famous, or eminent black Americans of those decades was often subjected to incidents that might run the gamut from a verbal racial insult to physical violence. Indeed, the renowned black entertainers, writers, and athletes were often targeted for a special intense fury, no doubt fueled by a deep resentment that they had been able to raise themselves up and out of the poverty and deprivation from which they had sprung.

Singer Nat "King" Cole, arguably the best of the American song stylists of his time, was giving a concert in his hometown of Birmingham, Alabama. All of the codes for the presentation of a black performer in the South, written and unwritten, had been followed to the letter. The audience was segregated, whites downstairs, blacks in the balcony. Cole's orchestra, which included some whites, had to be hidden from the audience by a screen.

Cole appeared alone onstage.

While he was singing, three white thugs came onstage, beat him to the floor and tried to drag him off the stage. The audience witnessed all of it.

American tenor Roland Hayes, critically acclaimed for concerts on the great stages in Europe, had to perform in American movie houses behind a scrim. One day in 1942, following the musical successes he had enjoyed in the great cities around the world, he entered a shoe store in his hometown in Georgia and mistakenly sat in one of the chairs near the front of the store. He had apparently forgotten that blacks were required to sit in the back. For that momentary lapse, he was attacked and severely beaten.

Half of LeRoy Walker's life and work has to be viewed against the backdrop of America's overt racism, the other half against a more subtle form. He chose to live and work in the South, even after having experienced as a youth the sanctuary of Harlem.

A memorable incident occurred during his college days: Following a concert by Duke Ellington in Columbia, South Carolina, Walker and his friends walked back to their campus at Benedict College. They noticed a young white man walking toward them with his date. They quickly gave up the sidewalk and walked on the curb. As they passed, the white youth stopped and said to his companion,

"Just a minute, let me go back there and put this nigger in his place." Walker remembers: "He came over and pushed me into the street. We had already given them the whole sidewalk and were within twenty meters of our own campus." Now angered beyond turning away, Walker prevailed in the fist fight that followed.

That cities north of the Mason-Dixon line were racially tolerant was simply a cruel myth. During the Summer following his junior year in high school, when Walker was working as valet for the Jimmy Lunceford Orchestra, an incident took place that is described by Walker as "my first encounter with the 'City Of Brotherly Love.'"

Following a band date in Hershey, Pennsylvania, the band bus pulled over at a "hamburger restaurant" in Philadelphia. Lunceford sent LeRoy inside to order two burgers each for about twenty people. The band members stayed on the bus to rest and play cards. When enough time had elapsed for the order to have been prepared, the musicians started to enter the restaurant, only to be stopped by a manager screaming that he didn't allow "colored" to eat inside. They would have to take the order with them.

"Many of the Lunceford players were from Fisk University in Tennessee and had, like myself, put up with so much of this kind of thing in the South," said Walker. "And as hungry as we were, we left those forty hamburgers and some of the guys left a few words with the management that described how they felt about the situation."

Some young people these days might be tempted to rush to the conclusion that Walker and others may have leaned toward capitulation rather than confrontation. However, physical confrontations between the two races in those days often resulted in blacks being seriously injured or killed. Yet it would be a mistake to conclude that Walker would not fight. When those times came he was formidable, as revealed in another incident, this time in Prairie View, Texas.

The town of Prairie View, a college village, offered very limited shopping facilities. Most faculty members shopped in the little town of Hempstead, not far from the campus. About equal distance down the road the other way was the town of Waller, Texas. But Hempstead boasted the largest general store, named for its white owner Mr. Burnett. Burnett's store featured a great variety of food and merchandise and it was the store of choice for many of the college faculty. LeRoy did most of the grocery shopping for the family while Katherine stayed at home with LeRoy, Jr.

Occasionally when the whole family came to the store, Burnett's granddaughter and LeRoy, Jr., both toddlers, played together inside the store or on the wide, safe, walkway at the entrance One day, after several of these brief play periods, the grandmother came out, picked up the little girl and left with her. The child was crying to be allowed to continue to play.

"I later said to Katherine.," Walker recalled, "that is going to be that child's first exercise in prejudice, because the woman is going to have to give the child some reason why she can no longer play with LeRoy, Jr."

Some time later, while shopping, Walker was approached by Burnett who abruptly told him that his wife had run up a bill there of close to forty dollars that needed to be paid. LeRoy knew that Katherine had not been in the store recently, but, giving Burnett the benefit of the doubt, considered that she may have taken the college shuttle bus out to shop while he had been on the road. He told Burnett he was without his checkbook and promised he would pay the bill on the next visit. Later, when LeRoy asked his wife about the bill, she said there must be a mistake; she had not been in the store for some time. The couple theorized there might be some other Walker family shopping there, hence the mix-up.

On LeRoy's next shopping trip, in the company of other coaches from the campus, Walker explained to Burnett that his wife had not been in to run up a bill of any amount so there must be a mistake. Burnett, now agitated and angry, yelled out, "That's the way it is with you people, we let you have credit and then you won't pay." Walker tried to reason, "Mr. Burnett, wait; my wife says it is not that she has forgotten a bill, she has not even been in the store for a long time." When Burnett continued his verbal attack, Walker replied, "Sir, you need to understand that you are calling my wife a liar."

"It got more and more heated," said Walker. "Burnett was now making remarks about my race and how we could never be trusted." Walker then told the raging Burnett that he didn't intend to let him continue to verbally abuse him or his wife.

When Burnett began walking in the direction of the meat counter, Walker figured he was going for a knife and he grabbed a mop handle from a bundle close by and cut off Burnett's path. Each time Burnett tried to take a step forward, Walker swung the mop handle at him. "I never hit him, but each time I swung, he would stop and take a step back," Walker recalled, "but I was mad enough to have decapitated him with that mop handle. I had enough of it."

The other coaches talked Walker into leaving the store and getting back on campus.

At the same time, Prairie View was preparing for a big track meet. Many of the members of the college staff had been trained to serve as officials for the meet and would assist as volunteers. Other track-meet volunteers from the community joined them. At a meeting of the volunteer officiating team, Walker stood and related the incident at Burnett's store. He told the group, "I don't know why we are abused in Hempstead when a study was done that showed that we, the faculty and staff here, account for almost ninety percent of that town's financial support." Someone asked, "What can we do?"

"I said it's very simple. When you leave the campus and get to the corner, instead of turning right to Hempstead, just go left to Waller. And that's what we did. The boycott was not yet known as a tool for change in those days, but that is exactly what it was."

The word spread and the plan worked. The Waller merchants were ecstatic while the Hempstead businesses began to feel the pinch—so much so that Burnett came to the campus to meet with the President of Prairie View to complain that Walker had called the faculty together and organized them to hurt his business.

The President of the college immediately called Walker in to explain on what authority he had called a meeting of the faculty. LeRoy explained that it was a meeting of volunteers who would officiate at the track meet, not an official meeting of the faculty.

"I explained to him what had happened and added that we were citizens of a town and simply deserved better treatment," Walker said. Within days, the other merchants of Hempstead, who were continuing to lose business, put pressure on Burnett and insisted that he drive out and personally apologize to Katherine. He did.

"But we never went back to Hempstead, nor did many others," said Walker.

"I kid Jesse Jackson that he was late with the economic boycott in the Civil Rights Movement. We did it first, many years ago, in a little Texas town called Hempstead."

The incident at Burnett's store did not offset the positives for Walker during his stay at Prairie View.

During that time had the good fortune to be in the general vicinity of one of the brilliant minds in all of collegiate football, former Nebraska and Texas icon Dana Bible. Walker knew that the old coach had retired in Austin and "I went to him and introduced myself." Walker was a back coach who was determined to learn all the positions. "I wanted to be a complete football coach and I knew Bible was one of the geniuses of line-play."

Bible liked the young, aggressive coach and unlocked the wealth of his knowledge and experience gained over a lifetime of coaching successful programs.

Walker would travel to Bible's home in Austin, and occasionally Bible would come to Prairie View.

"He taught me all of the intricacies of line-play, and I was so far ahead because of that," recalled Walker.

The War Ends

Just before 6 p.m. on April 12, 1945, the bulletin hit the wires, "FDR Dead." The world held its breath. Franklin Delano Roosevelt had died suddenly at the "Little White House" in Warm Springs, Georgia shortly after complaining of a severe headache.

Vice President Harry S. Truman was called out of a meeting to the White House where he was met by the President's wife, Eleanor, who said to him, "Harry, the President is dead."

America's warrior President had not lived to see the end of the war. A strong man, loved and vilified, FDR had stood fast in the teeth of the pressures of rebuilding the economy following the Great Depression, and led the nation during the agonies and bloodletting of World War II. The burdens he had carried were clearly stamped on his face in the last photographs taken of him. The country and the world were now without one of the strongest human forces of the first half of the twentieth century.

African-Americans had lost a man in the White House in whom they had seen hope for change, driven, in great measure, by Eleanor who championed many of their causes. LeRoy and Katherine Walker were "deeply saddened" by the news of the President's death. The grief of the nation seemed to be bound up in the face of a black man photographed and published by Life Magazine.

As the president's body was being carried from Warm Springs, Chief Petty Officer Graham Jackson, with tears streaming down his face, began to play his accordion. The song was "Going Home."

Walker remembered Jackson. During his senior year at Booker T. Washington High School in Atlanta, Jackson had been the music teacher.

In the Spring of 1945, Germany surrendered. Hitler and his lover killed themselves in their Berlin bunker as the Russians closed in on them. Hitler's master plan had failed, but he had scorched the earth in Europe and Africa and murdered millions of Jews.

Japan had yet to be defeated. It dug in for a fight to the finish while America and its allies focused on a master plan to invade the Japanese mainland.

Facing casualty estimates that went into the hundreds of thousands, President Truman gave the nod to drop the world's first atomic bomb on the Japanese city of Hiroshima on August 6, 1945. When an offer of surrender was not forthcoming, three days later, another atomic bomb was released over Nagasaki. On August 14, Japan surrendered.

With the end of the war LeRoy Walker's work at Prairie View, Texas was finished. His next step would put him in the place that has remained his home for more than a half century.

When the war ended, Walker quickly pondered his options. The one he favored most was to return to New York. He was drawn to the idea of continuing his studies toward a doctorate degree from Columbia, when a coaching position became available at North Carolina College for Negroes in Durham.

Walker had met basketball coach John McLendon, now heading the physical education department at the college. McLendon offered him a job as assistant to head football coach Herman Riddick. Walker harbored positive and pleasant memories of his visit to the beautiful Durham campus and he agreed to come.

At the end of the Summer, Walker drove the family Chevrolet to Durham where, a half century later, he lives today.

The beginning of Walker's remarkable career must be viewed in context with the force of the personality around which it was launched. A man of intense determination, focus, and drive, his tenacity is legend. Early in his development, he equipped himself with a weapon that eludes most people: the ability to purge from his thinking that which is unimportant.

"My philosophy of life has not permitted me to spend time nor energy on people who simply, for whatever reason, did not like me," he said.

The House That Shepard Built

LeRoy Walker initially had no intentions of spending his entire career in Durham. It was there, however, that he became famous and further illuminated a school that has a unique history.

When the Civil War ended, the multitudes of former slaves rejoiced in spontaneous celebrations throughout the South before the realization set in that they had become America's unwanted.

The victorious North had no clue about what to do with the freedmen, most of whom were uneducated and unqualified for the job markets of the times.

In the South, there was no inclination by the defeated white power structure to provide anything for the former slaves. Many of them, fearing the unknown, stayed on the plantations.

In the decades that followed, black parents knew that if their children were to be educated, they would have to see to it themselves. Their leaders began to search for ways to establish schools, colleges, and training facilities. The premiere predominantly-black institutions in America today were founded out of an uncompromising necessity.

"When the Civil War was over, my history tells me that the education of blacks was illegal," said B.T. McMillon, professor and school historian at North Carolina Central University. "There were some slaves who were educated, depending on their circumstances with their masters." He said. "But as far as formal education was concerned, it did not exist. It was difficult for blacks to understand what freedom meant, or where to go, or what to do."

In 1894, James A. Shepard, the son of a Baptist preacher, earned his degree at Shaw University in Raleigh and became one of the area's first black pharmacists. For several years, Shepard worked with the Baptist associations that had headquarters in Chicago. Shepard was a liaison between the organization and the ministers in the field. He was assigned the Southern district.

In his travels, Shepard determined that in nearly every community of black people in the South, it was the preacher who held the most influence and potential for leadership. He found, too, that most were uneducated and without job skills to earn a living independently of the meager financial resources of their congregations. "They were dedicated preachers of the bible but Shepard was looking beyond that to a broader area of leadership," said McMillon. This was his motivation for starting a school. He thought the ministers should be able to support themselves."

With the financial help of Brodie Duke, of the powerful Duke tobacco family, and wide support among the black and white leadership in Durham, Shepard acquired twenty-five acres of land, built the first structures and, in 1910, opened the National Religious Training School and Chautauqua.

Insisting on a rigid curriculum of classical studies for men and women, Shepard placed heavy emphasis on vocational training, skills that could earn money. There were courses in sewing, wagon-making, carpentry, bricklaying, paper hanging, and dress- and hat-making.

From that meager start, Shepard led his institution into a position of prominence among black schools in the South and the nation. By 1912, ten buildings had been constructed on the site.

Shepard was a powerful personality with keen political instincts. When the school faced financial disaster in the early years, it was Shepard, through his contacts and persuasive skills, who kept the institution alive.

In 1922, now with some state support, it became Durham State Normal School, three years later the name was changed to North Carolina College for Negroes when it became one of the nation's first state-supported liberal arts college for African-Americans. Before Shepard died in 1947, the school became North Carolina College at Durham, later North Carolina Central, and finally North Carolina Central University as a part of the restructured University of North Carolina system in 1972.

The decades have not been without struggle for the institution, financially or academically, however, today NCCU is a healthy and vital link in the UNC chain, enrolling more than 5,000 students in a diverse curriculum that offers degrees in education, business, law, and nursing.

From the beginning, the school was Shepard's home. He took enormous pride in its appearance and beauty. Stories abound about his insistence on meticulous grounds keeping. Shrubs and trees planted on his campus had to be plum-lined for precise alignment, grass edged perfectly at the sidewalks, and the most visible sections of the campus were graced with an abundance of flowering plants and shrubs. Neatness and cleanliness were the orders of the day and many a visitor, before any other impression had developed, was first struck by the physical beauty of the campus on the hill. Shepard's wife, Annie, wrote the school's Alma Mater that began, "The sloping hills, the verdant green. The lovely blossoms' beauteous sheen."

Shepard was willing to guarantee the parents of his students, especially the mothers and fathers of the girls, that they would be safe in every respect in his care. He would keep the men and women separated, except for very specific times of the day during which time they would be chaperoned.

While demanding the very best comportment from his students, both on and off the campus, Shepard had higher expectations of his faculty and staff. Walker, in temperament and training, would find the campus atmosphere very much to his liking.

Dynamics of Durham

The city of Durham has one of the more interesting histories among the cities of the South. Unique events and powerful personalities came together to define the city's economics, politics, race relations, and culture. African-Americans have always played a pivotal role in determining the character of the city. Durham has produced an array of renowned black leaders in a diversity of categories.

It would be difficult to overestimate the influence of Charles Clifford Spaulding and his family. Spaulding was hired by another ambitious black man, John Merrick, who, during the last decade of the Nineteenth Century, saw the need to make insurance available to a very large group of people who were basically ignored. The intelligent and resourceful Merrick formed the North Carolina Mutual and Provident Society. It became the legendary North Carolina Mutual.

Among other prominent black leaders and entrepreneurs of the time in Durham were: Dr. Aaron McDuffie Moore; William Gaston Pearson; and the young educator, James E. Shepard.

In the earlier years of the tobacco factories of Washington Duke, black people were hired for the most difficult, labor-intensive jobs. However, many of them saw this as their opportunity to escape the agonies of the hot farm fields.

When LeRoy Walker moved his family to Durham in the Summer of 1945, the city, like the others in the South, practiced total segregation. Black citizens were, for the most part, confined to the southwest quadrant that was, and is, called "Hayti," pronounced *hay-tie.* By the war's end that section of town was enjoying spirited commerce in a business district that offered, in the words of more than one resident, "everything we needed." Some observers would describe Hayti as "the Harlem of the South."

The stresses of racial laws, policies, and customs were ever-present, and were exacerbated by the return of young black men from World War II. Once again, as they had in World War I, black troops who were allowed to fight had distinguished themselves, and returned to the South to find themselves immediately segregated, mired in the agony of second-class citizenship, and the subjects of racial hostility. Their understandable impatience was even more acute because they had received little or no recognition for their sacrifices in battle.

In Bayeux, France, stands an enormous museum dedicated to the allied invasion of Europe that began on the beaches of

Normandy, raged into the Battle of the Bulge and on into Germany. Running the entire length of the museum exhibits are the framed front pages of London newspapers, chronological accounts of the Allies' bloody fighting across the continent for nearly a year after the invasion before Germany surrendered.

There, for the world to see, are a number of front-page stories and pictures of black American soldiers meeting the enemy. One picture is that of a black soldier leveling his 45-caliber side-arm at German troops he had just captured, along with an accompanying story. Few of those stories were carried by major American newspapers. In the South they were virtually avoided.

Another example of the slight is the story of the courageous Tuskeegee airmen, a black fighter squadron. It was a long time in the telling.

It would be 1996 before America would consider that of the great number of blacks who served the country in World War II, many of them were courageous in combat roles, and yet, not one of them had been recommended for the Congressional Medal of Honor. It was only after an exhaustive study by professor Daniel Gibran of Shaw University, who gathered records and interviews corroborating acts of great courage among black combatants, that seven of their names were sent to Washington and approved for the medal. Only one was still alive to witness the end of the fifty-year oversight and receive the medal from President Clinton.

When the African-American fighting men returned, they were expected to fall back in step with the "Jim Crow" culture they had left behind and to refrain from getting "uppity" about it.

The city of Durham was dealing with the many issues of the times, as well as those of a growing city, when the Walkers arrived. While the college was building faculty housing on the campus, it was not completed in time for the Walkers' occupancy.

After a short stay in the home of football coach Herman Riddick, the family found quarters near the campus in the home of Mr. and Mrs. Fordice Jeffers. The older couple loved having the new coach and his family sharing part of their home. They were especially fond of the lively little boy who brought energy to the household. It was a sad day for the Jeffers when the Walkers moved into the new campus faculty quarters.

Katherine Walker enjoyed her life on campus in a safe and culturally-oriented environment. A college campus is something of an island set apart from the real world—intellectually energized and secure in its cocoon.

Faculty families could enjoy the company of other families much like themselves in a world far removed from the separate drinking fountains, the movie theater balconies, the back of the bus and the restaurants and public facilities closed to them in town.

LeRoy went to work.

"Johnny Mac"

Of all the personality forces that surrounded Walker when he walked onto the campus, none was more positively influential than that of John McLendon, the man who hired him.

John McLendon came to NC College in 1937 as an assistant coach. A Kansan who earned his undergraduate degree from Kansas University and a master's degree from Iowa, he came to Durham as the result of a pact with a friend in graduate school.

McLendon had met William F. Burghardt while both were pursuing their Master's program at Iowa. They were quartered in the same rooming house, "only a bathroom separated our rooms, we had all our classes together, and became great friends," said McLendon. That friendship led to an agreement that the first to be hired would provide a job for the other. When Burghardt was hired by NC College as head coach of all sports in 1937, he sent for his friend.

McLendon's small, spidery physique and ready smile masked the heart of a competitor. He was, in every sense of the word, a fighter. The sport in that he excelled was boxing. "I loved it," he said, "I thought that if I didn't box every day the world would come to an end."

Since the age of ten he wanted to become a coach and would become a genius at basketball during a career that would span thirty-four years in the collegiate ranks. At the outset, however, he was brought in to help Burghardt coach all sports. McLendon was paid two dollars a day plus room and board. He ate in the dining hall and lived in a faculty cottage on campus.

Not long removed from student days himself, McLendon's strikingly youthful appearance caused President Shepard to remark later, "John, had I known you were so young I probably wouldn't have hired you." Shepard was concerned about the possibility of female students' flirtations with such an attractive and youthful member of the faculty. Any minor reservation about his hiring was quickly dispelled by the comportment of the coach who "looked like a student."

According to Alex Rivera, longtime head of the school's news bureau and public relations department, "Mac was a person of high character who didn't drink, smoke, or curse. You could bring your wife or daughter out to any of his practices without fear of hearing any foul language whatsoever."

McLendon quickly established his impact as a recruiter, observed Rivera, "because he had a charisma that mothers liked."

In 1940, Burghardt split football and basketball into separate programs and named McLendon head basketball coach. During his remarkable career, he would become one of the most creative of his time and a brilliant game strategist.

Dean Smith, the retired basketball coaching legend at the University of North Carolina at Chapel Hill, is credited with inventing the "four corners" offensive play.

Smith was never known to have made the claim. According to John McLendon, network sportscaster and former coach, Al McGuire named the play and indicated to his nationwide audiences that it was a Smith innovation.

The play was conceived by McLendon who first used it in the CIAA tournament in 1946. "I had been experimenting with it," he recalled "and when we went into the third overtime period we went into the 'corners.' We out scored them eight to nothing in that overtime and one player scored all eight points!

"I taught it to Dean Smith in 1970 in Estes Park, Colorado. I had given a lecture to a coach's meeting and Dean came up and wanted to know more about it. We were up in a mountainside cabin and stayed up several hours working out variations of the corners." According to McLendon, even after his friends made McGuire aware of the origins of the now-famous play, "he never corrected it."

By 1940 Burghardt was eager to pursue his doctoral studies and when he resigned, McLendon was the unanimous choice to succeed him. By now he was a tried-and-true ally of President Shepard and had established impeccable credentials as a coach and administrator.

In the mid-forties, few black colleges offered a degree in physical education. Among them were Howard University in Washington, D.C., Hampton University in Virginia, and North Carolina College for Negroes in Durham where the trust and respect earned by McLendon was rewarded when college President James Shepard chose him to establish and to chair the school's first Department of Physical Education in 1944. The appointment was a wise one. McLendon hired the best he could find. His excellent faculty included teachers from Duke and the University of North Carolina along with those selected from some of the top black colleges. Alex Rivera said, " We had one of the best faculties in the country in that department; they were renowned teachers."

The PE department quickly established an enviable reputation for producing graduates of quality and commitment. Floyd Brown, a star athlete, was the first to earn a degree. For the first seven years of the department's existence, every single graduate was placed in jobs. Rivera recalled. "Just as fast as we could graduate them, other schools were hiring our people in Virginia, North and South Carolina, Georgia, Alabama, and Florida."

LeRoy Walker and John McLendon were, in some respects, of one mind. They believed that character and integrity were essential qualities to the success of their students and athletes, and they taught by example. Neither drank, smoked, nor swore. They were fair but demanding in their expectations of their charges, sympathetic to their problems and, sensitive to the influences of the environment from which many of the students had come. Many were in college on a financial shoestring, or were there because they qualified for athletic scholarship aid. The frustrations with the bigotry the youngsters faced off the campus, and the ever-present weight of the laws of segregation were important aspects of the dynamic of dealing with black students. Walker once told a reporter, "I spent a lot of my time trying to keep my athletes from getting killed."

The beginning years of Walker's coaching career at North Carolina College were marked with frustration. His conflict with the head football coach, for whom he worked, became both a burden and a blessing. Herman Riddick did not foresee the coming clash with his new assistant.

Herman Riddick

World War II had thinned the college ranks of draft eligible males so drastically that it was impossible for many small colleges to sustain a football program following the 1942 season. NC College abandoned football for the duration. McLendon was one of the few coaches left in the predominately black colleges. "I got out of the service by being declared 'essential' because I was about the only one left around here in the coaching business," he said.

McLendon found that when he was looking for a new football coach after the war, it was difficult to ignore a high school coach across town at Hillside, Durham's high school for African-American students. Herman Riddick had amassed an amazing record and had become one of the most successful high school coaches in the country.

McLendon hired Walker to assist Riddick in re-establishing and fielding the college's first post-war football team in the Fall of 1945. Walker would also look after the school's fledgling track program.

"The colleges' track program at the time was more in name than substance," said McLendon, "however, there were a few strong individual track athletes." Riddick took over NC College football with a deficit of coaching experience at the collegiate level. McLendon was counting on Walker's experience at Benedict, Prairie View, and Bishop to shore up that deficiency. In the beginning, the Riddick-Walker coalition seemed ideal. That first season the NC College Eagles win column was impressive. They defeated Shaw University of Raleigh 54 to 0; A&T of Greensboro 47 to 0; Winston-Salem 34 to 0; Bluefield 23 to 0; and Virginia Union 34 to 14. The next year was even more impressive. The offense scored 230 total points against their opponents in 1946 while the defense allowed only 24 points. Before Riddick's career was over he would become the school's winningest coach and later a member of the North Carolina Sports Hall of Fame. Despite the success on the field, the stage was being set for a collision of personalities.

By all accounts a good man, according to Alex Rivera, "Riddick, on game day would almost be in rigor mortis, and in my opinion, coaching killed him." Rivera's assessment of the coming conflict was that "when Walker came here he was way ahead of those who were over him in football, so that was his problem." At first the "problem" was over-shadowed by the football program's great success. Rivera recalled, for example, a game that will be forever etched in the memories of all who saw it. The game between NC College and Tennessee State was part of what was called "Capital Classics" held in Washington D.C. The games were designed to pit some of the best teams of the black colleges, schools that would attract the most fans. "We were there because we were a good draw, but no one thought we would beat Tennessee State," said Rivera. "But LeRoy was there to put in his defensive stuff."

The powerful opposing team got all of the pre-game breaks according to Rivera, "and when we got to the park that was supposed to be open to us for a pre-game practice, it was locked up and all the while everything was being done for the glamorous Tennessee State squad." Rivera's version of Walker's line strategy, based on his memory of the event, was that he instructed his linemen to tackle every back that came through the line with his head down and "I guarantee you that one of them will have the ball. Don't try to figure out what they are doing; you'll never be able to do that. Just hit them! Well," said Rivera, "they started hitting those backs so hard that they began to come through the line exposing their hands if they weren't carrying the ball so they wouldn't be hit. When the Tennessee coach complained to an official about the tackling, LeRoy told him that his boys were not too sophisticated and didn't know how to tell who had the ball so they just tackled anyone who came through with his head down." "We won the game and when it was over some of the Washington Redskin coaches who were in the stands followed LeRoy into the dressing room and asked him to explain to them the line play he was using. What they were doing is commonplace now, called stunts and different things, but it was new then."

"We didn't have the luxury of specialty coaches then," recalled Walker. "When I got to NC College, there were Head Football Coach Riddick, Backfield Coach Pops Turner, and John McLendon, the basketball coach who had no assistant, and me. That was it. "Not long after he arrived, Walker asked if he could assist McLendon with the basketball team. "That's how he got to be my assistant," said McLendon. "He would come directly off the football field to the gym and help me. "In those days Walker was getting home in the evenings between nine and ten o'clock.

"The truth is," McLendon said, "Walker would have been a super coach in any sport because he is a student of the games and one of his strongest skills is to read young people, to understand what they are thinking, and to have good answers for their problems both on and off the field." McLendon and Walker set the highest of standards of behavior, for themselves and their athletes. In contrast to today's chair-throwing, profanity-riddled coaching styles, the athletes under their care were not subjected to that. It is surely a measure of McLendon's character that in thirty-four years of coaching basketball he was never called for a technical foul. "That's one of the things I like to feel good about," he said. "Neither Walker nor I ever used profanity nor called people names."

§

The first few years in Durham brought many changes for Katherine Walker as well. She devoted all of her time to making a home on another campus in a new city, caring for her husband and little son. By Spring of 1946 she was pregnant again.

Carolyn Walker was born on January 5, 1947 in Lincoln Hospital in Durham. There was not the technology for advanced notification of the sex of an expected child and Katherine was thrilled to have given birth to a daughter. LeRoy was "overjoyed." However, for the second time he had not been present at the birth of a child. Now assisting John McLendon with basketball, LeRoy was on a trip with the team for post-holiday games. He called, sent flowers, and got home as soon as he could to behold the beautiful and healthy infant daughter he and Katherine had so wished for.

A few weeks after the Fall semester got underway, the college's beloved founder and president James Shepard died on October 6, 1947 following complications from injuries suffered in a fall. His funeral was attended by far more people than could get inside the auditorium on campus. Among the mourners were many of North Carolina's leaders in education, industry, and politics.

Shepard had become a champion for the education and enlightenment of young African-Americans. His legacy was an institution of higher learning that had produced legions of outstanding alumni. When he died he could be assured that the house of learning he had built was secured for the generations of students to follow. After Shepard's death, the college was governed by an interim committee. Dr. Alfonso Elder was selected the school's second president. He had been on the faculty and with Shepard since 1924. Elder's installation was held January 20, 1948 and he would hold the office for fifteen years.

The football and basketball programs at NC College were enjoying tremendous success. McLendon was producing championship teams. The success the football team was having on the field in no way telegraphed to those on the outside the growing tension between Riddick and Walker.

However, it was obvious to insiders that the conflict was becoming more difficult to conceal. The souring of the relationship reached its climax with Walker's growing perception that Riddick was "playing favorites" with those athletes who followed him over from Hillside High. Walker, who had contacts in the New York-New Jersey area, was tracking some of the outstanding high school athletes there, recruited some of them, and was convinced that they were more advanced than some of the Hillside players. "Riddick was a fine man with a great record," said Walker, "and I didn't want to air my differences with him in public. I didn't blame Riddick for those difficulties as much as I did those around him who were constantly planting the idea in his mind that I was trying to take over and run the team. I wasn't going for the glory but his friends kept pressing that concept. They would ask him 'who is running this team anyway, you or Walker?' At that point I just wanted to get out."

Walker aired his frustrations in a private meeting President Elder in 1949, and concluded by asking permission to be relieved of his duties in the football program. Elder refused, ending his response with, "I want you to stay out there even if you don't do anything but hold the chains." Walker was crestfallen and now desperate. He asked for and was later granted permission to pursue a doctorate degree.

As a part of that, Walker would be allowed to drop football, concentrate on the school's track program, and prepare for a required year's residency for doctoral studies.

"Pursuing studies was a goal," said Walker, "but I mainly wanted out of football." What came next would result in one of the greatest disappointments of his life.

❖

❖

CHAPTER THREE

THE FIFTIES

Cold Shoulder

While the incidents of overt racial hatred had to be feared and faced, other forms of it were employed to bedevil blacks, especially those who aspired to reach for a higher road. Many whites in powerful positions devised schemes to subvert black people in more quiet and subtle ways. It is useful, in demonstration, to follow the story of the resistance Walker encountered in the pursuit of his doctorate degree.

His high school record showed two Bs. The rest were As. With virtually the same scholastic record, he finished his undergraduate studies at Benedict College. "I was no genius, but I prepared myself." During his master's program at Columbia University, Walker established himself scholastically as one of the rising young stars. Columbia had always been an important institution in his life. "Early on Columbia was one of the leading institutions in the country in my field and there had never been a black to get a Ph.D. from there in my field," said Walker. His grades were excellent. He had already completed many courses required for the doctoral program there, and he had quality experience. What he did not have, as it turned out, was what he needed most: an unbiased and fair-minded department chairman. At the time Dr. Clifford Brownell had taken over the department following the retirement of the highly respected and revered Jesse Feiring Williams. "Williams was the Pope, so to speak, in his field," said Walker. "All of the people who had been the leaders and the great writers in the discipline studied under him."

Walker had every right to conclude that he would be accepted in a doctoral program at the same school where he had flourished and had established an excellent scholastic reputation. Even before he applied Walker had heard the rumors of other black students difficulties with the man who now headed the department. "Somehow I didn't think it would happened to me," said Walker, "because of my status there." He was wrong. Early in 1953, Walker wrote to Brownell with questions regarding a course of study and to ask for a faculty advisor. When an answer was not forthcoming, LeRoy wrote down ten questions, made an appointment with Brownell, and flew to New York on a Friday morning.

He was greeted by Miss Montgomery in Brownell's outer office. She was a long-term employee of the University and knew Walker very well. Her cordiality was warm and sincere. She was glad to see him again. The door between the two offices remained open so without eavesdropping, Montgomery could easily see and hear anything that took place in the inner office.

Walker began the meeting by starting at the top of his list of questions. Shortly, Brownell began to make excuses that he was needed upstairs to help a colleague. Walker reminded the professor that the only reason he had taken the day from his work and gone to the expense to fly to New York was to get the answers he needed. When Brownell repeated that he was needed upstairs, Walker replied that he would wait. Brownell then indicated that he really did not know how long he would be gone. "Are you telling me that I have come here for this specific information and you are not going to help me?" asked Walker. By this time Miss Montgomery, hearing their voices rising, began trying to motion Walker out of Brownell's office. Brownell then stated that the only time Walker would need the answers to the questions he had posed was "after you have passed the comprehensive exam and the language exams." Walker replied: "Dr. Brownell, have you even checked my records? I have already passed the comprehensive and I have already passed the French and German exams. Why don't you just ask Miss Montgomery there to show you my records? " Brownell answered that with a question of his own. "Are you suggesting that I am being prejudicial toward you?" he said.

"I am not suggesting," replied Walker, "I am telling you. There is no suggestion to this whatsoever. I am telling you there is something wrong when I, a Negro, can't get answers to questions that you seem to be able to answer for everybody else." Without responding, Brownell left the room.

Walker then walked directly to the office of Dean Russell of the school of education. When he finished relating the story, Russell shocked him by picking up the phone and ordering Brownell to his office immediately. He did not mention that Walker was present. As soon as Brownell entered the room, Russell began to berate him for his treatment of Walker and reminded the professor that Walker had been a star student and as such deserved fair and equitable treatment. Walker sadly recalled, "But that was the end of it. Up until that moment, I might have been able to persuade Brownell that I was a worthy doctoral candidate, but not now after he had been dressed down by Russell right in front of me."

Walking through the tunnel back to the main building, Walker made his decision to give up on Columbia and immediately placed a call to J. B. Nash, department head at New York University. Walker set up an appointment for Monday morning, then phoned Katherine to tell her what had developed. Walker and Nash had met on several professional occasions. Nash was receptive to the young coach's dogged determination and accepted his application. However, as is often the case in transfers, LeRoy's excellent transcript from Columbia was gutted. NYU gave him credit for only a few of the thirty extra hours he had completed at Columbia in preparation for a Ph.D. program. In addition, "I had to pass the comprehensive again, pass the language exams again, and develop a proposal for a dissertation."

Walker comes as close to harboring bitterness over this devastating incident as he does over any of the myriad racial barriers he has faced during his life. He said: "It hurt to have to get practically the equivalent of two doctorates in order to achieve one." The depth of his indignation can perhaps be measured conversely by the importance he places on fairness in his dealings with others. Drawing on all the determination and resolve within his soul, he began again. It was a struggle.

His daughter Carolyn remembers those years. "When I was a little girl, the greatest gauge of how things were going was my mother Katherine. If she had a smile on her face and talked very casually and leisurely about things, we knew everything was O.K." The child adored her father and was acutely aware that he was often away from home. She recalled a day when, as a second-grader, she confronted her mother about his absence.Katherine replied that he was busy working on his dissertation." That was the first time I had ever heard that word," Carolyn said, "and I proceeded to question Mother about what it meant and why, since my father already worked at a college couldn't he do his thesis here. Mother said it had to be earned at other universities and told me he was going to get the highest degree that he could have in his field."

Katherine would meet Carolyn at her neighborhood school to walk her home, then the little girl would accompany her mother to the mail box. On a particular day Carolyn noticed that her mother became very agitated after opening a brown envelope. The envelope contained pages of LeRoy's dissertation that were being returned, as Carolyn recalled, "all marked up in red. Mother was really angry, swinging that envelope and swinging her hands. I thought I heard her say the word 'rat.' I said, 'Who's a rat?' She just looked at me for a moment and said, 'Dr. Raths.'"

It was NYU professor Louis Raths who was marking up LeRoy's dissertation and returning it for corrections or restructuring. Dr. Raths was a specialist in the "needs" theory of human behavior, a major component of Walker's thesis. Little Carolyn decided then that she would always accompany her mother to the mail box in order to "comfort her when those brown envelopes arrived." As time went on there were fewer and fewer corrections, however, three whole chapters were lost in the mail with no back-up copies to restore them. It happened when Walker was on a three-week trip to the West coast for a series of competitions. Katherine decided to forward three chapters that had been returned from NYU so her husband could work on them in the evenings while on his trip. He was lodging at the Naval Training Center in San Diego. At the end of the three weeks they had not arrived. Without backup copies Walker was frantic. He contacted the post office with no results. Three months later, after Walker had rewritten and gotten approval for the lost chapters, the packet arrived at his home in Durham. Postmarks indicated that it had gone to every naval training center in the United States before being sent back to his home.

Carolyn said, "I realized later how important this goal was to both my parents. My father was working full-time and when these setbacks occurred, my mother just kept seeing his goal pushed farther into the future. I can see her now, sitting at the kitchen table...typing...typing....typing." As always, Walker refused to entertain defeat and in 1957 received his doctorate degree in Health and Physical Education, Exercise Physiology, and Bio-Mechanics.

The Coach

If ever a college coach started an athletic program "from scratch" it was surely LeRoy Walker at NC College. He began with a piece of ground the school referred to as the track, plenty of lime to draw the lanes, and five hurdles. There was one meet where a pair of track shoes was passed from one athlete who had completed his event, to another who was about to run. The dearth of facilities was a test of Walker's resolve and tenacity. The building of an internationally recognized track program, given the obstacles that faced him, is a prime example of his lifelong ability to brush aside adversity and focus on the goal. "Donald Leek from Gary, Indiana, was my very first national indoor champion in the hurdles and "Lover" Foster from Virginia was my first champion distance runner," he said. "The makeshift track was placed where the gymnasium is today. When they put that track down, I began serious recruiting for the program." But just as Walker was beginning to enjoy some success in his embryonic track effort, a turn of events involving his friend and mentor John McLendon would cause him to consider turning in his resignation.

McLendon Resigns

President Alfonso Elder, a highly qualified and experienced academician, faced a crucial decision that impacted the entire athletic program at his school. Around 1950, the North Carolina General Assembly had ruled that state money was not to be used for athletic programs. While a hardship for the large schools, the decision was devastating for the smaller ones. At the end of the Spring semester of 1953 North Carolina College President Alfonso Elder announced that all athletic scholarships were voided and that if those students returned in the Fall they would be required to pay full tuition, at the time more than $300.

"That wrecked my team," said athletic director and basketball coach John McLendon, "and they waited until the kids went home for the Summer to tell them." McLendon was devastated, mainly for his athletes, and it appeared to him that the school had not looked at enough alternatives. "In those days we couldn't write up an athletic scholarship agreement as you can today," said McLendon. "All the kids had to go on was your word. Coaches built their reputations on how well they kept their word without a written agreement and in terms of recruiting, that was the essence of your program."

McLendon resigned in protest. Walker's reaction was swift. He immediately came to McLendon and expressed his intention of resigning in support. "I remember that LeRoy was ready to go with me, but I asked him to stay because he was bringing tremendous prestige to the college. I told him that only one of us was needed to make the point." The intensity of the students' rage reached a dangerous level and had to be diffused by the coaches. The students agreed to a nondestructive protest that resulted in a sit-down strike they vowed would last until the coach returned to the campus." McLendon released a seventeen-point manifesto that he would require signed by Elder as the only circumstance under which he would return. The enormous pressure was intensified by the actions of a committee of 100 students who circled the President's home in their cars all day and night. Subsequently, McLendon decided that because of "philosophical differences" with Elder he would not return to the campus under any circumstances and was quickly hired by Hampton University in Virginia.

Following McLendon's departure, NC College contacted its very first physical education graduate, Floyd Brown, who was coaching at Texas Southern, and hired him as athletics director. "As it turned out, Floyd Brown not only got everything back that had caused McLendon to leave, he got more!" recalled Walker. Following the loss of one of his greatest mentors, and the upheaval in the wake of McLendon's departure, Walker turned all of his energies into the track program. McLendon said of Walker:

"It is his interest to help people reach their goals in life as well as on the field of competition. When you are coaching you are taking young men into manhood and there are special people who can be very helpful in the lives of youth at that stage. LeRoy had a knack for it. He helped them make that passage and to continue on to other successes, he probably had every problem to deal with as any of them, and more."

§

Athletes who excel in the events bunched into the general heading of "track and field" are of a different, if not unique, mindset from those who are drawn to the court, the gridiron, or the diamond. While the team concept constitutes the basic structure for the sport, the athlete is in constant competition with himself, or herself. The quest is a never-ending reach to best himself or herself. Track events are of such diversity that a marathon runner and a sprinter require a different character athlete and customized coaching. The skills of the sprinter, who explodes in a short burst of maximum energy are at variance with those of the distance runner whose goal is to mete out that energy over an extended period of time during which pacing is of paramount importance. What they have in common is that at the end of either event, a total expenditure of energy should have taken place. Practice sessions can begin only after all the important warm-up has been completed. These routines include a variety of exercises, including butt kicks, both physical and mental. Within certain parameters, individual athletes are free to customize their warm-ups, resulting in some athletes taking longer than others to accomplish that most important prelude. Walker's athletes learned to back-time their warm-ups to conclude precisely at the moment his practice sessions were scheduled to begin.

As with all sports, track practice involves a "grind it out" regimen. Routines vary little and the acceptance of that must be a part of the athlete's commitment and a challenge for the coach. A practice has to be tolerable, hopefully satisfying, and optimally fun. Unlike football, filled with shouts, grunts, and violent clashes, a track practice is quiet. The prominent sound is that of the voice of the head coach to which the hearing of the athletes and assistant coaches are finely attuned, even across the field, and on days of competition, one that penetrates the din of cheering spectators. Aside from winning medals and titles, the greatest reward for the track athlete is that of traceable progress. The stopwatch and the measuring devices are undeniable instruments of proof of performance. From the beginning of a collegiate track season to the end, there should be, with quality coaching, a line graph of progress that follows a continuous upward track.

With an eagle-eye and a stopwatch, Walker demanded the best from his young men on and off the field. A key factor to his success was his skill at spotting talent that often was not obvious to others. In the later years, following his coaching triumphs, he would often use this phrase at coaching clinics: "If you want to make a rabbit stew, you first have to get yourself a rabbit." Walker possessed an uncanny talent for snaring the "rabbits."

Lee Calhoun

Walker first saw Lee Calhoun at the Indiana High School Championship meet held in Mishawaka. He had flown there at the urging of a friend to view the field of high school track athletes competing at the state championship level with the idea of recruiting for his college team. It would become a day of destiny for a distraught teenager and a wise, young coach. Walker approached a weeping athlete beside the track who had just finished last in his event. The youth asked why the coach would be interested after seeing his performance.

It was Walker's keen eye that would lift the fallen young athlete from his despair and change his life forever. Calhoun, in return, would allow Walker to take the first step of a pilgrimage into the realm of the Olympics and international competition from which he would never return. It was during the warm-ups that day in Indiana, that Walker had observed in Calhoun what he describes as "those God-given gifts of height and split." Walker recruited Calhoun and never looked back.

It was Fall of 1952 that the future two-time Olympic Gold medalist walked onto the campus of NC College in Durham and began working with a coach with facilities so sparse that it consisted of half a track and only five hurdles. Before his association with Walker was over, the word "champion" would appear beside Calhoun's name. Then, the irony: Fate would have the coach outlive the slender teenager who first stood before him that day in Indiana.

Coaching Philosophy

I believe in the four Fs of coaching: I am firm, fair, and friendly.
If that doesn't work, then it's farewell.

—LeRoy T. Walker

A friend of LeRoy Walker called him the track coach of the century. In every Olympic Games from 1956 to 1980, there have been athletes on the field from NCCU.

Divining the secrets of his success as a renowned track coach is a multilayered journey that began in Atlanta during his boyhood years. Walker credited two men at Morehouse College, two blocks from his boyhood home with defining his initial attitudes toward sport, Charlie Clark and Frank Forbes.

Later, when the lad moved to Harlem, there were other adults willing to spend the time and effort it took to inspire and motivate him in the city's athletic youth leagues. Next to substantially impact Walker's developing philosophy of coaching was his beloved high school coach at Booker T. Washington High School, Thelman Hope Giles Crawford, who also coached him at Benedict College. Then there was the influence of Dana Bible, the football wizard, and John McLendon, the basketball coaching legend at North Carolina College. Each of these men impacted Walker's philosophy in various ways but the overview, as Walker describes it is that "you tend to teach as you have been taught and to coach as you have been coached."

Walker said of basketball coach McLendon: "He taught me the important lesson that the subtleties of coaching would only come after a total dedication and commitment to the fundamentals of the game," said Walker. He credited McLendon with teaching him how to best get a point across to his athletes. Walker became a master of that important coaching skill. Walker also credited J.J. Starks at Benedict during his student years. Walker's position of campus leader often brought him in contact with Starks, a conservative educator and administrator "from the old school." From Sumpter, South Carolina, Starks was a highly skilled evaluator of people and their potential. He employed various ways of testing a young person's mettle. The following incident is an example: As president of his class Walker made an appointment with Starks to discuss a student proposal. "Dr. Starks had a bad habit, but I think too it was to test you, of continuing to read while you were trying to talk with him" said Walker. "If you continued to talk he might just glance up at you, but on this particular occasion I just stopped talking." Starks put the paper down and asked, "What's wrong?" Walker boldly told Starks that he had something important to talk about for the benefit of his class and for the college, but added "if it isn't important enough to be heard now perhaps I can come back some other time." Starks seemed pleased.

Walker soon began to form his own methods and philosophies of coaching and classroom instruction. "I learned how to integrate my disciplines, how to transfer the subtleties into coaching different sports. From the influences of Bible and McLendon, Walker was anchored to the principle of fundamentals.

"Most of my coaching has not been done on frills," said Walker, "but it has been based on understanding every single move you make as an athlete." Another significant factor in Walker's coaching success has been his study of science and bio-mechanics. He consistently related what he learned in the sciences to his work in the field. He was able to grasp the theories of science and to make them his bedrock for coaching track. "I had the advantage of fully understanding the laws of motion," said Walker. "For instance, the theory that for every action there is an opposite and equal action is the whole basis for jumping. Another applicable law is that once something is started in a direction, unless another force intervenes, it will continue in the same direction," said Walker.

Many of his athletes recall the classroom sessions before practice with Walker at the blackboard, often teaching the scientific theories supporting the drills he would ask them to perform on the field. This element, perhaps more than any other facet of his coaching, reveals Walker's constant striving to answer for his athletes, the question, "why?" The classroom sessions paid dividends for the athletes. Because he added this scientific approach to athletics, Walker was able to get them to perform better in their other classes as well. Those student-athletes who became coaches were better prepared to meet the challenges of their careers. One of his champions, hurdler Charles W. Foster, remembers that there was never a question, of the multitude that he presented the coach, that was not answered by Walker. "I was one of these guys," said Foster, "who always wanted to know why." Walker believed, above all, that there was no substitute for work, for himself and his athletes. Foster recalled that when the coach was writing on the chalkboard exactly what was to be accomplished on the field on a particular day that the athletes, "behind his back, we would be looking at each other with grimacing expressions as the drills were being quickly scribbled on the board at the front of the room." Foster said, "We thought it was easy for him to put them on the board but we were the ones who were going to have to break our hearts and lungs on the field." Walker, from the beginning, held to the theory that athletes perform better if they understand why a particular drill will make them better. "If they don't understand how it works," he said, "then it is hard to get them to relate to the practice."

Walker was the first to show the great Norman Tate what the triple jump was. He broke it down for him and so thoroughly coached him in the event that Tate became a national champion in the triple and the long jump. Once when Walker was forced to cancel a scheduled lecture on the triple jump, he sent Tate to substitute for him. "The truly great coaches in any sport, I believe, are those who do not depend on frills," said Walker. "The coaching of the late professional football coach Vince Lombardi, or former UNC basketball coach Dean Smith is based on fundamentals and the ability to motivate. But if the athletes have not been properly prepared it is impossible, no matter how many motivational speeches you make, to get them to believe they can win."

Walker talked with young people often about dealing with the world when they stepped off the field of play. He prepared them for the reaction to the David-Goliath events when his team from the little college in North Carolina would upset such giants as Michigan or Southern California.. He would always warn the members of his small team "that some people and surely some members of the press would say you were just lucky." Walker advised, in those cases, that the athletes just agree with that assessment. "Go ahead and admit it to them," he would say, "but in your heart just remember that luck is when preparation and opportunity meet. Just remember that we were right beside them when they might have bobbled the stick just a bit,.and because we were there, we were able pass them." Just as Walker had never asked for an advantage in his own life and career, he has consistently rejected the idea that any group of Americans be insulted by separate standards or requirements. In later years he vehemently fought efforts to single out black youth for "special" or lower academic standards of admission or scholastic performance. "I had student-athletes who bought into my philosophy," he said, "I told them that I was working to make them good enough that they would never have to have an advantage given to them in order to succeed." When the NCAA was considering Proposition 48, which would standardize scholastic requirements for collegiate athletes, there was plenty of opposition. Walker took a stand that was not at all popular with many other coaches, especially those representing predominantly black institutions, when he said to the delegates, "I want it understood that I will never (be for anything) that treats one race as secondary to another."

§

Walker employed a methodical, step-by-step technique in developing his track champions. His work with hurdler Lee Calhoun is instructive. "I knew what had to be done in coordinating his lead leg, trail leg and hips," said Walker. "But you can't correct all the body parts collectively, so you first have to take the one that impacts his performance the most negatively. You get that one out of the way without worrying about the other three right then. Then, building on that, you proceed to keep correcting."

When his sprint-medley relay team set the world record competing in Madison Square Garden, Walker's assessment of how that was accomplished goes back to his theory of coaching fundamentals. He said, "we passed the stick better." From Vince Lombardi, Walker honed his theory on the dangers of "over-coaching." When Lombardi was explaining what he looked for in the great assistant coaches surrounding him, he said he looked for someone who could determine "when it was exactly right." When multiple corrections seemed to be indicated for a gifted athlete Walker was careful "not to destroy the athlete's natural skill projections." Often when other coaches would ask him to assess their training of a particular athlete, his advice was "Why don't you just leave that kid alone and let him make you a great coach?"

Al Buehler Friendship

LeRoy and I made a good blend....we were Barnum and Bailey. Once on a trip, when he had a change of plans after releasing his hotel room, and I still had my room for another night....we slept in the same bed. My God...in those days in the South you could get killed for that if anybody had ever found out!

—Al Buehler, head track coach and Chairman of the
Department of Physical Eduction, Duke University

LeRoy Walker's association with Duke University has been one of the more enduring connections of his career, beginning in the Forties. When Al Buehler came to Duke University in 1955, Bob Chambers was head track coach and head trainer at the prestigious private school. Chambers hired the skinny young man who grew up in Hagerstown, Maryland, to help with the distance runners. Buehler had been a star at the University of Maryland from 1948 to 1952, where he had twice been the 800-meter Southern Conference outdoor and indoor champion. That, of course, drew the attention of coaches and athletic departments around the country, especially since he was not only a gifted athlete but possessed all the necessary talent and skill needed in coaching.

The disciplined young man had gained valuable experience as a coach of the Maryland cross-country freshmen. Al was a solid student and finished with a major in math and history, plus an Air Force ROTC commission. He was activated in April of 1953. He truly loved working with the latest military electronics and was sent to Korea near the end of the war. When Duke's assistant track coach Red

Lewis needed to take care of his critically ill wife, Buehler was recommended and Chambers asked him to come to Durham.

Some time before Buehler arrived, Bob Chambers and Walker developed a relationship that was both professional and personal. Chambers knew of Walker's growing reputation at NC College and the success he was having recruiting and training premiere athletes showing up in championship categories. "Bob liked me, had seen some of my performers, and asked me why I wasn't competing in the AAU," said Walker, "and I told him I had tried, without success to be allowed to enter the AAU meets." Duke had excellent track facilities and Al Buehler recalled with astonishment that Walker "was actually training one of his greatest discoveries, Lee Calhoun, with five hurdles."

Without fanfare, Chambers invited Walker to hold his practices at Duke, launching one the great sports stories in history. It was not the first time Duke had involved itself with an athletic team from North Carolina College. In the Spring of 1944, when integration was against the law, a basketball game was arranged and played in secret on the NC College campus. John McLendon's Eagles defeated an all-white Duke medical school team, 88 to 44. While the invitation Bob Chambers had issued to Walker and his track team was not a secret, it nevertheless did not go through a formal battery of approvals, since Duke had the autonomy of a private institution. It was more or less viewed and accepted as one track coach helping another. Buehler said: "That was an unusual situation at that time—a white coach at the private school, working with a black coach from another school." The Chambers-Walker coaching coalition and later the Buehler-Walker track meet triumphs would bring undreamed-of accolades to both institutions, the city of Durham, the State of North Carolina and the United States.

Chambers and Walker traded coaching techniques and the athletes from the two schools began to help each other while developing friendships. At the time, training film and slow motion video tape were not available to track coaches. Chambers and

Walker relied on "eyeballing," each one gifted in picking up flaws and then formulating drills to correct them.

There was an acceleration drill. Hurdles are three steps and up. If the athlete hits the hurdle, the next first stride is shortened, leaving only two steps to make up for the loss. In drills, the acceleration distance was cut in half. Instead of the usual fifteen yards to the first hurdle, for instance, the approach would be limited to seven-and-one-half in an effort to get the same momentum in half the distance. This enabled athletes to regenerate the energy and the flow if they hit a hurdle. It was a very tough drill. "It was one of Walker's specialty drills in developing hurdlers," said Buehler.

Walker had a rising star in Lee Calhoun but Duke had two: Joel Shankle and Dave Sime. Shankle was a Methodist preacher's son from Front Royal, Virginia, and as such he was able to attend Duke tuition-free. Eventually he was put on full athletic scholarship. Meanwhile high school baseball sensation Dave Sime from Fairlawn, New Jersey was a student at Duke on a scholarship provided by the New York Yankees. It was before the big league clubs were allowed to sign a youngster who was in school. The best way to develop loyalty from a kid was to provide a scholarship, with the hope that it would later lead the way to a contract.

Duke's Fall baseball program at the time was modest but Chambers worked out some fitness drills to keep them in shape for Spring. When Sime came down, the track coaches got an eye-full. When Chambers asked Buehler to clock Sime out of the blocks for 100 yards "Lo and behold, in a warm-up suit, on a cinder track, Dave ran 9.8, which showed right away that he was one fantastic athlete!" recalled Buehler. "So you had Lee Calhoun, Dave Sime, and Joel Shankle all working out together and there was never any problem at all," said Buehler. The combination produced very positive results.

That cooperative spirit led the way for the coaches and athletes from the two schools to gain from the experience. "Shankle had speed, Calhoun had finesse over the hurdles and Sime was the best sprinter. It all worked because they helped each other," said Buehler. Walker assisted in coaching the Duke sprinters and hurdlers, while his athletes were turning in better performances on Duke's superior track, all the while using Calhoun and Shankle to challenge each other. "I knew if I could get Shankle to the point of staying close to Calhoun, they both could medal," said Walker.

In preparation for the 1956 Olympic Games in Melbourne, Australia, the U.S. trials were held in Los Angeles and in a photo finish, first place in the 110-meter hurdles went to USC's Jack Davis. Lee Calhoun was second, Joel Shankle third. "The race was so close that some thought I should protest the decision," said Walker, "but I was happy. I knew that Calhoun was either first or second, a toss-up, and that Shankle was a strong third."

The pay-off came in Melbourne when Lee Calhoun thundered into the world's sports spotlight. In a thrilling race, he shaved past Jack Davis, set a record and took the gold medal. "Calhoun, from a small NAIA school, beating Davis, the best hurdler in the NCAA," said Al Buehler, "was like Kentucky being beaten by Fort Hayes State in basketball." Duke's Joel Shankle came in third for the bronze.

In preparing Calhoun for the Olympic Games in Melbourne, Walker recalled: "I'll never forget that at a meet in Quantico, Virginia, Jack Davis told the press that Lee would never be strong enough to be a great hurdler. All I did was tape that article to the door of Calhoun's locker so he would see it every day. So, when I kept pushing him—and it was tough—for more and more preparation for the Olympic trials, I didn't have to motivate him. Jack Davis had done that. Davis was so sure that he would win the Melbourne race. When he lost, he took off his spikes and never ran again."

That thrilling moment for athlete and coach would mark the point from which LeRoy Walker launched the twenty years of competition that would make him a coaching legend. When the triumphant teams returned from Melbourne, Durham Mayor E. J. Evans and the city put together a victory parade to honor the athletes and coaches who had put their schools and Durham in the spotlight. In one convertible rode LeRoy Walker and Lee Calhoun, in another was Joel Shankle. In Bob Chamber's absence, Al Buehler was asked to ride in the car with Duke star Shankle. Pride crossed racial lines and the people of Durham turned out for the returning heroes. The event was bringing the community together. The press pictures, published locally and across the country showed Walker and Buehler shaking hands and Calhoun shaking hands with Shankle. While that kind of solidarity seemed "unusual" at the time to some of the media, "that part of it was nothing new to us," said Buehler. "It was great, LeRoy was so proud of Lee and proud for North Carolina College."

Calhoun's victory in Melbourne added Walker's name to that exalted list of coaches to be reckoned with in international competition.

§

Duke's Bob Chambers was 58-years-old when he died suddenly on February 11, 1964. Al Buehler, then in his early thirties, remembers "just walking around in that stadium trying to deal with the great personal loss." He was named head track and field coach at Duke, a job he holds today, in addition to that of chairman of the Department of Physical Education. Following Chamber's death, Walker and Buehler continued their supportive collaborations and became life-long friends. From 1969 to 1996, they would make track-meet history.

Growing Up In the Shadow

Among LeRoy Walker, Jr.'s earliest memories were the warnings from his mother in Prairie View to stay in the yard to "avoid being bitten by one of those Texas rattlesnakes!" When the family moved to Durham, LeRoy, Jr. was enrolled at W.D. Pearson Elementary on Merrick Street, not far from the college campus. His school days were pleasant, especially those during third grade when he became a member of the school safety patrol. "Mr. Roach, the sixth-grade teacher, was in charge of the patrol, a nice but very disciplined guy who handled the patrol in a military style. I loved it for three reasons. It was companionship, it was organized, and it was recognized."

Each year the children on the patrol were treated to a trip to Washington, D.C. where the national organization of school patrols rewarded them with sightseeing tours, concluding with a big parade in which every child was allowed to march. In the sixth grade, LeRoy, Jr. met up with a teacher whom he considered the "meanest, toughest, person I had ever encountered."

Mrs. Morrison's reputation as a tough disciplinarian was one she had earned over the years, at least from the students, in her quest to prepare them for the tougher academic years ahead of them. "It turned out she was the best thing that ever happened to me and to many others," LeRoy, Jr. said. "Anyone who was going on to higher studies really benefited by having her as a teacher. One of Mrs. Morrison's requirements was that each student keep a color-coded notebook in green, blue, and red ink. She constantly checked the books to see that everyone was keeping up with the program. Her serious approach to the discipline of study was most beneficial by the time we reached the tenth and eleventh grades in high school."

It was Mrs. Morrison who inadvertently bestowed upon LeRoy, Jr. the nickname "Cush," one that he carries to this day. As recess began one day, the physical education teacher had not arrived, so Mrs. Morrison instructed the children to stay in line until the other teacher arrived. Naturally, when she was out of sight, the boys began to break ranks and play. Just before the physical education teacher arrived, LeRoy, Jr. got back in line. When play period was over and the kids got back into their home room with Mrs. Morrison "some of the girls began to snitch on us and pointed out to Mrs. Morrison which boys had violated her orders to stay in line."

The teacher proceeded to take the perpetrators to the boys' bathroom, where she prepared to spank them. In a desperate effort to avoid the impending punishment, LeRoy, Jr. said, "Miss Morrison I did get out of line but I was the very first one to get back in my place before the teacher came." LeRoy, Jr. has a vivid memory of her reply: "Walker, it is not going to do you any good to make up something because I am still going to spank you on your "cushion." Other boys thought that hilarious and later, some of them began to call him "Cushion." In high school it was shortened to "Cush."

When they weren't in school, the Walker children lived a different kind of life from that of their school chums. While at the time they accepted it as a the norm, the fact that they lived on a college campus offered varied and exciting experiences for them. The access to the energy of football Saturdays, pep rallies, bands and a surrogate family of several thousand older brothers and sisters was a world of special privilege for the Walker children.

"Being black in Durham during segregation was a lot better than being black anywhere else in North Carolina and other parts of the South," said LeRoy Walker, Jr., who grew up during the transitional period from segregation to integration. His experience was far more positive than many other youngsters who bore the full force of a cruel atmosphere that permitted whites to add to the suffering of blacks in any way they pleased. In the movie theaters of small towns, blacks sat in a hot, cramped area up next to the roof, adjacent to the projection booth. To add to the discomfort, they were often provided only backless wooden benches on which to sit. The price of their admission ticket was the same as that of the whites.

If blacks were allowed to buy a hot dog at a roadside stand, then their window was placed in the side or the back of the building. When LeRoy, Jr. was 9, the family traveled to a meeting in Texas. Long family trips had to be carefully planned. Blacks were not permitted in public restaurants, motels or hotels. Therefore, a trip often might take them hundreds of miles out of their way in order to lodge with relatives, friends or fraternity brothers. Many of the great black fraternities were initially formed to provide a way for black families to cross the country by car and plot out a route that would pass through the town of a brother, who might someday need reciprocal considerations for his family. The Walkers' route to Texas had zigzagged through some rural country in Alabama where at one point father LeRoy stopped for gas. LeRoy, Jr. saw that people were ordering hot dogs from a screened-in window-counter at the front of the building. When he announced that he wanted a hot dog, mother Katherine said to him, "we can't get a hot dog here." The boy argued that he certainly could because he could see other people doing it right in front of him.

Perhaps he wore his mother down or perhaps she decided he needed to learn a bitter lesson. When he asked again she did not move to stop him. Approaching the window LeRoy, Jr. was confronted with a sullen white man who asked what he wanted. "A hot dog," said LeRoy, Jr. "just a hot dog."

"You'll have to go around to the back," said the man. From the slit in the back wall, LeRoy, Jr. could see all the way through the room and observed the man serving people at the front window. When everyone in the front of the building had been served, the same man walked to the back and again asked LeRoy what he wanted. The boy just stared at the man for a moment and replied, "Nothing." Seeking solace from his mother, she said quietly, "You are colored and they won't serve you the same way they serve whites. That's the way life is."

LeRoy, Jr. recalled, "That's the first time I was really hurt. There were incidents in college when I began to realize that anything I did would reflect on my father" said LeRoy, Jr. "It was not until my last years in college that I fully realized he was not just a good coach but a very smart man. LeRoy Walker, Jr. claims that he never felt the sting of walking in the ominous shadow that sons of other powerful men have suffered. He felt a strong sense of duty to "behave" himself but did "not see that as undue pressure; it was more of a nuisance." Walker's only son claims he was never pressured by his father, with one notable exception. "In a heart-to-heart talk he insisted that I finish college." When he dropped out of NC State's School of Engineering in Raleigh after two-and-a-half years, his father quickly intervened.

LeRoy, Jr. had dropped out of school for a number of reasons but his grades were not one of them. He was having "trouble" with at least one professor and there was the isolation he and other black students suffered when they found themselves among the first waves of the few students who were experiencing the integrating of institutions of higher education. A good athlete, but not gifted as his father had been, LeRoy, Jr. had entertained the idea of a career in coaching only to be persuaded by his father that there was a glut of teachers and coaches entering the work force and, while he could probably be a good coach, colleges usually were attracted to those who had been great players. Following his troubles at State and with some initial reluctance, "Cush" enrolled at North Carolina Central University with a math major and business minor. While studying computer programming, he discovered it was a perfect match. Following graduation, he joined IBM for "twenty-five-and-a-half great years of working with one of the great companies of the world in its field."

State Department Recruits Walker

LeRoy Walker was able to persuade the administration at NC College to relieve him of Summer duties so he would be free to study, travel with his family, or accept other temporary coaching assignments. That decision by the college, however reluctant at the time, would eventually bring the school into a sphere of recognition that it had never before imagined. The arrangement rankled some of the other faculty members, some of whom expressed their displeasure to Walker. He would simply reply, "That is my agreement with the college. I am sorry you don't like it." Walker was called out of a professional meeting at Howard University in Washington to take a call from Ross Merrick, executive director of the National Association of Sport and Physical Education. The U.S. State Department at the time had implemented an exchange program that, among other things, provided an opportunity for smaller countries around the world to benefit from the expertise of some of America's best teachers and coaches. Merrick wanted to recommend Walker for an assignment in Africa. His tour would take him to Syria, then Ethiopia, then Israel. Walker's reality check for that part of the world began when he asked why, if he were in Syria first, he could not go to nearby Israel instead of traveling down the continent to Ethiopia and then doubling back. "That's when they told me you couldn't get into Israel from Syria," said Walker. That answer was the beginning of Walker's struggle with the sensitive politics and emotions in that part of the world.

Walker arrived in North Africa in the Summer of 1959. Since he could offer expertise in both education and coaching, the countries divided his work day. The mornings were spent in the classrooms of the high schools and universities, his afternoons working with track teams. In Ethiopia, the American coach discovered a virtual gold mine of talent in distance runners. Their lifestyle and the high altitude in which they lived combined to produce runners of superior stamina and speed. Walker recalled that when an Ethiopian said he believed he would "run over" to another town, the Ethiopian meant it in the literal sense. If school happened to be ten miles away and there were no buses, the youth were able to run all the way, and enjoyed doing it. Even their exhibitions were scaled to distance. Walker noted that at half-times during athletic events such as soccer matches, the Ethiopians would often sponsor a distance run.

As he left Ethiopia for Israel, Walker took with him the impressions of the distance-running talent he had seen in that country. In turn, the Ethiopians revered the American coach, later making him an honorary citizen. In Israel, Walker taught at the prestigious Wingate Institute, on the outskirts of Tel Aviv, the country's center for physical education studies. While there, he made a judgment call that endeared him to the population at large. The U.S. had backed a dam project in the area of Haifa and during Walker's working tour, the American ambassador, along with some Israeli officials, asked that he attend dedication ceremonies on the same Saturday Walker had been scheduled to conduct a workshop for teachers and coaches of physical education and track from around the country. He politely declined, explaining to the U.S. and

Israeli government officials that he did not want to disappoint those who had set aside the time to come to his workshop. "To me," he recalls, "I would touch many more lives by being with those young teachers than by going to the dedication of the dam, because they would be able to take back to their schools some of the things they would learn in my classroom and on the field of play." The next day, Walker saw his picture on the front page of the papers with a story written in Hebrew. Before it was translated for him' he "figured that the story might be critical of my declining the invitation to the official event at the dam." Instead, the words were in high praise of his greater concern for the youth and the teachers in the country. Today, a tree grows on the Wingate campus, planted as a sapling many years ago with a dedication plaque honoring LeRoy T. Walker.

The State Department had instituted a rule that neither Walker nor any of the other representatives of the program could revisit a country. This was to avoid the appearance of favoritism. However, it wasn't long before both Israel and Ethiopia were calling for his return. Before he returned home from his first visit, Walker devised a complete Olympic training program for the Ethiopians. He had no idea that they would follow through. When he returned several years later they handed him a thick book with complete records of how they had worked diligently on his detailed instructions. Working with the African youth was both enlightening and challenging for Walker. They were extremely cooperative and very coachable.

An incident involving a distance runner in Ethiopia proved that the quiet young men did not share all their secrets with their coach. "When one very strong and dominate runner who lived in Addis Ababa fell out during a practice session, I was perplexed and confused," said Walker, "and I took him to the medical facility for a complete examination where nothing turned up in the tests." Addis Ababa was thirty miles away from the practice site. The youth hitched a ride to practice each day and Walker was providing bus fare for his return in the evenings. Finally one of the boy's teammates told Walker the story. In addition to fulfilling Walker's "full work load" on the track, the athlete was pocketing the bus fare and running the thirty miles back to town! "He literally ran himself into the ground."

All of Walker's coaching and consulting work in Africa and around the world was done as a volunteer. The State Department paid expenses and a daily per diem. Walker's mission in Africa was not finished. His concept of a Pan-Africa team had come from his belief that if the countries of Africa could put their best athletes together on a unified team, the results on field would be formidable. "Any one of those countries working alone would not be able to mount so great a challenge. "Their natural abilities were in distance running," he said, " but they did not have the good coaching it takes to develop their sprinters and hurdlers. All of my good field people came from above the Sahara, the distance runners primarily from below the Sahara in East and West Africa."

By 1965, he was in charge of programming and training for the entire continent, with the exception of South Africa. Criticism came to Walker from what he described as "a few narrow-minded Americans who were upset at the success the Africans were having against the US. athletes." His proposal to assemble a Pan-Africa team was met with some resistance, and it was an idea that astounded some of his associates. One of them, with whom Walker shared his idea while they sat in a sauna in Oslo, replied, "Your brain has surely been softened by this intense heat."

The Organization of African States often had difficulty bringing the diverse and divided countries together on almost any issue. Yet Walker was able to persuade many of them to put aside their conflicts for sport. He insisted that the Pan-Africa team wear a common uniform and use a common musical flourish. Division was not an acceptable format for Walker's concept of a team that, by all reasoning, ought to present itself on the field of sport as a cohesive unit. "I knew all of the top sports councils there. "Walker was able to put together a team in 1971 with the help and support of the Supreme Council of Sport for Africa, made up of talented athletes from 27 different countries on the continent. He noted that they were from "north of the Sahara, south of the Sahara, East Africa,

West Africa, and when they came together "it created a tolerance for one another. We even got two warring factions out of Nigeria to meet face to face at a hotel in Uganda," Walker remembered, "I said, 'Look at each other; you people are brothers.'"

Personal Matters

In 1959, LeRoy and Katherine built their home in a quiet neighborhood in West Durham, only five minutes from the college. "It was nothing real fancy," said LeRoy, "but a home that was comfortable and that suited us." The ranch-style home on Red Oak Avenue remains the hearth and touchstone for LeRoy and the extended family. In money matters, Walker's frugality became legend among some of his friends and athletes. Hurdler Charles Foster recalled that "'Doc' sure knew how to hold onto a dollar." In contrast, those who know, trumpet his generosity to his family, his church and his university. After careful study, he made wise investments. In searching for a place he thought suitable for his mother, at the time in failing health and in need of a place where she could be properly cared for, he found that rest homes for minorities were nearly nonexistent. In the late-Fifties, he was able to find the financing for construction of the first of several rest homes he would build over the next few years. The first one, Pine Knoll, was constructed on Highway 55 in Durham. The rest homes would prove to be an excellent financial venture and the homes were filled to capacity. Walker later was able to sell the facilities for a substantial profit.

❖

CHAPTER FOUR

THE SIXTIES

Climate of the Times

The year 1960 ushered in one of America's most turbulent decades. Black Americans were not only voicing their concerns about the oppression they were suffering in a segregated society, they had now found the courage to act. On February 1, 1960, a few weeks after the inauguration of President John F. Kennedy, four students from North Carolina A&T in Greensboro, at great personal risk, took seats at the lunch counter at the Woolworth store downtown and asked to be served. Franklin McCain, Ezell Blair, Jr., Joseph McNeil and David Richmond gave birth to the "sit-in."

Their courage emboldened students across the South and around the country to put themselves forward in nonviolent protests. Drawing inspiration and resolve from Martin Luther King Jr., demonstrations were staged throughout the South in the form of sit-ins, marches, rallies and sit-downs.

In North Carolina's triangle towns of Raleigh, Durham and Chapel Hill, students on the campuses of the black colleges were organizing and planning strategy. Leading the way were North Carolina Central in Durham and Shaw and St. Augustines in Raleigh. White youth were welcomed, even encouraged, to join the movement and many did. The initial phase of the movement could not foretell the struggles and violence that would follow across the land. The press turned the spotlight on the South as it was entering a convulsive state of rioting, shootings, church bombings and martial law. In many cases, school systems would be integrated by force of the military. Pictures of black schoolchildren walking past a gauntlet of screaming white tormentors at the schoolhouse door were being flashed around the world. The tensions that gripped the land were particularly frightening to African-American children, including a future mayor of Atlanta whose father had become a courageous challenger of the status quo.

In Raleigh, North Carolina, Ralph Campbell, Sr. told his little son Bill one night in September 1960 that the next day he would be going to a different school. "My father has always been my hero because of the role that he played," said William "Bill" Campbell, now mayor of Atlanta. "He was confrontational, he insisted on equal rights, he believed in education and was a ferocious advocate for the disadvantaged until the moment he died of a heart attack. It was September 7, 1960. My father was president of the NAACP in Wake County and for as long as I could remember, as soon as he came home from work at the post office, we would gather on the campuses of Shaw or St. Augustines colleges and march up and down the streets of Raleigh, lying down in front of movie theaters and hotels we could not enter. So when my dad said I would be leaving the school I was already enrolled in and would be going to Murphy Elementary, we assumed there would be a number of other children to go along with me on the crusade to desegregate the schools. However, one by one all of the other parents decided they did not want to expose their children to the kinds of hardships that were inevitable. So, I ended up being the only black child to integrate the schools. It was very difficult. We had a caravan of cars that would take me back and forth. There were crowds of people, a lot of parents withdrew their children because of the commotion of the protests. We had police protection, but the Raleigh Police Department did not have the racial make-up it has now. My father was always suspicious of their protection because he knew most were not sympathetic to our cause; in fact many of them were very much opposed to integration. We largely relied on the security of our own community, ministers, community leaders, and student leaders. Terry Sanford, who was North Carolina's governor at the time, put his children into Murphy school with me. The school was only two blocks from the governor's mansion. My second grade teacher, Mrs. Nell Abbott, with whom I still correspond, was enormously helpful. She always treated me the same as the others. For the next five years at that school I was the only black child, even though some of the other schools were later integrated. It was a lonely existence for a seven-year-old. Virtually all the other integration that took place in the South was done with groups of children. The Little Rock Nine were Arkansas High School students and had a sense of solidarity by being together. I was alone. "But we lived through it and even then I believe I understood the importance of it. It was a complex time in America's history, a nonviolent revolution that changed the essential fabric of our society."

§

If the fabric was changing, the weaving was difficult. LeRoy Walker was fighting battles on the inside, coming from a bedrock of experience that had convinced him that it was possible to form positive alliances, if not friendships, within the white power structure for the greater good. He is, to this day, convinced that his method of "beating the system" was the proper course to pursue.

Walker's track team was not allowed to compete in the North Carolina-South Carolina combined AAU track events often held in nearby North Carolina State in Raleigh. "They refused to let us in," said Walker, "because even though they knew I had some of the finest athletes, we were from North Carolina College, a black school. Bob Chambers of Duke communicated a message for me. He told them: 'LeRoy doesn't want to dress in your dressing room, they can dress in Durham, which is only twenty-five minutes away. He doesn't request that his team eat in your cafeteria; they will bring their food.' Well, they finally let us in. We then opened up two other Southern track meets. The meets at Furman and South Carolina let us come and open the meets to blacks. Many of the people were not happy when we came out ahead of South Carolina or the University of Georgia. I told my team that some people would be saying, 'Look at those niggers run and jump and throw.' But I stressed that at least some of them would applaud excellence. I told them that if we were to succeed we would have to beat them on the field. All of those things hurt to the core, but I couldn't let it affect me then, because if I had, the young men on my team would not know how to respond to it properly. At the time, every educational body had two organizations: one for whites, one for blacks. Believe it or not, the National Education Association at the time had a white-only clause for membership. I was nominated for the presidency of the North Carolina Association of Health, Physical Education and Recreation. At the time I was functioning more at the national level than the state. C. D. Henry, who was at Grambling at the time and later became associate commissioner of the Big Ten Conference, began breaking the barriers. It just didn't make sense. I was lecturing at the national level but couldn't do it here in North Carolina."

"When I became chairman of the Department of Physical Education at North Carolina Central, there was a big professional meeting at North Carolina State. I got a busload of my students, drove over there, and just entered the room. I took my best students. I had lectured them to offer no resistance if they were stopped. When they saw us they were confused at first and they didn't know what to do with us. We were well-dressed and orderly. They asked me what we wanted and I replied that some of our favorite people were lecturing there and that we wanted to hear them, too. They didn't put us out and that started the breaking down of the racial barrier."

"I never became impervious to it but some of the stuff just got comical. We went to Mississippi to deal with the situation and there was this nice, white lady with whom I had served at the national level. In her best Southern accent she said to me, 'Now, LeRoy, you know that we wouldn't have any problem with this if all of your people were like you and C.D. Henry.' I replied, 'Since you have implied that we are exceptional, why don't you just get a lot of average blacks just like all of the average whites you have in there and then we will have a good mix? She said, 'I get your point.'"

Rome 1960

Following his work under the auspices of the U.S. State Department, two countries, Israel and Ethiopia, asked Walker to coach their national teams for the upcoming Olympic Games in Rome in 1960. He considered it an honor and accepted. "I did not want to have the title of head coach out of deference to their primary coaches who had worked so hard," he said. Walker was also coaching and consulting for Lee Calhoun, who successfully made his second run for the gold in the 110-meter hurdles, the first back-to-back gold medalist in the history of that event. By now Walker had coached two other athletes at North Carolina College to All-America titles: Vance Robinson in the 220-dash and Walter Johnson in the 440.

When he flew to Rome three weeks before the opening of the Olympic Games for final workouts and preparations of the teams of Israel and Ethiopia, he encountered a modern-day manifestation of ancient hatred. He was handling an extremely diverse group of athletes, simultaneously coaching Jews and Arabs. "I ran into trouble because I was also helping a Syrian shot-putter, Saleem el Jisk and, of course, I also had the Israeli shot-putter, Gideon Ariel. Members of the local organizing committees demanded separate practice sites. Some of those venues were two hours apart. In reasoning with them I asked a simple question: 'What happens if they are in the same flight when the Games start? Are you going to ask them to cancel the flight?' I felt the same way many years later in 1994 at Lillehammer when some people were suggesting that we provide separate practice sites for Nancy Kerrigan and Tonya Harding." Walker reminded those protesting that in the ancient Games, warring factions ceased all hostilities for the duration of the competition. That reasoning carried the day. Though small in number, the teams from Israel and Ethiopia competed with confidence.

An unknown marathoner from Ethiopia, Abebe Bikila, took the race away from the favorites. In bare feet, he became the first black African to win a gold medal. He and his coach, Onni Niskanen, Ethiopian Emperor Haile Selassie and LeRoy Walker were among the few people who knew Bikila had the potential to win. Before coming to Rome, Walker had intervened when Ethiopian track officials were about to scuttle their participation in the marathon. According to Walker, "They didn't like that the finish line for the race was not in the grand stadium in Rome but on the more obscure Appian Way." Walker asked for and was granted an audience with Emperor Selassie.

"When the emperor received, he was usually seated," recalled Walker, "a concession to his sensitivity about his height. If more than one English-speaking person at a time met with His Majesty, who spoke several languages, the conversation was interpreted. One-on-one he would converse in English directly without the intervention of interpretation.

"I told him that it was my opinion that the Ethiopian team would have an excellent chance to finish in the top ten, bringing honor and acclaim to his country." Selassie ordered his country's participation in the marathon and Ethiopia became a track power in international competition.

The U.S. took thirty-four gold medals in Rome and enjoyed outstanding performances among its black athletes. Track star Wilma Rudolph turned in three gold medal performances. Rafer Johnson won the gold in the decathlon. Among the most talkative and talked-about Americans was a brash 18-year-old boxer named Cassius Clay. A gifted and superbly trained athlete, he took the gold with seeming ease in the light heavyweight division. The teenager would later change his name to Muhammad Ali and become the most recognized and beloved athlete in the world.

In Rome, Walker continued to make friends among the coaches and athletes around the world. His now growing reputation for sharing his coaching talent and experience with smaller nations, particularly on the continent of Africa, was being noted in many capitals. Yet, some U.S. coaches were viewing his success with some trepidation. At first Walker ignored the remarks that suggested that he was, in effect, working against his own country's Olympic effort. The comments were finally put to rest when Walker, in a flash of anger, shouted, "What do you expect me to do, coach them to lose?"

Mama Dies

When Mary Walker died in the Spring of 1961, she had lived to see the beginning of her youngest son's accomplishments in education and athletics. While she was supportive of all her children, it was LeRoy in whom she had invested her grandest dreams of success and accomplishment. She had observed in him the intellect and the will of an achiever. He had not disappointed her. She had looked on with typical motherly pride as LeRoy distinguished himself as an athlete, scholar, coach of Olympians, and a father and husband in a loving marriage. Not long before Mary Walker died, LeRoy visited her in Atlanta where they shared conversation on the front porch of his childhood home. His memory of that last visit was that Mary was "really feeling good about me and the family." As old age approached, she was steadfast in her desire to stay in the home where she had reared her large family. Following a short illness, Mary died at home. She was buried next to her beloved Willie.

Mary Walker never knew the extent of her influence on LeRoy nor how often he would draw on her simple teachings. He would, for the rest of his life, revere her name, and forever credit her with providing the bedrock of his strength. In an interview with the author in Atlanta on the morning following the closing ceremonies of the Olympic Games and thirty-five years after Mary's death, he said:

> Throughout my life, when things got roughest, I would just remember some simple saying from this little, uneducated, but wise woman I called 'Mama,' and it would help me through the difficulty.

§

The Sixties were a turbulent time for America and LeRoy Walker. They also proved very productive for him. One of the most frequent comments about Walker relates to the way he runs his meetings. He honed his skills with the gavel because he saw it as a necessity for forceful leadership. He studied until he had mastered the very nuances of parliamentary procedure. His preparation for any event over which he was presiding was complete and he is seldom caught off guard. Shortly after returning from Rome he was elected President of the Central Intercollegiate Athletic Association. His leadership skills now recognized, he would spend the rest of his life in executive positions of professional organizations representing athletics or education. In 1961, the first of several books he would author over the decades of his career, *A Manual In Adapted-Advanced Physical Education* was published. In the Summer of 1962 he was invited again by the State Department to participate in an exchange program, this time to Haiti and Jamaica.

By the Summer of 1963, Martin Luther King Jr. had galvanized the Civil Rights Movement when a quarter-of-a-million people joined him at the Lincoln Memorial in Washington, D.C., to hear his immortal "I Have a Dream" speech. There was a stirring in the country. Voices, both eloquent and angry, were beginning to move people to action. Martin Luther King was recruiting some of the brightest and best of the black youth to his side. Among them were Andrew Young, Jesse Jackson and Ralph Abernathy. In a bewildering mix of ideologies, young blacks were exposed to the emerging philosophies of Malcolm X, Stokely Carmichael, LeRoi Jones and Eldridge Cleaver. From King to Cleaver—however different their solutions—there was a common cry: The time for action was now. Events and the winds of change would combine to alter the course of history.

On Friday, November 22, 1963 the nation was deeply traumatized by the assassination of President John F. Kennedy by a disturbed young man named Lee Harvey Oswald. Oswald shot the President from a sixth-floor window of a schoolbook depository building in Dallas, Texas as Kennedy rode past in an open car. The young President had been especially appealing to the youth of America, having stimulated their sense of responsibility to a world community by creating the Peace Corps, sending workaday American ambassadors to the far corners of the globe. From pre-Thanksgiving holiday week exuberance, Americans everywhere were suddenly plunged into shock, sorrow and confusion, and nowhere more than on college campuses. At North Carolina College in Durham, the faculty attempted to be of some comfort to the students while they themselves were devastated. Walker remembers: "Many of us gathered on the floor of the gym. We just looked at each other. There was not much talking, just stunned disbelief." The climate of the times affected nearly every American in some way. College staff and faculty braced for an unprecedented and sustained period of student unrest.

Coaching Recognition

The track program at North Carolina Central University was now boasting a coach of international reputation and Walker's recruiting could begin at another level. He no longer had to begin an interview by explaining who he was. From Trinidad, Walker recruited a formidable sprinter named Edwin Roberts. The foundation of Walker's relationship with his athletes was multifaceted, but rooted in the deep respect the young men had for a coach who was showing them a record of proven results. There was also the fear of going against him and his policies. Walker has always operated on the theory that a successful program is not possible unless the coach holds all the power and that no single athlete, no matter how accomplished, be allowed to jeopardize the team. He was a stickler for the rules and regulations under which his athletes lived and performed. An infraction, depending on its severity, was sure to result in punishment.

As an enforcer, he had no peer. As competitive as he was, Walker would not hesitate to suspend an athlete from a track meet, sometimes more than one, even if the decision meant certain defeat in specific events. While making sure his rules were applied fairly and evenly, Walker was superbly gifted at customizing his treatment of athletes as individuals. "As a track coach, I could not treat everybody alike," he said. "I had guys on my team who, if I talked above a whisper, they would go to pieces. They did not want to see me upset. If I yelled at them, they could not even come out of the blocks. There were others that I could yell at and they not only could take that, but responded to it. But I was always fair with them." Could Walker coach the athletes of a modern-day track team with the same firm, if not dictatorial, methods today? He smiled and replied, "They would either abide by the rules or they wouldn't be on my team."

While the Sixties ushered in a wide range of permissiveness, Walker was steadfast in his insistence for order, restraint, adherence to rules and discipline. He abhorred what he saw as a capitulation of authority by many college administrators. Edwin Roberts qualified for the 1964 Olympic team in the 200-meter and in Tokyo he won the bronze medal. Walker was in Tokyo in the capacity of consultant to the teams of Trinidad and Tobago. Superstar that he was, Roberts was not above the disciplines laid down by his coach. Once when the athlete abruptly left for a surprise visit to Trinidad, Walker's response was swift. "I took Edwin off the team," said Walker, "but I didn't remove his scholarship. He was a three-time winner in the Penn relays, three-time winner at the CIAA as well as an Olympic Bronze medalist. "I made that decision because of what he had done to his teammates. He had let themdown." In a later incident, Walker would leave hurdle and relay star Melvin Bassett on the sidelines at the prestigious Milrose Games "as a disciplinary action."

It was also during the early Sixties that Walker recruited the man he still considers to be the best all-round athlete he ever coached, Norman Tate from New Jersey. Tate became a national champion in the long and triple jump. In 1968, he became another of Walker's illustrious Olympians when he represented the United States in the triple jump at the 1968 Games in Mexico City.

Assassinations of MLK & JFK

It was in the Spring of 1968 that Martin Luther King Jr. became embroiled in a dispute involving garbage workers in Memphis, Tennessee. In his quest for equality for African-Americans, the young preacher had been jailed, spat upon, reviled and stoned. He had also received the Nobel Peace Prize and, like Gandhi, was securing a place in history reserved for those who become the champions of the oppressed.

Americans were witnessing a frightening escalation of racial violence. The world watched the pathetic spectacle of young, black, civil rights protesters being shot, beaten, attacked by police dogs, sprayed with powerful fire hoses, and arrested and jailed by the hundreds for daring to ask for basic civil rights, in a country founded on a document declaring that all men were created equal.

Television news, which had established a new level of excellence in both technology and journalistic commitment during and following the John Kennedy assassination, was placing the country's trauma directly into America's living room. King was steadfast in preaching to the young that the only acceptable response to their enemies was nonviolence. The chant, "We ain't gonna let nobody turn us around" spoke to the movement's resolve.

King had ignited a fire that could neither be doused nor drowned in the tears that followed his murder in Memphis. A few days before King went to Memphis, Walker was in Philadelphia for a meeting. King was in the city and Walker, through a minister friend, was included as an invited guest at a late dinner. King discussed his upcoming trip to Memphis and when others expressed fear for his safety, Walker recalled. "I had the feeling that Martin had already prepared himself for what might happen to him." On April 4, when James Earl Ray fired the bullet that killed King, he set off a seething rage that quickly enveloped the country. Riots broke out in the major cities and the burning of city blocks was commonplace.

In Raleigh, North Carolina, a curfew was imposed and martial law declared. On the campus of North Carolina Central and the other black colleges in the state and nation, administrators tried to cool the inflamed passions of their students. President Lyndon Johnson implored, "Let us, for God's sake, resolve to live under the law."He and many leaders around the country, white and black, knew the tension had reached a flash point. Two months later, a Jordanian immigrant shot and killed Robert Kennedy, the slain President's brother, shortly after a speech to political supporters in Los Angeles. The nation's anxiety was heightened by the growing opposition to America's escalating involvement in the Vietnam War. It was an angry and confusing time, but yet an opportunity for charismatic activists to vie for the political hearts and souls of the nation's youth.

Harry Edwards, an activist from California, went to the training site at Lake Tahoe and urged black athletes representing the United States to boycott the 1968 Olympic Games to express opposition to the oppressive treatment of American blacks. Unable to achieve that, he exhorted them to make some visible display of protest during the Games.

Olympic Backlash

It was against this backdrop that the U.S. Olympic Team prepared for the Games in Mexico City. The Games were among the most unusual and controversial in Olympic history. The chapter describing them in the USOC publication "Athens to Atlanta" is titled "Attitude and Altitude," a reference to the two-pronged atmosphere that marked the Games.

The thin air at 7,000 feet allowed athletes to break an amazing number of Olympic and world records.U.S. long-jumper Bob Beamon took flight to soar almost two feet beyond the previous world record and runners from the high-altitude regions of Africa did particularly well. Even before the Games, the U.S. coaches, the International Olympic Committee and its American president, Avery Brundage, were worried about the rumors of demonstrations by the black athletes. At the training camp Walker had a chance to talk with some of them. "When I talked with John Carlos, Tommie

Smith, Lee Evans and the other people there, I was trying to get them to understand that they must be ready to pay the price for whatever they were getting ready to do," said Walker. "'Because if you falter', I told them, 'whatever good you think is going to come of this is not going to happen.' I knew what the price was going to be. I knew they would be expelled. Now, they never told me what they intended to do. I didn't learn that until it actually happened." Walker urged that dignity be one of their considerations, "and then be willing to pay the price to the end," he told them."They did, and it affected them for a long time. John Carlos hasn't recovered yet in many ways."

The Olympic world was shocked at the demonstration that took place at the medal peristyle when American athletes Tommie Smith and John Carlos were receiving their gold and bronze medals for the 200-meter. When the national anthem was played, they made their move. With heads bowed, they raised gloved, clenched fists. The images shot around the world on television; the still pictures made every news publication on the planet. Avery Brundage and the IOC were furious. They took the athletes' medals and banished them from the Games.

Walker and others, including Jesse Owens, who had tried to reason with the athletes felt the brunt of a backlash. "We were called 'Uncle Toms,' recalled Walker. "They indicated they thought Jesse and I were trying to get them to forego the protest because we had been influenced by Brundage and others. I never even talked with the leaders. But it was implicit with some and explicit with others that Jesse and I had fallen victim to the power structure. It hurt."

Walker Joins the Peace Corps

In the mid-Sixties, Walker considered resigning from North Carolina College. No one except Katherine knew about his thoughts. Considering the success he was enjoying as a coach and the recognition he was receiving for his track program, it is difficult to imagine that anything could turn his head. The seducer was the Peace Corps. "I was granted a leave of absence from the college when Jack Vaughn, head of the Peace Corps, Sargent Shriver and Marie Gasden said they needed me to head up programming and training for the Corps on the continent of Africa.After being there for nearly two years, I was ready to resign from the college and stay with the Corps on a permanent basis. I loved the work. "We would train individuals in language in the three-week period, even taught them to speak it with the proper dialects. Our training center was in the Virgin Islands. We totally immersed them in the spoken language, no writing, no conjugation of verbs, just oral communication. The immersion theory meant you had to learn to speak it to survive. A lot of colleges and universities picked that up from the Peace Corps.

"There were two things that bothered me in those days about how we were conducting the work of the organization. In every country there was an assigned group called the 'host-country nationals.' No one from that group held a responsible position but simply performed menial tasks for us. So I posed the question, 'Why?' We had a document called the "104," a program proposal submitted by the country's director, that I could use on Capitol Hill to ask for money to support those projects around the world.The problem was that the same American directors were filling out the "104" with their pet projects with little or no regard for what a particular country needed.

"I changed three things: We began doing our language immersion training in the host countries, the host country nationals were allowed to have a greater leadership role and we stopped having directors' meetings in Washington. (The first meeting we had had there was a disaster. Everybody was running back and forth to Capitol Hill to see their congressman or senator. One year I moved the meeting to a remote location in Virginia. It was a place so isolated that if you couldn't find the person who brought you there, you could not find your way out. They didn't like it there so we began to hold directors' meetings in host countries.)

"In the Peace Corps, the most distasteful thing I dealt with was when the civil war broke out in Nigeria. I had to move 600 Peace

Corps volunteers out of there to, of all places, Uganda. At the time one of my best directors was in Uganda. It was before Idi Amin came to power. (When I had known him he was just a sergeant, not a powerful person in the country.) "We even had the warring factions meet in Kampala. I will never forget that. That is where we had the first meeting—trying to negotiate. Of course they stayed at two separate hotels.

"I loved the Peace Corps. I could see the positive changes it was making. I enjoyed the people I worked with. I became friends with C. Paine Lucas who became the head of Afri-Care. I was prepared to submit my resignation to the college when the White House decided to get rid of Jack Vaughn. When I returned from the Games in Mexico City, I had decided by then that I would not resign since I was not sure now of the direction of the Peace Corps."

The Peace Corps experience, now combined with that of the State Department's exchange programs, made Walker popular in scores of countries where his hard work as a volunteer had been greatly appreciated and recognized for its impact. Walker was building a network of friends around the world and other international contacts that would bode well for him in so many ways in the coming decades.

The Bridal Suite

Walker believed that involvement in local and national educational organizations was important to growth and progress, a chance to mingle with other professionals, attend lectures and exchange ideas. Organizations began taking notice of his growing reputation and, as a result, electing him to leadership positions. He was elected president of the Southern District of the African Alliance for Health, Physical Education and Recreation. During the time he was an officer in his state organization, Walker flew to Gainesville, Florida as a delegate to a conference. While his reservations had been made and confirmed in advance, he was not allowed to register when he reached the hotel. "When they saw that a black face belonged to the name on their reservations list, they weren't interested in having me for a customer," said Walker.

Upon learning of the situation, the other delegates went to the hotel's management and threatened to leave en masse if the hotel refused Walker lodging. The manager agreed to put him in the most isolated room on the premises—the bridal suite on the top floor. The black members of the hotel staff, no doubt taking the cue from management, treated Walker just as shabbily. They refused to handle his luggage and the elevator operator balked at taking him upstairs. Walker endured the insults and before the convention was over, "the hotel staff would learn that I was just as civilized and genteel as anyone else."

In his own city of Durham, North Carolina, when he stepped off the campus, he and all other blacks were required to drink from separate water fountains. There, and in public places throughout the South, fountains were marked "colored" and "whites."

The passage of the Civil Rights Act of 1964 did not have an immediate impact in many parts of the South. On a trip to Greenville, South Carolina where his was the first black team to participate in the Furman Relays, LeRoy and Katherine joined their friends Al Buehler, track coach at Duke, and his wife, Delaina, for breakfast at a restaurant that was a part of a national chain. "We sat there for forty-five minutes until it dawned on us that they were dodging around our table and did not intend to serve us," recalled Buehler, "This was in the Sixties. I came from another part of the country and had never seen that."

"You sometimes just forgot that you might be subjected to those things even though you were guests of the universities," Walker said. Walker never dwelled on the incidents, nor allowed his energy to be drained by them. "I just try to find a solution as quickly as possible." While Walker deflects bitterness and rancor associated with the racism he has encountered, there are some scars he cannot erase. "You know I still feel a little shiver going up to Stone Mountain, Georgia," he said. The mountain of solid granite, a half-hour's drive from Atlanta, came to represent for African-Americans the impenetrable rock of racism in America.

The Ku Klux Klan was first organized shortly after the Civil War but was reborn on the night before Thanksgiving 1915 on top of Stone Mountain when a group of white supremacists gathered to launch a campaign of acts, words and deeds that would fulfill the Klan's original goal to "terrify darkies and keep them in their place." One of the delegates that night wrote, "Under a blazing cross, the invisible empire was called from its slumber." The Venable family owned the mountain and gave the north face of it to the United Daughters of the Confederacy for the sole purpose of carving a monument to three confederate heroes, Jefferson Davis, president of the confederacy, and the generals Robert E. Lee and "Stonewall" Jackson. The magnificent work was the largest bas-relief sculpture in the world, but for some the gray stone stands for a place where violence against them originated. "Think of all the scars we got while I was growing up," said Walker, "reading about the lynchings, and the black people who simply disappeared, never to be heard of again."

As often as they happened to Walker in those days, the nasty incidents were never discussed by him in public. In all the times during long car trips, track meets or social occasions with his good friend Al Buehler, Walker never mentioned the racist incidents, even though some of them occurred in Buehler's presence. "The thing I like and respect about LeRoy is that even after the Civil Rights legislation, he never attempted to take advantage of the politics of race," said Buehler. "There are others who used the clout of affirmative action, but LeRoy never went that way at all. That is why he is held with such respect. That is why he became President of the United States Olympic Committee."

Walker was reluctant to share these stories with the author. He was never able to insulate the pain. But when times were hardest I could hear my mother saying, "Don't allow this environment to determine what you do. Be the best person you can be, do the best job you can possibly do, and you will find that there are enough fair-minded people in the world who will finally recognize it."

Cush and Judi

For several years, beginning in high school, LeRoy Walker, Jr. dated a pretty young lady from Greensboro who had enrolled at North Carolina Central. She was a frequent visitor in the Walker home and Katherine's affection for her grew and was strengthened by the possibility that the young woman would be her future daughter-in-law.

LeRoy, Jr. also had enjoyed a friendship with schoolmate Judith "Judi" Burton since sixth grade. Their "buddy" relationship continued into the college years and according to LeRoy, Jr. could not be considered initially, in any respect, to be "romantic."

However, on one autumn afternoon, following a homecoming football game, feelings would change quickly and dramatically. LeRoy, Jr. recalled: "I was talking with a friend when Judi walked up wearing a lavender outfit. It was as if I had never seen her before in my life. Alarms went off, bells began to ring, and I asked her for a date!" A year later Judi accepted his engagement ring. Katherine had difficulty accepting the idea that her son's affections had been turned from the girl in Greensboro. "My mother was a wonderful person, but hard-headed," said LeRoy, Jr. As hard as he tried he could not bring together the two most important women in his life. His father finally advised him to let go, and to stop trying to force a relationship. He said, "Give it time and it will either come about or not but you can't keep forcing it." The young man took the advice and began to view the situation with some hopelessness. LeRoy, Jr. and Judi were married on July 30, 1969 following a three-year engagement.

Later, in the last few weeks of Judi's pregnancy with their first child Shawn, Katherine volunteered to come to their home in Queens, New York to be with them during the time surrounding the birth. She was very helpful and supportive during that time, but LeRoy, Jr. could see that the healing of the relationship between the two women had not occurred. He could recognize, however, that his mother absolutely cherished her grandson.

Nearly four years later when their second child, Melodie, was born, Katherine asked if she could return to help out. This time LeRoy, Jr. was less than receptive to the idea. He related to his mother his disappointment in the tone of her previous "nursing" visit. Then, in a frank discussion with his wife about his reluctance to have his mother come again, Judi, in her forgiving way, urged LeRoy, Jr. to invite her. "It was like night and day. My mother and Judi became the very best of friends and loved each other dearly from that day forward. It was a burden lifted," LeRoy, Jr. recalled. "It did my heart good." Judi would become Katherine's friend, confidante and defender.

❖

CHAPTER FIVE

THE SEVENTIES

The Pan-Africa-USA Games—1971

The decade of the Seventies would further define LeRoy Walker's talents and career as a coach and administrator. Teaming up with Duke's Al Buehler the two would make history by staging some of the most exciting and successful track meets on record. By now Buehler was well established as head track coach with considerable skill and one who had already coordinated large meets. For years he staged an event called the Duke-Durham Relays, which drew thousands of athletes from a half-dozen states.

Walker's work on the African continent had been a catalyst and a unifying force in his being able to persuade belligerent African countries to come together for the greater good of their continent's athletic representation in international competition. This was a giant step for the Africans. Walker's contacts resulted in plans for the Pan-Africa vs. USA meet at Duke on July 16-17, 1971. African athletes would have the opportunity to travel, as part of a united team to the United States. The event would mark the first two-day international meet presented at Duke's Wallace Wade Stadium.

The meet attracted 52,000 spectators! The fans were treated to memorable sports' moments. In the 5,000-meter run, the great Oregon runner Steve Prefontaine defeated Miruts Yifter the beloved distance runner and national sports hero from Ethiopia. Yifter, confused by the language differences, was not sure of the printed lap signs and to the horror of his coaches, began his sprint with two laps to go, believing it to be his last. He passed Prefontaine, heading toward the finish line to break the tape. There was no tape. Realizing he was a lap short of the race, the exhausted Ethiopian struggled on, to be passed up quickly by Prefontaine now in full sprint.

The next day Yifter entered the 10,000-meter race against the great American runner Frank Shorter, just out of Yale, who would, in 1972, win the marathon in Munich. Buehler now had to make sure Yifter would hear a bell, as he had in Europe, and see the signs with huge numbers designating laps to go. The older man beat the younger Shorter, and the crowd, aware of what had happened to Yifter the day before, "went wild" cheering him to victory. The visitors from Africa, in colorful native dress, brought their drums to the stands, held up their scoreboards titled "Black vs. White," and had a marvelous time of it. Nothing like this had ever taken place before and the impact was overwhelmingly positive. Walker and Buehler were elated, as were their respective schools and, for the city of Durham, the Games were credited for having had a unifying effect on the people.

§

In the euphoric afterglow of that success in Durham, Walker and Buehler looked forward to the 1972 Olympic Games in Munich, West Germany. Buehler was selected to serve as team manager for the U.S. Track and Field Team while Walker would again be associated with a foreign team. The national team of Kenya asked him to serve as consultant.His connection to that African nation had been strengthened by his recruiting and coaching to stardom two of Kenya's native sons, Robert Ouko and Julius Sang. A strong stable of track stars came out of Walker's program in the Seventies. He sent three athletes to the Games in Munich: Larry Black and the two Kenyans, Ouko and Sang. All would come home with medals.

The head track and field coach for the U.S. at Munich was Bill Bowerman from the University of Oregon who had earned outstanding credentials, as had his assistant, an outstanding African-American coach named Stan Wright. In some ways Wright's career had paralleled that of LeRoy Walker. Beginning in 1950 at Texas Southern, over the next seventeen years he produced more than thirty All-American track stars and two Olympians, he served as assistant coach for the Pan-American Team and moved to Western Illinois, the first African-American in the department. Munich was not Wright's first experience as an assistant at the Olympic level.

"In 1968, I was the only black coach on the track staff in Mexico City," he said, "and I got involved in the athletes' protest. It was so intense because I was against the boycott. LeRoy Walker supported me. I caught hell. Harry Edwards, who was inciting the boycott, threatened me. He told me if I showed up for the trials I would be shot. Athlete Lee Evans wrote to ask me not to come to the trials in Los Angeles because he was afraid I would be killed. At the Coliseum in 1968 I had bodyguards all the time." Wright's dream was to become head coach for the U.S. Track and Field Team." I should have been head coach in Munich. It was a tie vote between Bowerman and me. So the New York Athletic Club, which was making the selection, told me they wanted co-coaches. I refused.They then held a telephone vote and Bowerman won by a single vote. It was politics. I was black."

Walker, Buehler, Bowerman and Wright departed their respective campuses in a high state of anticipation. Each had every reason to believe the Games in Munich would be memorable. They were.

September 5, 1972...Olympic Village...Munich, Germany

He held back the tears until he reached his room. Now, LeRoy Walker wept alone. His anguish and pain came in waves, as did the questions. Why had this unspeakable horror taken the lives of his friends? How could the blood of athletes and coaches be flowing at the Olympic Games, the time set aside for the youth of the world to gather for competition in peace and friendship? Why must the purity and tradition of the Games be sacrificed now at this time and place? Walker had so believed in, and held sacred, the sanctity of the Olympic spirit. Had he not personally volunteered much of his professional life to the ideal of international sport competition in a number of countries around the world? Now the ideal lay as shattered as the bodies of the victims. How did his Israeli friends die? Were they shot, burned, or blown up? How much terror and pain did they endure before the cloak of death had relieved them?

As Walker wept in his room, tears flowed in many quarters as details of the Palestinian terrorist attack on the Israelis were flashed around the world. Walker thought about the families of the victims. He thought about his wife, Katherine, and their two children, safe at home in Durham, North Carolina. He was suddenly lonely and heartsick. Since 1956 he had been a part of the Olympic Games. "I sat there and tried hard to keep my composure," he recalled, "but I was so sad and stricken by this that I wanted to go home. To hell with the Games." Walker's revulsion at the news of the massacre was the same gut-wrenching feeling he had experienced when hearing of the assassination of Martin Luther King Jr. and President John Kennedy. "Initially I no longer had that inner feeling of why we were there, or why we could go on," he said.

Meanwhile, Avery Brundage, the only American to have served as President of the International Olympic Committee, and other IOC officials quickly called a meeting and decided to continue the Games, following a day of mourning for the eleven Israelis. It was a controversial decision. Many, particularly in Israel, thought the Games should have been called off. Several of the surviving Israeli athletes, however, including their team leader, argued that if the Games were canceled, then the terrorists had won. Walker would also come around to that conclusion.

At the memorial service the next day Walker sat close to what was left of the Israeli delegation, some of whom were afraid to show up. American swimming sensation Mark Spitz, a Jew, had already completed his events, winning a record-breaking seven gold medals, and was quickly flown out of Germany under heavy security.

In a somber ceremony, the International Olympic family grieved for the murdered athletes and coaches. As Walker sat there contemplating his loss of friends, he also realized that the days of free movement and safety that had been enjoyed during the Games, the passes that allowed spectators to walk freely about Olympic Village, the mixing with athletes for autographs and picture taking, were now lost forever. He thought too, of the possibility that he might have been caught in the violent trap with the Israelis.

The story of the slaughter is one of shock and disbelief. The killings took place on the world's stage. Arab terrorists stormed the Israeli dormitory at 31 Connollystrasse in Olympic Village in the early morning hours of September 5. The eight young gunmen killed two Israelis on their way into the quarters. About twenty hours later, at a near-by military airport, nine other helpless Israeli athletes and coaches, some tied inside helicopters, died writhing and screaming in a hail of bullets and fire.

Golda Meir was Prime Minister of Israel. That country always sent a small but enthusiastic group of athletes to the Games. Many in the delegation were well-known to LeRoy Walker. In 1960 he had coached the Israeli Olympic Track and Field Team in Rome. The relatively small numbers of people created an atmosphere for close personal relationships. Walker looked forward to seeing some of the coaches he had worked with, some of them former athletes. An informal reunion was planned for the American coach and his Israeli friends for the evening of September 4.

"We were going to get together in the quarters of the Israeli Team in Olympic Village," recalled Walker, "we had already gotten together some food, fruit, and soft drinks from the cafeteria for the occasion. We looked forward to being with each other again and sharing memories. As it turned out, I was probably spared when we postponed our get-together in order to watch an Israeli athlete who had made it to the semifinals in her event."

When the decision was made to bring the Games to Munich, Willy Brandt and his West German government were elated that one of their cities would be the focus of positive international attention. The Germans were acutely sensitive to considerations of image. The last time the Games had been held in Germany, Adolf Hitler and the Nazis were in control.

This time, security enforcement would be laced with a goodly measure of concern for public relations. Uniforms were to be minimized so that many security people in civilian clothing would blend into the crowd. Athletes' living quarters had been surrounded by fences of a height that, in some places, presented little challenge for healthy young athletes and coaches. It was not unusual to observe scalings of the fence by athletes wanting to party in town after curfew. While security guards were stationed at the gates of the fences, some had been known to turn their heads, as the more aggressive young people stole some night life by violating the curfew and the barrier.

The Games had not been presented on German soil since 1936 when American Jesse Owens was shunned by Hitler. Hitler had counted on representatives of the German "super-race" to outperform the rest of the world. Hitler saw the Games as a golden opportunity for public relations and a propaganda forum for his dogma.

By the time the Games ended, the name Jesse Owens was on the lips of countless millions around the globe. In performances that electrified the world, Owens, a young African-American athlete, swept gold medals in the 100- and 200-meter sprints, the long jump, and the 4 x 100 meter relay. Hitler sat in his track side box in the stadium and congratulated each medalist with a handshake, adding a special flourish of enthusiasm for those from Germany. It was only when Owens won his first gold medal that Hitler found an excuse to leave the stadium. It was widely theorized that Hitler did not want to put himself in the position of congratulating and shaking hands with the black American. 1936 ended Germany's chances of hosting the Games until 1972. After World War II, the Games resumed in

London in 1948, the city still bearing massive scars of Hitler's bombs. As the West Germans planned for the 1972 Games, they wanted Munich to show the world that it was a place of friendship and hospitality, and there would be nothing to remind visitors of the War or the Nazis. In Olympic Village, the Israeli athletes were assigned to Building 31, a three-story structure, and most of the delegation, fifteen of them, had rooms there.

Among the victims were friends of Walker. There was 40-year-old Coach Amitzur Shapira, who had called Walker to share his excitement at being selected. "I recall that he was in a state of ecstasy over his rising to the position of coach since the days we first met in 1960," said Walker. Moshe Weinberg, 33-year-old wrestling coach, had been a competitor in Rome in 1960 and he and Walker had become friends. It is thought that Weinberg was killed first in the attack.

At the time of the massacre, the Israelis had won no medals nor distinguished themselves in the contests with the exception of Esther Shahmorov. In the early hours of the night of the terrorist attack, she reached the semifinals in the women's 100-meter dash. Walker had gone to watch her compete. "While I was there they asked me to analyze the race for broadcast to Israel," recalled Walker. In the wake of the massacre, instead of competing in the upcoming finals the next day, Shahmorov would find herself flying home with a coffin containing her murdered coach.

According to wire reports and *Time Magazine*, at just before 4:30 on the morning of September 5, there was a tap on the door of Moshe Weinberg's three-room apartment he shared with others. Weinberg cracked the door, saw hooded gunmen, and in a final act of courage, flattened his body against the door and began yelling for the others to get out. Some did. Weinberg died in a hail of gunfire that poured through the door from the outside.

Wrestler Joseph Romano was beaten and stabbed, but not before putting up a fight. He collapsed and died.

The Arabs quickly seized nine others: 18-year-old wrestler Mark Slavin; 27-year-old fencing coach Andre Spitzer; 53-year-old shooting coach Kehat Shorr; 24-year-old wrestler Eliezer Halfin; 28-year-old weight lifter David Berger; 28-year-old weight lifter Ze'ev Friedman; 52-year-old weightlifting referee Ya'acov Springer; 40-year-old track and field coach Amitzur Shapira; and 40-year-old wrestling referee Yosef Gottbreund, who, like Weinberg, held the door to his apartment shut as long as he could so others could escape.

About 9 a.m., the Arabs made their demands known to the West German authorities in a note they threw from a window. The guerrilla group identified itself as Black September and demanded the immediate release of 200 Arab guerrillas being held in Israeli prisons and vowed to kill the hostages if their demands were not met. As the Olympic day began, most of the thousands of athletes, coaches, and spectators were not aware of the attack. As the day wore on, more and more people at the Games became aware of the crisis through the live radio and television reports being broadcast to the world. When we learned about the hostages being taken," Walker said, "we could look up and see the terrorists in their hoods walking around in the rooms. We were all asking each other what the demands might be, but at that time we felt confident it could be worked out."

Israeli Prime Minister Golda Meir and her government in Tel Aviv, true to national policy of never giving in to terrorists, rejected the demand. To buy time, negotiators in Munich led the kidnappers to believe that their demands were being worked out. In truth, an ambush was being planned. The Germans brought up sharpshooters, police, and troops in armored vehicles and sealed off that part of the Olympic Village. The Germans' immediate goal was to get the Arabs to move themselves and their captives out of Olympic Village. Negotiations went on throughout the day with the terrorists setting deadlines, then moving them forward in the belief that Israel would capitulate.

That night the captors ordered a bus to the compound to take them and their hostages to waiting helicopters nearby. Just after ten o'clock, three helicopters lifted out of Olympic Village, two containing the Arabs and hostages, the third German officials and negotiators. They flew to a military airport fifteen miles away in Furstenfeldbruck, where a Lufthansa jet was waiting on the runway, ostensibly to take them to Cairo. The Germans, however, had already privately resolved that no matter what developed, the plane would never leave the ground. The airfield would be the site of the ambush. West German officials had already "considered the Israeli hostages dead" the moment they learned that Tel Aviv had privately refused the terrorists' demands.

There was, and still is, controversy and mixed opinions about the decisions that led to the events that followed. Shortly after the helicopters landed near the jet at the military field, several of the terrorists got out and began to move about the tarmac. In the dark beyond the spotlighted plane and helicopters, crouched the German forces that would execute the ambush. Among them were five sharpshooters assigned to kill the eight terrorists at the first opportunity. The first shot set off a firefight that ended only after five of the Arabs were killed and the other three surrendered. When the smoke cleared, all of the Israelis were dead, some of them machine-gunned by the guerrillas as soon as the shooting started, others burned to death when, it was theorized, a terrorist threw a hand-grenade into one of the helicopters carrying the bound athletes and coaches.

Back at Olympic Village, Walker and thousands of others were holding out hope for the safe release of the hostages. A rumor surfaced that a rescue by the Germans had been successful and that the captives were safe. Later came the devastating news of the massacre. Walker had gone to bed with confidence that the hostages would somehow be saved, only to be awakened in the wee hours and told that all of them were dead.

The memorial service was attended by 80,000 people. A German symphony orchestra played Beethoven's "Eroica" while the crowd sat in stunned silence, many quietly weeping. Walker sat in despair with the Israelis. "At that moment the Games were no longer important to me."

Martin Luther King Games

Durham drew 20,000 people for the one-day track meet. That was unheard of.

—Al Buehler, Duke University

Following the assassination of Martin Luther King Jr., a track meet was organized in his name to honor his contribution to America's black youth. For the first few years the Games were held in Philadelphia. As attendance and sponsorships began to wane, organizers looked elsewhere. LeRoy Walker, whose reputation and credentials were now nationally recognized, was approached about the possibility of staging the 1973 games at Duke's facility, now named Wallace Wade Stadium in honor of the school's legendary football coach.

The response to the request was met with enthusiasm by Al Buehler. All parties involved saw the opportunity to reach out in a spirit of cooperation and unity to perhaps defuse some racial tension that had reached powder-keg proportions in America. The unrest on the college campuses in North Carolina was a part of what was taking place across the nation. Administrators at both private and state-supported institutions struggled with a new and much more strident development of the movement: black power.

Some students occupied Duke University's administration building, and supported by hundreds of others, fought back at police until tear gas was finally used. At UNC Chapel Hill, the students organized to support a cafeteria worker's strike. The confrontation resulted in a melee, resulting in the closing of one of the main campus cafeterias. Students at North Carolina Central and other black colleges in the area, Shaw University and St. Augustines in Raleigh, organized protest marches. It was into this general climate that Al Buehler and LeRoy Walker accepted the challenge of staging the Martin Luther King Games in Durham.

The coaches in tandem were impressive and their enthusiasm and positive approach to the project gained support from academicians. A noted sociologist on the faculty at Duke helped sell the idea to the university and found compassion for the project. The city of Durham and its mayor were supportive and, in retrospect, it was with considerable courage on the part of all factions involved that this event was launched in a Southern city during such a racially volatile period. Buehler believes that "Duke is not credited for some of the things it did at that time very quietly." The two coaches went to work. While Duke would donate the facilities, they figured they needed $20,000 for expenses to put on the Games. The two of them appeared together to request $10,000 from the city, and another $10,000 from the Durham Merchants Bureau. They were convincing. "We were Barnum and Bailey," said Buehler. "LeRoy was beating the drum and I was there representing Duke." Buehler's title was Meet Director, Walker was Meet Coordinator. "Walker's job was to get the athletes there," said Buehler, "and my job was to run the show."

The MLK Games were staged on May 12, 1973 and were a colossal success. The official attendance figure of 20,600 was astounding. "For a one-day track meet," Buehler said, "that was unheard of! Philadelphia had drawn only 8,000 to 10,000." The success of the Games had many positive implications for the two coaches, the two schools, the city of Durham, and the state of North Carolina. The teaming of the coaches and the resources from black and white schools in a Southern city during a racially volatile time for an event that saluted King and the black movement was unique.

Charles Foster

I wasn't a bad guy, I was spirited, let's just put it that way. Today Dr. Walker is my chief confidante, daddy, the whole works—everything.

—Charles Wayne Foster,
former NCCU track star and World Champion

In 1976, upon the occasion of receiving UNC's coveted O. Max Gardner Award, "for contributions to the welfare of the human race," LeRoy Walker's remarks shed illuminating insight into his teaching philosophy and his encompassing love for young people and sports.

"Sport and physical education are the microcosm of life itself and thus serve as a laboratory where a positive value system may be formulated and developed." He continued, "What a joy of effort there is in observing students, the gifted and not so gifted, the typical and the atypical, discover that the most precious gift of all possessions is the power over themselves, the power to withstand trial, to bear suffering, to front danger, power over pleasure and pain, power to follow convictions however resisted by menace and scorn.

The power of calm reliance in scenes of darkness and storm." Scattered around the United States and in some of the far corners of the world are adults who spent part of their youth under the direct influence of LeRoy Walker. Their successes and their contributions to their communities are the source of Walker's greatest professional satisfaction. They are his legacy. Among them are physicians, attorneys, professors, coaches or chieftains in government and industry. Entering college, most had two things in common—they were African-Americans, and they came from families at the lower end of the economic scale.

In his decades of coaching and teaching at North Carolina Central, Walker dealt with a different kind of youngster from, for instance, those enrolled across town at the Duke University. Walker's charges, money aside, were perhaps in other ways even more needful. They needed more reassurance, a way to build more confidence, a way to earn a living, a guideline for attaining independence, and in many cases they needed a surrogate parent. If our soul is mirrored by those we have impacted, then the story of one of Walker's liveliest athletes is instructive.

If there is a living, breathing, embodiment of the essence of LeRoy Walker it is Charles Wayne Foster. By the time he was 19, Walker had coached him to the exalted plateau of fastest human being in the world in the sixty-yard indoor high hurdles. Foster's energy, intellect and confidence burst from him like a volcanic shower. Now in his forties, he has an athletic body. His eyes constantly sweep his surroundings and he is eager for action and prepared for anything.

Foster is at once affectionate and wary, relaxed and taut, friendly and gregarious but still, if necessary, willing to deal with any physical challenge. "I came to college in 1971, following the '68 riots and the rise of the Black Panthers. It was a time when if you said something to me, I would just say, 'Let's fight.' Even now I am ready. Any time you are ready to go a few rounds, no problem, just step right on up. If you want to get physical with me I'm down for it. I'm not walking away." Foster, somewhat wistfully, acknowledged that his former coach had the strength take the higher road. "He will just say, I don't want to deal with it and walk away. I am probably not as integrity oriented as he is. I don't know if I can muster that up." Then with telling insight Foster said, "I am probably more scared of that kind of integrity than he is. "Foster's memory of his first contact with LeRoy Walker was that it was casual, almost accidental. It was not.

Quite some time before the youngster and Walker met, Foster's high school track coach in Gaffney, South Carolina, had been sharing with Walker the ticks of the stopwatch he had been clicking on the fleet teenager. The talent was raw but the times were impressive. Walker, in turn, had begun advising the coach on techniques and conditioning routines for the boy. "Coach Walker had been talking to my coach all the while," said Foster. "My coach never told me anything about that until after I had signed with North Carolina Central." Gaffney, a small town largely dependent on textiles for its economic health, was a big football town. Foster had played and performed well but he absolutely hated Spring practice. With characteristic independent reasoning, he decided that if he went out for track in the Spring, that would take care of it. After an initial failure to make the team, Foster, an admitted workaholic, improved his performance so quickly that his speed took him to the star level and his team to the state championship. Gaffney High

School had no track. The team worked out on the football field. The coach had little experience in teaching hurdlers. He was doing the best he could and, like all committed coaches, looked out for his athletes. Above all, he wanted the talented Foster to get noticed. Because of his performance in the South Carolina High School State Championship Meet, Foster suddenly found himself in the glare of the recruiting searchlight.

It was late afternoon. Foster was still on the practice field. His teammates were in the showers. His extra effort was partly driven by the realization that the only way he would get to college was to be faster than other people. "I looked up at the bank and saw this guy walking around, and then he sat down. He was just watching,. I had no idea who he was. He didn't look like a coach. He was dressed in a suit and I said to myself, 'Who's this guy?' Later, my coach got me out of the locker room and introduced us. That same night he came to my parent's house and we talked, not very much at all, something like, 'How are you doing? I'm Dr. LeRoy Walker. I coach at a school you probably haven't ever heard about.' He didn't talk long and then he left."

By this time, Foster had received letters from, talked with or had visited schools such as Michigan State, UCLA, Nebraska and others. Coach John West of the University of South Carolina wanted Foster there, of course. The Governor personally called to urge the high school star to join the Gamecocks. Foster was also being recruited for football. His good grades made him a premiere candidate for any school in the country. He held all the cards. "A month or so later," Foster said, "Dr. Walker showed up again and this time we sat at our kitchen table." Walker looked across the table and said, "I know that to you, I'm just another black man coming from a small school that you never heard of, but I am going places and if you want to go with me, just grab onto this coattail and let's go."

When Foster went for his visit to North Carolina Central University, he was not impressed. He had just returned from a recruiting visit to UCLA and the Gamecock "roost" at the University of South Carolina where they had rolled out the red carpet. Walker made a point to tell Foster that they didn't lay out the red carpet at Central and that was the way it was. "I didn't like it at all," Foster thought. "It was real 'college.' I mean, real down-home. I wanted something bigger and more modern. I didn't know about this atmosphere." What Foster did know was "When I was talking with Dr. Walker, it seemed like I was talking with my father."

When it was time for him to choose, Foster narrowed it down to two schools and Central was one of them. His parents did not want to make the decision for him but they advised, "We think Coach Walker is going to take care of you. But go with your gut feeling. " Foster's gut feeling was Walker and North Carolina Central. His decision set off a backlash of anger. The Mayor of Gaffney was furious. Said Foster, "So was the powerful black director of the funeral home in Gaffney, who was also the cornerstone of social life there. The Governor had gotten next to him and he had sat at my house pleading with me to go to South Carolina." Foster's decision had been made.

The country boy's entry on the Central campus would be marked by an accidental violation of NCAA rules, not by the athlete but by his coach. It was Spring of 1971. Walker's NCC team was competing at a relay meet at Quantico, Virginia. He wanted Foster to observe the competition. Walker had picked the boy up at his home in Gaffney the day before the meet, brought him to the Walker home in Durham where Foster spent the night. The next morning the two of them headed out for Quantico in Walker's car. About halfway there, according to Foster, "Dr. Walker jumped like he had been startled and said, 'Oh, dad gummit.' I said, 'What is it?' He paused and then said, 'Nothing, nothing.'"

A short time later Walker stopped to make a phone call, got back in the car and continued to Quantico. One of the first people Foster saw at the meet was South Carolina track coach John West who inquired how he got there. Foster told him he had come up with Dr. Walker. West headed for the nearest phone.

According to Walker, when West called to report Walker's infraction of the NCAA rule that a coach is not permitted to take a potential recruit more than thirty miles away from the school, he learned that Walker had already called in his own infraction and had discussed whether to turn back or go on. Since the rule had already been violated, it was decided they might as well go on to the relays. It was later that Foster learned of this and it explained why Walker had stopped abruptly during the trip to make the call. "He had already beaten West to the punch. At the time Dr. Walker never told me any of this, but as soon as I got to Central, it all hit," recalled Foster. The headlines in the local Durham paper trumpeted the story of Walker's track program at NCCU being put on probation. Later, when Charles Foster walked into the cafeteria he could hear the buzzing. "They were looking at me and saying, 'Who is this new cat who has the school on probation?' So now I am already the bad guy." Foster was truly innocent in the incident. At that point he knew little of the NCAA rules that governed the athletes and coaches. He remembers, "It must have been just a slap on the wrist because we still went to the NCAA and the NAIA my freshman year. I never got penalized for the Quantico incident. "

The first action Walker took was to get Foster started in a scholastic program and schedule. The fact that fewer than a dozen of all the athletes he ever coached "ran out of eligibility before they graduated" is often mentioned by Walker as an important component of his coaching legacy and a source of great professional and personal satisfaction. He never wavered from his strong convictions regarding "student" athletes. Foster recalled that he was ill-equipped for his first day's practice. "I really did not know the basics of how to hurdle. All I knew was that if you set up ten sticks, I was going to get past the ten sticks faster than the rest of them." Walker knew that the boy was "green" and assured him that he could show him how to get from one end of the sticks to the other faster. In the same freshman lineup was another All-American high school hurdler, Charles Johnson. Foster recalled, "Charlie had come down from a specialized school in Washington, D.C. from a more refined and organized program. No one had yet been able to really teach me how to run the hurdles." Walker gave Foster some basic drills that he was unable to accomplish "...and Charles Johnson was just 'whipping' and 'whipping' and I just could not pick it up." Foster was second string at the first meet during his freshman year. But when they lined them all up and the gun sounded, it was the kid from Gaffney who crossed the finish line first. Walker knew he had a competitor and a worker. Foster said, "I just knew how to beat you down there."

"Coach Walker never contested my commitment to winning, because he knew that regardless of who it was, I was going to give them my best shot, and I did," said Foster. "In my freshman year, 'Doc' said to me, 'I am going to put you in the thick of it. I am going to race you against the big boys and you are going to have to take your lumps.'"

Charles was 18-years-old and Walker was pitting him against the best in the world. Foster said, "I was never doing anything right, never. But when the gun sounded, 'Pow.' I was giving it all I had. I have pictures of it right now that shows these world-class guys crossing the finish line while I was still coming over the last hurdle, still giving it all I had but I just couldn't muster it up, and I could not understand how they could do it like that and I couldn't."

Walker knew why the determined young athlete, who gave everything he had in him, was unable to beat the best. The coach carefully laid out the concept of the scissors action in the hurdle drills. Foster recalled, "I could not grasp what he was trying to get across to me." Walker gave Foster hurdles to take home for training. "He said to me, 'You now understand the concept but the reason you can't do it is that you haven't practiced it enough.' He told me that if I kept working the drill, something would click. "I'll never forget. I was out one Sunday repeating the routine in a big field and all of a sudden I could do it!" The "click" took place just after Foster's parents returned from church and were preparing the Sunday meal. They were startled by their son who approached them in a euphoric state of energy and excitement. They didn't quite understand what he was talking about but what he discovered was the finesse that would, in a short time, make him a world champion. "Doc was right, it just clicked in. I don't know where coach came up with it," said Foster, "but he showed it to Lee Calhoun, Ron Draper, Ben Lee and the line of hurdlers coming directly from under him with the same basic philosophy of how to get it done. The guy I am coaching right now, Alan Johnson, is another one down the line from Coach Walker. All the credit goes back to Dr. Walker. That is what I am passing on."

Walker's track stars were attracting attention around the country and around the world. Track meet directors were seeking the team out, often as a drawing card. Even so, Walker faced a very limited budget at North Carolina Central. Foster recalled, "Dr. Walker would take his own credit card and pay for our rooms because he refused to put us in the cheap rooms." In his junior year Foster was No. 1 in the world, bringing him international attention as an athlete and he was also recognized as a personality to be reckoned with.

Walker called him to his office one day to ask if he would go to Italy for a meet during the coming weekend. The Italians wanted to run their best against Foster at an indoor meet in Genoa. Walker explained it would be a match race and Foster would be going against the Italian champion. Walker told his star that he would be traveling alone and was to compete the race and come right back. All arrangements had been made. Foster's response: "No problem. When am I leaving?" Following last-minute coaching instructions, Walker said that the Italian officials would be handing Foster some expense money that he was to deliver to Walker as soon as he got back. Foster would leave Friday, arrive Saturday, run Saturday, and fly directly back to Durham.

With a few hours of fitful sleep on the overnight Atlantic crossing, Foster faced a long day on Saturday. "I get off the plane, hop a bus and go straight to the arena. It was full of Italians all pumping up their champion. They were holding up the race until I got there. They saw me come in and I wave. I had a signature hat that I wore and they had seen newspaper pictures of me wearing that hat. They knew I was there. The place was packed." After a short warm-up, Foster was ready. When asked by the officials if he needed more warm-up time, the answer was, "Let's get it over." Foster ran a remarkable race. "I am telling you, I never checked into a hotel, never put my bags down, never did anything or saw anything except the airport and the arena. I ran the race, kicked his butt, set the fastest time they ever ran in Italy, without any sleep. After the award ceremony, and a couple of pictures taken with me and their champion, they whisked me back to the airport and I flew back to America."

When Foster arrived on the Central campus, he went to Walker's office with the expense money the Italians had given him, just over $300, and learned that the coach would be away for a week. The situation proved too much for the kid. "I came from a poor family. The clothes I had were really ragged and worn," said Foster, "and here I had just set the Italian indoor record wearing a ragged shirt." Unable to stop himself, Foster went to a clothing store and spent all of the money. "I don't know how I worked it to come out even but I spent every single dime on clothes, every single dime."

Foster agonized for the rest of the week over his inevitable meeting with the coach. The following Monday he spent the day avoiding Walker, but while changing classes ran into him and was summoned to the coach's office.

"When I walk in, Dr. Walker is sitting at his table, writing. Without looking up at me he said, 'Where's the money?' I said, 'I spent it.' He stopped writing and looked up at me with those eyes of his and I just about crumpled. I said, 'Dr. Walker, you know my situation. You know that I don't have any clothes. People are laughing at me because I have holes in my clothes.' Walker said, 'OK, how much of it did you spend?' I said, 'All of it.' He began writing again and said, 'Leave my office.' And to this day, he has never mentioned it to me again." The young man made a solemn vow that from that day forward he would never again wear ragged clothes.

Foster's respect for Walker did not preclude his challenging his coach on many issues. "I have been one of those people who has really put Dr. Walker to the test. I was the guy who always asked him, 'Why?' Yeah, we would get into some heat. I remember his discussion about the technique of snapping your lead leg down a certain way and I started telling him that you can't snap it down like that. He would say, 'Yes, you can.' We would go back and forth with it. I would say, 'You are looking at it from a purely scientific standpoint' and in my frustration I said once, 'The problem with you is that you know everything.' "Then I would say, 'But this is what I can do' and he would say, 'That makes sense; let's try it.' He always seemed to know that his job was to answer the question 'Why?' He always knew that when he could do that then everybody on the team would be satisfied."

Walker required Foster and his five teammates to run the 100, the 4 x 1, the 4 x 2, the sprint medley, and the mile relay. Questions among them would abound when, after Walker's workouts, the athletes would, as Foster put it, be "dragging themselves into the cafeteria." They knew they were being called on to do much more than any average track team. Foster said, "It always proved itself at the meets. He told us, time and again, that everything in the universe worked on the law of cause and effect. My dad, who was a preacher, was saying in the pulpit that you reap what you sow. Dr. Walker was saying the same thing to me. To this day I live and die by that. "

Because the college athletes were not allowed to receive money, many of them, especially those from poor families were broke. Among the athletes there were always rumors that other teams were able to get money "under the table" but knowing that Walker adhered strictly to the rules and regulations, Charles Foster was well aware that "If I screwed up, his reputation was on the line." Foster, however, would devise a ploy for pin money that he would set in motion when Walker was in a public place and in the company of other coaches.

In 1976, in a bar near the training camp at Plattsburgh, New York, preceding the Olympic Games in Montreal, Foster remembers: "All the fellows are sitting around, all the big cheeses with 'Doc,' who is the head track and field coach for the U.S. Olympic Team. With him are all his assistants, his managers, and some members of the International Olympic Committee. You hardly ever see 'Doc' with a drink, but to be polite he might nurse one drink all night long and then still leave most of it on the table. On this night he is 'hanging out with the fellows.' So with all his fellow coaches gathered around him, I walk in and say, in a tone loud enough for everybody to hear me, 'Excuse me, Dr. Walker but I need a couple of dollars.' Onto my scheme, he looks up at me and reaches for his wallet. He hands me exactly $2. Now, I'm depending on the others to say something. Stan Wright, the great coach says, 'Give your boy some money. Isn't that your star?' Now coach has to dig deeper still. They lean on him a second time, 'That's not enough; come on, give your boy some money.' Now you've got to understand that 'Doc' is close with a dollar—I mean he can save a dollar bill. Now you can see him squirming in his seat. Then he straightened up in his chair and sat back. You know that you have gotten the best of Dr. Walker when you see him sit back, because you know he is getting ready to come back at you. I got away with it then, but later he pulled me aside and said, 'Don't put me in that situation anymore.'"

When Foster speaks of his old coach, it is with warmth, love and affection, but above all, respect. "I have never seen him panic. He always told us, 'Don't panic until you see me panic. I have remembered that in my coaching career. My athletes think my blood just runs cold in my veins. I learned it from Walker. He always said you don't have to panic if you are looking at the big picture. What may be taking place at the moment, compared with the big picture may be very small, so why would you worry about it?" Foster's propensity for showboating was never condoned by Walker. On occasion when Foster would find it irresistible to show off during a meet, he paid for it in practice. "You would have a hell of a practice the next week if you were guilty of bush-leaguing. I would show off in Europe sometimes when I knew there were 3,000 miles of water between me and the coach. I would say to the coach that I was just trying to create a means by which the crowd would recognize me. He would say, 'You just cross the finish line first, then they will recognize you.' That was his answer. He had an answer for everything."

The Foster-Walker relationship was not atypical of that of most father-figure coaches and their young college athletes who perform and live at a high-octane level of energy. Either by happenstance or by design, Charles Foster managed to place himself at the very center of the coach's attention. On a motor trip to a meet in Virginia during Foster's freshman year, the team was riding up in two of the university's nine-passenger station wagons. Foster recalled, "We were a quality team on a low budget. It was only because of Doc's wheeling and dealing that we were able to use those vehicles. They belonged to the college but some of the other athletic teams were not allowed to use them."

Foster was driving one of the crowded vehicles with Walker sitting in the center seat next to him. Either the vehicle's suspension system was out of line or the sway bars were broken, but try as he might Foster could not keep the car from swaying back and forth in the driving lane.

"Doc's shoulder was right next to mine so I am really being put to the test. Then he starts looking at me and finally asked me why I could not hold the car in the road, and then asked if I had my driver's license. I just said, 'Yes, sir.' A short time later he asked me to pull over and he took the wheel. Now he's fighting the steering wheel and can't hold the car straight. So I say, 'Dr. Walker, can't you hold this car in the road?' The car exploded with laughter. The payback was just great."

Foster had another chance to showboat when Walker could not go with the team to an early Spring meet at William and Mary. It was so cold in Williamsburg the team would warm up inside, rush out for the races, and come right back in. Coaching the NC Central team that day was Assistant Coach Ted Manley. Walker always wrote down exactly how his assistant would coach the team. So before his race Foster made his move. "I said, 'Ted, it is so cold I want to run in my sweats.'" It was either arrogance or, more than likely, his sincere belief that he could beat the competition even in sweats, but Foster knew he had put Coach Manley on the spot. "The coach said, 'I can't say no because I don't want to see you pull up out there, but you had better win, I mean you better win.'" While it would be against the rules today and perhaps it was then, Foster ran in his sweats with a cap pulled down over his ears and he set a record. The feat was not without its complications for the confident athlete. He had to gamble that his pants would not creep downward during the race. "The pants getting lower would have lengthened my crotch and would have become a hazard while trying to clear that forty-two inch hurdle every three steps." But that's another instance when superior training takes precedence over all other factors. His being able to clear the hurdles higher, to make up for the layer of clothing, allowed Foster to set a new mark.

Walker's coaching philosophy and techniques were those used by Foster in his own successful career. Conditioning was at the top of the list of disciplines. Foster was a good student. Walker made sure the young man kept his balance between the classroom and his success on the field of play. Following his degree at North Carolina Central University, Foster went on to graduate school at UNC-Chapel Hill, earned his master's degree in 1977, then returned as an assistant track coach from 1985 to 1992. "At UNC, we were ACC champions nine times of the ten championships that we ran." With unabashed pride, he points out that hurdlers and sprinters got the lion's share of the credit. Walker's theory that to consistently overload the body would make it stronger, more flexible and more resilient when injured, held up for Foster during the 1976 Olympic trials. With a torn hamstring he beat every other American at the trials. "That is where conditioning came in," Foster said. "I was in such good condition that the associated muscles covered the injury and I won the trials." At the time, the long practice-drill sessions, the extra burden of running in more events than other track athletes and the many times he and his teammates "dragged themselves to the cafeteria" often seemed unreasonable. Yet Foster credited Walker's demanding conditioning regimen for his success.

Years later when Charles Foster was on the coaching staff at UNC he would invite the old master to observe, "Dr. Walker would say to me, 'You know you wouldn't be having the problems you are having if you had your people in shape.' At the same time the head coach, Dennis Craddock, was telling me to back off. I would reply that 'We aren't even breaking the surface.' Dennis would say, 'Back off, you're trying to kill them.'" Among Walker's axioms for success on the field is that flexibility follows conditioning. "After that, rhythm, coordination, those other things can be learned. You can do it a lot easier without having to learn them while you are getting in shape," said Walker.

The coach held to another axiom. He would not tamper with success. When he was trying to change Foster's trail leg and his lead leg, he took into account that it was Foster who was getting himself across the finish line first. He told his athlete to continue what he was doing because he was winning with it. He also promised the young man he would look for other ways to make him faster. According to Foster, Walker increased his speed by first holding a classroom session before every practice to explain the scientific principles that supported the goals of acceleration, speed, strength and force. It was the coach's way of showing the athlete why he was asking them to perform certain drills. He sold them on the concept of conditioning first, followed by finesse and style.

Foster credited his former coach with much more than his success on the field of competition. Walker instilled in the younger man a life-lesson regarding racial prejudice. Charles Foster's description of the way he sees people of all races is one word: "clear." According to Foster that concept comes directly from Walker. "He instilled that in me, and when I tell people of my own race that I see them and everybody else as clear, some of them have a real problem with that. They tell me I have forgotten a lot. I tell them I haven't forgotten anything, and I understand everything."

Walker's analytical mind serves him well. As the coach explained to his athletes the specific techniques of how to win on the playing field, he was more aware than they of the brevity of their golden playing time and that he, as an educator, needed to leave them with life skills when their time came to walk off the field for the last time. Foster said, "When you are in the car for six hours with Dr. Walker on a return trip from, say, Atlanta to Durham following a meet, he is first going to ream you out. When that is over you know you are going to get to listen to the man down deeper." Walker stressed that some of the axioms he was sharing with the athletes perhaps didn't apply at the moment but would be there later in life. He told Foster, "I know you don't understand all the things I am telling you now, but when you have to apply these lessons, they will be there." Foster would call on those teachings many times.

In 1980, at Walker's recommendation, Foster was chosen by the U.S. Information Agency to spend a year in Kenya teaching coaches the American philosophy of training. Those coaches began working with seven-, eight-, and nine-year-olds. Foster believed that these coaching techniques of LeRoy Walker contributed significantly to Kenya's dominance in international competition.

In 1984, Foster was sent by the U.S. Information Agency to Harare, Zimbabwe to direct an African multinational track and field training camp to help prepare the coaches and athletes for the 1984 Olympic Games in Los Angeles. The countries sending participants to the training camp were: Zaire, Zambia, Mozambique, Tanzania, Lesotho, Malawi and Zimbabwe.

Tribal and political tensions were rampant among the delegations arriving at the camp. "I had coaches in there who wouldn't even speak to each other. And here I was supposed to teach them the American philosophy of sport and to acclimate them as to what to expect in Los Angeles." Foster's first attempts to gain control of the African coaches in his camp were disastrous. Arguments and disruptions during the meetings were frequent and heated. In a moment of desperation he resorted to a method he had not learned from Coach Walker. Foster put on what he called a physical "display." He grabbed one of the rebellious ring leaders who had left his seat to argue, lifted the man's feet off the floor, pinned him against the wall and held him there for a moment. Instead of throwing him down, Foster let him down easily, straightened him up and said, "Now sir, would you please have a seat?"

"Now I had everybody's attention," said Foster. "That alone did not iron out all my problems, but it let them know that I meant business." Foster's challenge with the athletes from various African countries was to get them to buy into a team concept, which was difficult for such diverse political factions. His attempts to bring them together were not productive. Foster was worried to the point of losing sleep. "Coach Walker always said that a person's best thinking took place in two places—in the shower and lying in bed with your head on the pillow, hands behind your head, staring at the ceiling. I was staring at my bedroom ceiling when his words came to me. 'Fatigue makes cowards of us all.' I thought, That's it!"

The next day, Foster grouped together the athletes from all the nations according to their specialties—all the sprinters, hurdlers, and the distance runners. He told them their workout would be five 200-meter sprints and that he wanted them done in 23.5 seconds. "That was just fast enough to let them know they were sprinting." Foster declared that he would time the last man and each time the last man failed to hit the 23.5 mark, they all would have to repeat the run. He told them to think of themselves as a part of a fleet, and that the fleet wouldn't be in until the last ship had docked. "They ran the first 200 and the last guy doesn't hit the time. He doesn't make it the second or the third time. Now they were getting unnerved. Now their legs were aching, their hearts were pounding and they still haven't finished their first sprint on time. They began to talk to that last guy, began to try to encourage him, and help him make the time. I know I'm getting somewhere. Doc was right. Fatigue makes cowards of us all and, at the same time, brings us all together."

Foster credited Walker with the past and present success of the African athletes in world competition. He points to the impact of Walker's coaching of African teams and the sharing of his techniques and philosophies with great numbers of African coaches. "Even those coming up now, the developing kids, are getting the benefits of Coach Walker's influence." When Walker sat at the kitchen table of Foster's home in Gaffney, South Carolina, and said to the high school boy, "I'm going places and if you hold on to my coattails you can go with me," the statement was prophetic. Charles Foster's accomplishments took him to the top.

Unfortunately, he pulled a hamstring just before the 1976 Olympics. He still doesn't like to talk about it. He pulled himself together following that injury and made a crucial decision to set his sights on 1980 and the Games in Moscow. "I was still at the top of my game between '76 and '80." Then came the devastating blow to American athletes across the country.

President Jimmy Carter decided that America would boycott the Moscow Games as a part of the administration's protest of the Soviet invasion of Afghanistan. Foster was forced to meet the press. "When it happened they came to my door. Sports reporters Rich Brenner at WRAL-TV in Raleigh, Don Shea at WTVD-TV in Durham, Woody Durham and a number of local radio stations were sticking a microphone in my face for a reaction." Walker's words again came to Foster: "Sometimes you have to bite your tongue." "I was very bitter, but knew this was one of those times I had to regroup." Foster made the following statement: "I am a proud citizen of the United States. I understand the freedoms that I enjoy here are not enjoyed by people in many other countries. I understand the political situation for our Chief Executive and I stand behind his decision one hundred percent." Foster recalled, "That's not what the press wanted to hear, of course, because they wanted me to say something controversial, but I had watched Dr. Walker many times with the press. He always knew when to bite his tongue and walk away."

Privately Foster was devastated. He had sacrificed another four years to amateur status so he could run for the gold. But there were highlights, too. His years on the coaching staff at UNC were successful and satisfying. LeRoy Walker had played a pivotal role in Foster's coaching experiences at home and abroad.

In 1991, Walker, then Vice President for Sport for the Atlanta Committee for the Olympic Games, offered his former star the opportunity to head up one of the five major divisions for the 1996 Olympic Games in Atlanta. Foster jumped at the chance. The twenty-six sports would be divided among five division planning managers. The elite planning managers would design, organize, administer and implement five of the Olympic sports. Foster said with pride, "When you are sitting in the stands at Olympic Stadium and looking out onto the playing field, just remember that I designed it. While I had to get it approved and passed by the Committee, I personally decided where the shot putt is, where the long jumps are, the radius of the track, how round the track is, how long the straightaway is. So it has been an equivalent or better than a doctorate degree in sports management."

His colleagues teased Foster about his unabashed affection for Walker. Foster said, "When they phoned me, looking for Dr. Walker, they would often say, 'Where's your daddy?' I even got it from Billy Payne, President and CEO of ACOG. I have met a lot of sharp people but Doc is the brightest person I have ever been around. He is a visionary. It is a compliment to me to be so closely associated with him and more importantly, everyone involved realized that he knew more than anybody else there, so we all had to deal with him on that level. Nobody at ACOG could match him when it came to the Olympics." Even to a casual observer, Foster's love and respect for his aging former coach is all encompassing. "There is no doubt about it," said Foster, "he is my chief confidante, Daddy, the whole works."

Foster's face saddens when discussing Walker's mortality. For the African-American community Foster believes that Walker's positive influence, while not as widely recognized, is as dynamic as that of Martin Luther King Jr. "When I think about Dr. Walker getting old, I think to myself' there is no one like him anywhere,"

Then Foster stares at the floor for a moment, lifts his head, eyes glistening, and with an expression of sudden discovery said, "But there is."

The Russians Are Coming

Following the success of the MLK Games, Walker and Al Buehler turned their energy and resources toward the Russians and a Cold War sports collaboration that is still talked about today. By 1974, the Soviet Union and the USA were the strongest powers in track and field. The Russians were the challengers to U.S. supremacy in international competition. Walker and Buehler were getting to know more of the Russian athletes and coaches, both having reached, by different routes, the international arena. They each had befriended Igor Ter-Ovanisyan, an outstanding athlete who headed the Soviet's track program. Walker and Buehler further solidified contacts with the Russians at Munich.

The Soviets were increasingly eager to have the world see their team and had already exchanged visits with the U.S. several times, the first time in Philadelphia. According to Buehler's estimate, when the Russians traveled abroad, about a third of the contingent consisted of KGB agents to thwart defections. Walker had earned the respect of the Russians, attending their clinics and professional meetings, and offering expertise when called upon. Walker knew of the Russian paranoia associated with possible defections. He was able, however, to persuade them that Durham, North Carolina would not likely be a city with the glamour conducive to defections by the young Russians. The American coaches theorized that the Russians would enjoy a much more relaxed and open visit unlike their trips to the big cities where their athletes were practically sequestered in their hotels at night. The Russians agreed to come to North Carolina and as Buehler remembered, "It was the time LeRoy and I really went to bat."

The two appeared together before the political, business and social power brokers to gain support for the meet. They visited the Durham County Commissioners, the Durham merchants group and heads of major corporations. The support was there. Durham city officials sensed that an event of this significance would be beneficial in terms of exposure and were supportive in helping raise the money. The academic communities at Duke and NC Central were eager and enthusiastic.

The Russians arrived in Durham the first week of July for a two-day meet beginning July 5, 1974. Excluding the Olympic Games, all previous track meet attendance records were shattered. In two days the USA-USSR meet drew more than 65,000 people. Terry Sanford, former governor of North Carolina and at the time president of Duke University, theorized that Durham's selection as an All-American City was directly related to the atmosphere spawned by the track meets. In enthusiastic preparation for the games, it was important to Walker that the stadium be full of people and that the curved end of the horseshoe-shaped stadium on the Duke campus also have people in it. North Carolina Governor Robert Scott had seen that $25,000 of state moneys went to support the event and asked if he could send over some young prison inmates to watch the games. Walker sent 2,000 complimentary tickets for youthful offenders in the state's prison system. "They were all dressed alike," said Buehler. "The Russians thought they were members of a large athletic club and were complimentary of their disciplined behavior."

§

Walker and Buehler wanted to assure that the Russian athletes and coaches were properly honored as guests in our country and would take with them a greater appreciation of "Southern hospitality." It was important to them that the Russians return to their homeland with positive evidence of their American experience. Several corporations were solicited to help accomplish that mission. A furniture company provided a magazine rack for each Russian athlete that could be easily folded to meet the requirements of air travel. Other corporations provided shirts and sweaters.

It was a manufacturer, Blue Bell, Inc., headquartered in Greensboro, North Carolina, however, that inadvertently became the cause of a minor Russian revolution with its gift product, Wrangler blue jeans outfits, jackets and pants! Youth from around the world had chosen blue denim as the wardrobe of choice. Young people from Russia regarded blue jeans as the ultimate youth fashion. "The jeans craze has hit that country as hard as it has in the U.S.," said one Blue Bell executive and, in a public relations coup, the company shipped to Durham boxes upon boxes of jeans and matching jackets in every conceivable size for every athlete, coach, male and female on the Russian team as well as for the Americans.

When the boxes of denim arrived they were stacked in the concourse of Duke's indoor stadium. There Buehler had arranged partitioned dressing facilities for the Russian athletes, women on one side, men on the other. No one knows exactly how the following incident began. It may be safely said, however, that one of the female Russian athletes "discovered" that the cardboard boxes stacked near their dressing area contained American blue jeans! The women began to dig into the cardboard boxes and, in a scene reminiscent of those famous Macy's sales, took matters into their own hands. In a frenzy of excitement, the shouting Russian women, pushing and shoving each other, quickly tore into some of the boxes of jeans, and stripping themselves down to their underwear, commenced trying them on. The Russian men, hearing the commotion, quickly responded by scurrying to the women's side of the stadium where they immediately began shoving the women aside in their own quest to gain possession of this prize of the Western world. Buehler remembered, "Then the men and women got to pushing and shoving over those blue jeans!"

A near riot ensued before the American officials were able to get the situation under control by assuring the athletes that there were plenty of jeans in all sizes, enough for each member of the team and staff. Following the blue jeans skirmish, representatives from Blue Bell arrived to mete out the clothing and supervise the sizing for the athletes. One recalled, "It was quite a feat for all those athletes." The Russian "family" conflict was put to rest.

Not put to rest was another Russian issue, which surfaced under more peaceful conditions at the home of Al and Delaina Buehler during a friendly social occasion. Feeling secure that there would be no athletes defecting from Durham, some of the KGB people and other members of the Russian staff joined Walker and the Americans for a reception at the comfortable home of the Buehlers, in a quiet neighborhood nestled in a forest not far from the Duke campus. The homes were lovely but not ostentatious. "LeRoy and I said to them, 'We are just having a friendly get-together at Al's house where we'll sit and talk and have some food,'" Buehler recalled.

When the head of the visiting delegation came into the home, he brought vodka but asked for bourbon for himself, candidly admitting that he did not like the famed Russian drink. Following a round of "toasting" he began to relax. "The Russians could clearly see there were no government officials among us; we were just ordinary people getting together for fellowship," said Buehler. A Russian visitor began to look around the Buehler residence with more than a normal curiosity and revealed what was on his mind in a series of questions of Al that began with, "Is this your home?" Al explained that, while there was a mortgage on it, which meant an ownership shared with a bank, it was their home. Seeing two cars in the garage, the Russian asked the same question about the ownership of the vehicles. He then asked his host to take him upstairs to see the children's rooms and, finally, asked to see Al's clothes closet. Perhaps emboldened by the bourbon, the visitor played his final card. He said, "Do you mind trying on one of your coats?" Buehler recalled, "The point was he thought this whole thing was a setup, a scam—even the clothing. He could simply not believe that LeRoy and I, track coaches and teachers, could have this quality of life and not be tied in with the government."

Later Walker took the man to his campus at North Carolina Central University to show him where he lived and worked. It was very difficult for the visitor to comprehend that, as Buehler

Photo Section

LeRoy and friend at Benedict

Mary Walker, LeRoy's Mother

At the Benedict Graduation

Katherine Walker, LeRoy's Wife   The Coach works out

At an early track meet

Lee Calhoun

Lee Calhoun laces up

photo: *Track and Field News*

Calhoun wins gold in Melbourne, 1956

Coach Walker and the Israeli team in Rome, 1960

Walker and the NC College Eagles

photo: U.S.M.C.

Walker's team wins the Marine
Corps Relays

Individual instruction

Coach Walker and team pose for the yearbook

President Gerald Ford visits the 1976 Olympics training site

Coach Walker presents the President with an
Olympics jacket, 1976

Carolyn Hopp and daughter
Wanda Wade

Adults, from left to right:
LeRoy, Jr., Katherine,Judi
and LeRoy, Sr.
Children: Melodie and Shawn

Walker in China

photo: *Track and Field News*

A big day for Duke, 1971

photo: *Track and Field News*

Directing the meet in Durham

photo: *Track and Field News*

Athletes perform before a packed stadium at Duke, 1971

Sharing laughs at a celebrity benefit

With President Carter, who declared the 1980 boycott of the Moscow Games

With friend William C. "Bill" Friday, President Emeritus, University of North Carolina

Friday, Walker, and South African Nobel Prize Laureate, Archbishop Desmond Tutu

Tutu, Carolyn Hopp, Walker

With Vice President Dan Quayle

photo: The White House

Chancellor Walker presides at NCCU graduation

A hug from Desmond Tutu

Three coaching legends, from left to right: Eddie Robinson of Grambling, Clarence "Big House" Gaines of Winston-Salem State, and Walker

At the memorial to Lee
Calhoun at Western
Illinois

With coaching icon
John McLendon

Paua Zahn presents an award

From left to right:
Bruce Hopp, Judi
Walker, Carolyn
Hopp, LeRoy Sr.,
and LeRoy Jr.

Walker receives the
Youthlinks Award

Entering the
Stadium at
Barcelona, 1992

photo: USOC

From left to right:
Jean Smith,
Walker, and
Olympic Champi-
ons Bonnie Blair
and Dan Jansen

With
President
Bill Clinton

photo: The White House

Presiding over
the Olympic
Congress,
Atlanta, 1995

photo: Charles Gaddy

With son and
grandchildren,
from left to
right:
LeRoy, Jr.,
Shawn Walker,
Melodie Walker,
"Papa" and
Wanda Wade

Official photo of the
USOC President

photo: Charles Gaddy
Friends Al and Delaina
Buehler following the
Olympic Torch Run at
Duke, 1996

At the Olympic Torch Run

photo: Charles Gaddy

Standing Next to IOC
President Juan Antonio
Samaranch following
the Olympic Order
Award, Atlanta, 1996

photo: Charles Gaddy

Montage by USOC

photo: Charles Gaddy
Construction at an Olympic
venue, Atlanta, 1995

photo: Charles Gaddy
Lighting the Olympic flame at
NCCU, 1996

photo: Charles Gaddy
Bill Friday presenting the Caroliniana Award

described it, "Two guys could be set up like this without some party line being infiltrated into it, that we could have a comfortable life and actually own things. In his country the government owned his car, controlled his life, and allowed him a brief yearly visit to a government-owned summer place." Walker and Buehler both understood that behind the Russian bluster was the sadness of a people with very limited opportunities or choices. Their view of America was so filtered through the party line that they were startled to see African-Americans in Durham out shopping. One was led to ask, "Why are they not out working in the fields of the plantations?"

The event became more than a track meet. Among the many benefits was the unifying effect it had on the community. Walker and Buehler enjoyed the support of 3,000 volunteers, black and white, working together for the success of the undertaking. The Russian athletes appeared at civic clubs, speaking through interpreters who were very often volunteers from the language studies department at Duke. Buehler said, "We had their athletes running around all over the place, and the communists were pleased to send them out, because these young Russians were first-rate, well-behaved and made very positive impressions on all the Americans who met them." The Soviet athletes were allowed to roam the shopping centers with a freedom they had not enjoyed at other meets.

They were taken to Durham's shopping centers, fortified with American money provided by their government, where they were observed "buying practically any item of apparel that had an alligator logo on it." The youth also swarmed the music stores to buy all of the latest American music. Through the Duke cultural exchange program the works of fine Russian artists were on display. The entire upper field near the stadium was devoted to attracting people interested in the cultural value of the visit. Russian dance troupes enthralled many Americans who came to the Duke campus. The arts community felt it had scored a coup.

Financially, the meet was a juggernaut. The gate receipts allowed an incredible $75,000 payback. "The AAU had paid for the expenses of the U.S. team and we gave them their money back with a big 'Thank you,'" said Buehler. "And we gave money to the Red Shield Boy's Club. It was the biggest money-maker that ever took place in track!" he said, "It just went great!"

Politicians and community leaders took many bows for the event that had attracted media attention around the world. Walker and Buehler, both volunteers, could not have been more pleased.

One year later, in 1975, Walker, Buehler and friends presented the Pan Africa and West Germany vs. USA Games. Kenya and other African nations were beginning to make their marks on the international track scene due in no small measure to the years of groundwork laid by Walker on the continent.

According to Buehler, Walker was concerned about attendance. Ernie Greup, then public affairs director for WTVD, the local television station in Durham, was, among other media supporters, credited with helping generate interest in the event by televising interviews with Walker and Buehler and producing free promotional spots to be aired throughout the broadcast day.

On July 18-19, 37,000 people turned out for the contests. Wallace Wade Stadium was colorful with the bright African clothing, and the sounds of bongo and conga drums added energy and excitement to the event. The City of Durham was a major benefactor of the highly visible series of meets. The merchants enjoyed a burst of economic stimulation provided by the influx of visitors. The impact of the two coaches, making speeches, raising money and working together, was not lost on the general population. The thousands of volunteers from all segments of the community came away with a sense that they had helped make something happen that they could look on with a great deal of pride. "LeRoy and I were actually bringing the people of Durham together," said Buehler. Given the makeup of the teams, the games enjoyed a media blitz, making the contests highly visible around the country.

Politically and culturally, LeRoy Walker was giving blacks in the town a new visibility and vitality. North Carolina Central University was now viewed with a more heightened realization that it held a treasure of highly capable and motivated people. Duke University, viewed by some as a bastion of elitism, took the opportunity to further display its willingness to reach out to the community.

The image of the city itself, too long that of a "tobacco town," was transformed to the extent that a movement developed to shed the slogan "Bull City," which had stuck tenaciously to the town that manufactured Bull Durham smoking tobacco, the smoke of choice for the soldiers of World War I, to the "City of Medicine," which highlighted the impact of the prestigious Duke Medical Center, other hospitals and the correlating medical research conducted in and around the Research Triangle Park. It was Walker's work through the State Department and the Peace Corps in the African countries that had enhanced his prestige in that part of the world. That became a key factor in opening new avenues of competition in sport. "LeRoy brought a lot of those countries together through athletics," said Buehler.

Among Walker's most endearing qualities, according to Buehler, is his ability to laugh at himself and with the athletes who have been a part of his life. Walker himself enjoys telling the story of athlete Vince Mathews' "attempted" arrival on the NCCU campus. Mathews was a premier high school athlete in New York City. Walker recruited him and looked forward to the young man's arrival in Durham. When Mathews rode south with some of his friends from Johnson C. Smith, an old and established college for black youth in Charlotte, North Carolina's largest city, they drove past Durham and took him on to Charlotte. All the while, on the campus of North Carolina Central, Coach Walker, who had made the proper preparations to receive and welcome Mathews to the Durham campus, remained perplexed and worried about his athlete, until receiving a phone call from an equally confused coach, Kenny Powell at Johnson C. Smith, inquiring if he knew Vince Mathews. The coach in Charlotte persuaded Mathews to remain at Johnson C. Smith where he became a champion track star and an Olympian, albeit a controversial one. Walker also laughs with Buehler about the time he recruited, sight unseen, another athlete from New York based solely on his running times. He confided to Buehler that "anyone with these times in high school has to be good." Meeting the plane in September, according to Buehler "with visions of another Lee Calhoun-type hurdler walking off the aircraft," Walker was greeted by a very nice, but very short young man. Walker, while masking his disappointment, knew immediately that the five-foot, nine-inch runner would have difficulty clearing a 42-inch hurdle.

Buehler's admiration for Walker comes from a deep respect that grows from close contact over an extended period of time and first-hand observance of the extra hardships that Walker had to face in his life and career.

"At the Penn Relays," recalled Buehler, "we all stayed in nice hotels and ate in the nice restaurants while LeRoy and his team had to be scattered out in individual homes in the black community."

Buehler recounts vivid memories of car trips with Walker when his faced outside "colored" and "white" drinking fountains. Once, when the "colored" fountain was out of order, both men knew that LeRoy could not take the few steps over to the other faucet and slake his thirst. Nor could he use the restroom. He walked back to the car and waited while Buehler went inside and returned with a soft drink for him. "Young people now, no matter what their race or background," said Buehler, "don't know what that is like to have that kind of insult. LeRoy and I also dealt with two different kinds of kids, as far as their backgrounds," said Buehler.

For all of his hard-nosed demands for discipline on and off the field, Walker would do anything to help the young people in his care to have confidence as athletes and as members of society.

When he noticed that an athlete on a competing team ate a complete meal in a hotel dining room with his spoon, he decided that his team should not be embarrassed in public, nor represent the university without the basic social graces. With touching sensitivity, Walker devised a lesson for the entire team in the proper use of an entire table setting of flatware. Careful not to embarrass anyone, he drew out a sketch, for each athlete, on those cardboard panels that came in the back of a freshly laundered shirt, which was the approximate width of a table setting. He occasionally paid for meals to be prepared by the home economics department, with a complete setup of proper flatware. The athletes were allowed to bring a guest for those meals during which Walker gave them instructions in etiquette. The Home Economics people realized that the coach's lessons were so valuable that they discontinued charging for them. Some of those former athletes, now in businesses and professions across the land, mention to their former coach the value of his instructions in the social graces. Buehler said: "Those coaches had to give kids food, clothing, and bus tickets—things that would be illegal today. Eddie Robinson, the great football coach at Grambling said, 'What do you do, walk away from a kid who is hungry, not work out a bus ticket, or (not) give them a ride home for a family funeral?'"

Respect flowed both ways in the Walker-Buehler friendship. The Duke coach considered it one of his highest honors to be invited to write two chapters on distance running in Walker's highly regarded book, *Championship Track and Field*.

The two were sought out for seminars and coaching clinics around the state and the country. Walker taught coaching techniques for sprinters and hurdlers while Buehler's expertise was distance running. Buehler recalled that "they held on to every word LeRoy uttered about coaching because he is a great speaker and a great teacher. Whenever he speaks, he is teaching."

Buehler said Walker "earned every honor and accolade he has received through knowledge, hard work and experience. LeRoy is not a powerful man in the way he sees himself," said Buehler, "but he has risen through the ranks, from assistant coach, to coach, to chairman of his department. He carried a full teaching load, and worked at physical education as hard as he did coaching, rising to the position of president of the American Alliance of Health, Physical Education, Recreation and Dance."

From the very beginning the two coaches enjoyed a unique relationship. Buehler said, "In those days, even the fact that we mixed socially was unique. We were two people from two different institutions, bound together by the same sport. LeRoy and I sat down and thought of all the great things he has done and of all the good things that have happened to me because of Duke. I didn't have to deal with all the things that he did, like segregation and racial hatreds. So, the big difference is, I had a great base, but LeRoy had to create his."

Probations

Walker's track program at North Carolina Central suffered two probations. The first came, as previously noted, in the Spring of 1971 when Walker inadvertently transported recruit Charles Foster past the thirty-mile NCAA limit from Durham to a track meet in Quantico, Virginia. "I wasn't thinking," said Walker.

The second probation was more serious.

When he recruited Kenyans Robert Ouko and Julius Sang, Kenyan President Jomo Kenyatta preferred that the athletes stay home. But Walker prevailed. When they arrived at NC Central campus they were a blessing. The shy, young Kenyans could run like the wind, were extremely coachable and were excellent students. Their undeniable success on the track and in the classroom was somewhat offset by some considerations of culture shock. The sudden shift to the rich American diet was difficult for them. Many of the other students at Central, instead of taking the opportunity to get to know and understand the African youth, began to treat them as "different." The Africans' shyness simply added to the complexities of their campus relationships. The two experienced isolation among their fellow students.

Walker, the friend and protector of all of his athletes, perhaps feeling an even keener sense of responsibility for the two youngsters he had talked into coming to Durham, was well aware that they had no money and a meager wardrobe. The totality of their subsistence rested on their athletic scholarship with the school. They were also a long way from home, thrust into a culture entirely new to them. The racist attitudes they found in the South were confusing and frightening. Walker's justifiable concerns for them following a robbery of their dorm room resulted in one of the most serious setbacks to his prestigious track program.

One afternoon while Ouko and Sang were at practice, thieves entered their dorm room and took everything they had. Robert and Julius were devastated. The only articles of clothing they had now were the track togs they were wearing. More serious than the loss of their possessions was the psychological trauma of being violated on their college campus. While no one was ever apprehended for the crime, the thinking was that the thieves were probably not fellow students but people who came off the city street that ran beside the men's dorm.

The two young men were frantic. Convinced that the criminal did not make a random selection of a room to rob and that they had been singled out because they were Africans, their fears over-whelmed them. Walker responded quickly and with the best intentions. Alex Rivera, head of public relations for the University at the time, recalled that, "What he was trying to do was help them."

Walker contacted friends and former athletes and asked them to donate clothing, which he would have altered at a local tailor shop to fit the two young men. "I also thought I had to get them out of that building," said Walker, "and I went to the administration to see if I could get their scholarship money combined and have enough to rent an apartment for them. I wrote to the dean of students to see if their student insurance would permit the restoration of what they had lost. The answer was 'No.'" Walker got meal tickets so they could eat in the dining hall and the two Africans moved off campus.

Walker is convinced that a good portion of the negative reaction he and his team were getting from opposing coaches stemmed from the fact that, "We were making a lot of noise on the track, beating up on some of the best teams in the country. They were trying to find some means of keeping Ouko and Sang out of the competition."

Another complaint that was filed concerned eligibility. "Robert and Julius had run on a junior team in Kenya," said Walker, "and the track coach at UCLA began to complain that I had all those 'foreigners.' He thought it was a detriment to track and field. His complaints came not long before UCLA had to face us on the field for the NCAA championship meet. I believe that because we were winners, there began to circulate reports that we were doing something illegal. At the Penn Relays, we had set three records, a world record and two collegiate records. Nobody could handle Larry Black in the 200, nor Ouko, nor Sang, nor Charles Foster and certainly nobody could handle our relay teams. And that is a lot of points, even though I only carried seven people. Although we were members of the NAIA, I was allowed to declare competition in Division One in the NCAA and that's what I did. We first had to finish in the top six in Division Two, then they let us in. We left here for the meets in Modesto, California, and a lot of people out there began to get nervous. In one write-up, we were favored to win the meet." Walker was handed a telegram on the way to the meet. "It was from the NCAA declaring Julius Sang and Robert Ouko ineligible to compete." After Walker told his team about the ruling, he phoned the Executive Director of the NAIA and was allowed to join that meet in Sioux Falls, South Dakota.

Whatever the factors, the complaints were formalized into a hearing before the NCAA's Committee on Infractions. The report stated: "North Carolina Central University in Durham has been placed on probation for a period of two years as a result of violations in the conduct of the University's intercollegiate track program." Spelling out the details of the findings, the report included a quote from Arthur Reynolds, the chairman of the NCAA Infractions Committee: "The committee found serious violations in this case."

The response from the administration of NC Central University was one of outrage. In a tersely worded statement, Chancellor Albert Whiting told the committee and the media what he thought of the imposed sanctions: "The circumstances surrounding the transgressions for which we are now being penalized related to emergencies and considerations overlaid with international consequences which could not have been wisely ignored," said Whiting. "These young men are natives of Kenya, East Africa, with no financial resources beyond those afforded by our institution." Whiting chided the committee for being "unreasonable and devoid of empathetic concern." The final sentence of his statement read: "Our comparatively tiny track and field program and the violations involved, particularly under the circumstances I had described, have attracted far more investigative attention than seems to be wise and we simply cannot resist the question, 'Why?'"

Eventually the eligibility of Ouko and Sang was restored. For his team and for himself, Walker was delighted when one newspaper reporter compared the NAIA scores of his team in events that NC Central led, against the scores of the same events in the NCAA meet. The reporter put the results on the front of the sports page. "By the score comparison, we would have beaten the NCAA by 33 points," said Walker.

§

By the Seventies, Walker had already become a world figure in sports. In 1970, he worked as a volunteer with athletes from France, Italy, Germany, the USSR and West Africa. He was a team leader in games involving England, Italy, Norway, Senegal, and Sweden. His accomplishments, now recognized at home, included:

1970 AND 1971

1970-71-and 1972 NAIA District 26 Coach of the Year
City of Durham, Distinguished Service Award
Kiwanis International, Distinguished Service Award
Helms Foundation, Sports Hall of Fame
Board of Directors, U.S. Collegiate Sports Council
Elected Chairman, College Commissioners Association

1972

Coach of the Year, National Track and Field Association
Coach of the Year, NAIA
Honor Award, AAHPERD
Executive Committee, NAIA

1973

Chairman, AAU Track and Field Committee
On his own campus, Walker was appointed Vice Chancellor of
University Relations

§

Montreal

*I guess they wanted me to serve my apprenticeship before they
chose me.*

—LeRoy T. Walker

Coach Stan Wright will tell you without hesitation that it was he
who should have been America's first African-American Olympic
head coach for track and field. Leading up to Munich in 1972, in a
protracted day of balloting during which there was one tie vote after
another, and a refusal by Wright to agree to co-coach the team with
Oregon's Bill Bowerman, the gridlock was finally broken by one vote
in Bowerman's favor. Walker had been interested in the head coach
position in 1972 but withdrew believing that Wright had the better
chance.

Bill Bowerman, head coach at the University of Oregon, had
amassed an impressive record of champions and championships.
Like Walker and Wright, he was a true student of the mechanics of
track and field. When Stan Wright confronted his own feeling
following the close vote, he was sadly convinced that another
element was involved.

"Our biggest problem as black guys was fighting the good-ol'-boy
system," said Wright. "We put up with it for the love of the sport,"
said Wright. "We hated what we had to go through; it was
dehumanizing. I cried many nights."

§

The rise of African-Americans among the ranks of the elite track
and field athletes over the decade leading up to the '76 Games had

been phenomenal. Not only had they posted exceptional performances on the field, the black athletes had become a political force. America was moving from the cloud of the Watergate scandal and the Nixon resignation into the sunshine of its Bicentennial celebration, a time to commemorate the best of its heritage.

Walker had never served as an assistant U.S. coach in the Olympics, yet when his name came up for vote before the selection committee, it was over in fewer than fifteen minutes, despite the competition of other prominent coaches in the running. Walker received a near unanimous vote. Some of his former champion athletes told the press outright that Walker's selection was long overdue. When pressed, Walker acknowledged that might have been the case but he couched it a different way: "I guess they wanted me to serve my apprenticeship," he said. Then he adds, "I was producing national champions as far back as 1956." While some would say his election was enhanced by political and racial considerations at the time, no one could dispute his coaching credentials. In truth, by any measurement, he had earned the top spot. The USOC selection committee developed a set of criteria, which when applied, placed Walker far above the other candidates.

The stress level in Montreal was enormous. The excitement of hosting the Games came with an under-layer of anxiety and fear on two fronts. These Games were the first since the horrible massacre at Munich and some critics had called for an outright dissolution of all Olympic Games. Montreal would spend $100 million on security alone. "It was an armed camp," said Walker, "Munich had changed the atmosphere of the Games forever." The other prevailing stressful issue was the total bill. While city taxpayers had been promised they would not be burdened with the costs, Montreal had spent $1.2 billion on the Games. Financial losses reached catastrophic proportions. For years to come, the city would be strangled with the debt. This had a chilling effect on other cities' bidding proposals.

In preparation for the Games, Walker quickly set about work on his strategy for the selection and training of the U.S. Team. His former gold medalist, Lee Calhoun, was one of his assistants. Walker instituted several changes: Up until that time, assistant Olympic coaches paid their expenses to meets and trials to observe athletes in preparation for the Olympic Games. Walker persuaded the USOC to reimburse them.

Traditionally the relay team was made up of the first four finishers of the 100-meter event only. Walker's sprint relay talent would be selected from all of the sprint-related events. He banished the athletes' individual coaches from the field. "I didn't want them coming in telling us what to do. I didn't let them come on the field."

Walker was convinced that in Munich there was a lack of team cohesiveness. He was so sure of his observation that he set up a camp at Plattsburgh, New York, an upstate facility two hours away from Montreal, and ordered the American athletes to report there. It was not long before all involved would get a clear demonstration of their coach's demand for discipline with no special treatment for anyone. Any of Walker's former athletes could have forewarned the Olympians. Walker recalled, "An assistant coach came to me and said that we had a problem. When I asked what it was he said one of the team members didn't want to come to the camp. I said to the coach, 'We don't have a problem, he has a problem. He either attends the camp or he doesn't jump in Montreal. Now you tell him— or I will tell him.'" The jumper reported to Plattsburgh with the others.

Bruce Jenner was among the athletes. Coaching a decathlete is an admitted challenge for any track and field coach. Walker recalled, "You have to persuade them to work on all ten events, otherwise they will tend to spend an inordinate amount of time on their weakest events at the expense of losing the edge on those in which they are strongest, where they are going to get the most points. Bruce had one of the most incredible work ethics I have ever encountered. From Munich, where he had finished tenth, until Montreal, he took everything else out of his life."

Walker also made sure that "everybody on my team lived in the Olympic Village." Throughout his career he would vehemently hold to the theory that unless an athlete lives in the Village with others from around the world, it was not possible to enjoy what he calls the "true Olympic experience."

Two days before the Games opened, international politics again moved from the wings to center stage. Twenty-four nations, mostly African, left Montreal, protesting New Zealand's admission to the Games. New Zealand had sent a rugby team on a tour of South Africa the year before. The African nations cited this in violation of a sports ban that had been imposed on South Africa because of its racial policies. Walker was approached and urged to join the boycott. His response was not surprising. "The Olympic Games are above politics," he said.

Once the Games were underway the world's athletes swept away the residue of the off-field struggles and performed brilliantly. A teenage gymnast from Romania became the sensation of the Games. Nadia Comaneci scored perfect tens in her routines. On the track, Bruce Jenner set a world record in the decathlon, to be crowned the world's greatest athlete after which he circled the track on his victory lap, waving the American flag. America won both the 400- and 1,600-meter relays, Arnie Robinson won the gold in the long jump and Mac Wilkins won the gold in the discus throw.

Perhaps Walker's greatest coaching triumph in Montreal involved the quiet young man in the 400-meter hurdles. It was Walker who persuaded Edwin Moses and his coach, Lloyd Jackson, that Moses had world-class potential in the intermediate hurdles. Only a few months prior to Montreal, Moses began to grind out the regimen that would ultimately lead him to athletic glories beyond his dreams. When Walker began to help prepare Moses for the Olympics, he strengthened the athlete with a most "demanding" cycle program. The drill involved sprinting around the track on the inside without taking the hurdles, then, after having energy drained by that, and without letting up, he would swerve into the lane and take five of the ten hurdles. In an interview with NBC's Tom Brokaw during the Atlanta Games in 1996, Moses recalled, "I thought at first Dr. Walker was trying to kill me! I was confused and it was Dr.

Walker who said this is what you have to do. He is modest, but those of us who know him think he is a genius. I began to improve by a half second a race starting at 50.1. When I got to 48.9, I knew I had a chance to strike for a world record." Moses' world record in Montreal was 47.64. Forced to skip the Moscow Games in 1980 because of the American boycott, he came to Los Angeles to win the gold and for the next ten years won every race he entered. "Dr. LeRoy Walker gets credit for my success," he said.

Montreal was a once-in-a-lifetime experience for Walker and his family. "They were all there. Katherine, the children and the grandchildren had shared an unforgettable family event and for the first time all of them observed, close-up, the full impact of LeRoy's accomplishments in international sport. Shortly after the Games, Walker, 58, ended his remarkable coaching career. He cited several reasons: "I wanted to leave the NC Central team at its peak. Out of seven people, I had two Olympians. Central was cutting back on track support, recruiting got to be tougher and I was losing a little zest."

Before the year was out, Walker was inducted into the North Carolina Sports Hall of Fame and received the highest honor bestowed by the University of North Carolina, the prestigious O. Max Gardner Award, named for the former governor associated with innovations in higher education.

For several years, Walker served on various committees of the USOC. In 1976, he was put on the Executive Board. His committee work included the awarding of grants to worthy grassroots programs that were developing Olympic athletes. It was here he began absorbing the money matters of budgets and allocations of the world's largest national Olympic committee. In 1977 he was elected to the presidency of an organization that had 50,000 members, the American Alliance for Health, Physical Education, Recreation and Dance. His legacy there would be the focus he brought to the further development of women's sports and his work to bring unity to the Southern states where there had been two separate professional organizations: black and white.

His predecessor at AAHPERD, Celeste Ulrich, "educator supreme" at UNC Greensboro and the University of Oregon and one of LeRoy's staunchest lifetime supporters, stood with him through many battles. She gave this touching tribute at the time of his retirement from North Carolina Central University, thanking him for his "caring concern for the weak, the misfit, the neglected; for the numerous opportunities to laugh and cry with you as problems were faced and challenges were undertaken; for the international example of excellence which you have set. And for your ability to walk with kings, yet not lose the common touch."

The Grandchildren

Katherine and LeRoy were doting grandparents. Shawn, first child of LeRoy, Jr. and Judi, was born in January 1969 in New Brunswick, New Jersey, where his father worked as a program analyst for IBM. Shawn's sister Melodie was born in September 1972. The family then lived in Maryland following an IBM transfer for LeRoy, Jr. Wanda Evon Wade was born in February 1971 "in the middle of an earthquake in Inglewood, California." She remains the only child of Carolyn Walker Hopp. When Carolyn and Clayton Wade were divorced, Carolyn moved with her child to Seattle, Washington where she met Bruce Hopp. "I was about 12 when mother and Bruce married," said Wanda Wade, "and I was really angry with my real father. I could never understand how he could have left his child. I later realized that he loved me, was not a bad person and was never trying to hurt me. From day one, Bruce has treated me like his daughter. He was there with me for every game, soccer, basketball, track; he was there for it all. It was later that I realized that Bruce was a good dad in every way and I let him know that now."

His grandchildren call LeRoy "Papa," which they pronounced "Pah-Pah." Walker made a special effort to take Katherine and the grandchildren on Summer trips. Those forays are the children's warmest memories of their childhood. "They were wonderful trips," said Wanda, "we probably hit every amusement park in America.

Once we flew to California and stayed three weeks!" LeRoy and Katherine had little or no discipline problems with the three grandchildren. They were respectful, fun-loving children who were easy to manage, even for a month's journey. Wanda, then, and perhaps now, the bravest risk-taker, recalled the infamous "Oreos cookie incident" when she tried to outsmart Papa. "Grandma always packed sandwiches and cookies. I was hungry and asked her for an Oreos cookie (that were in a bag near me in the back seat). She replied, 'No,' because we would be stopping soon for dinner. I am about six and I am being real sneaky. I pretend that I am coughing while I am going into the bag for the cookies. My cousins are watching and are having nothing to do with this. As I am coughing, I am saying, 'Pa-Pa, are we almost there?' Next I heard the turn signal blinker go on. Grandmother never even turned around. Grandfather gets out and proceeds to spank my little legs good, while reminding me that grandmother had said 'No' to the cookies. He told me much later that he had watched the whole episode in the rear-view mirror. (Thereafter) I hated Oreos. It took me ten years to begin eating them again." While initially enrolling at NC State University, Wanda got her degree in 1995 from Shaw University in Raleigh, where she starred on the basketball team. But she began to encounter racial pressures that she was not prepared for.

"It was culture shock. In Seattle, you didn't deal with any racial stuff. I was used to being around all kinds of people—it was never a big deal. When I came South, I was exposed to African-Americans en masse. Wanda inherited her grandfather's love of sports and, while small in stature like him, she relished the challenge of competition. She sought to be independent of his fame but was often unsuccessful.

"You would never hear me saying I was his granddaughter, but when I was at Shaw and his picture appeared on the cover of Ebony magazine it was devastating for me. The students started in on me, 'So, that's your Grandfather.' They would even ask me for tickets to the Olympics and would try to use me to get to him." Wanda first realized how famous her Grandfather had become when she attended a banquet in his honor and listened to the accolades. "I leaned over and said 'Papa, he is talking about you, right?' He said, 'Yes.' So I said, 'Well, that means you are really a neat guy.' He broke into laughter and said, 'Yeah, that means Papa is a neat guy.' I love him to death, but he will always be Papa before he is LeRoy T. Walker."

Wanda figures she inherited her analytical skills from her grandfather. But some of his lessons came the hard way. Once at the CIAA tournament, her team had the ball out-of-bounds and Wanda was to pass it in. Near the in-bounds play on press row sat Papa with the basketball coaching legend John McLendon. Wanda recalled: "Papa said to me, very quietly, Don't make a cross-court pass because that tall girl is going to pick it off.' I did, and she did, and scored. After the game, he walked over with a big smile, hugged me and said 'Precious' (that's what he calls me), 'I am proud of you for playing a good game.' Then he leaned over, kissed me on the cheek and whispered, 'But I told you not to throw that pass.'"

Wanda Wade has her mother's pretty features and a penchant for short hair, like her mother and grandmother. "My mother and my grandmother's names are tattooed to my heart; they are just the world to me."

Katherine Dies

She was an absolutely wonderful person.

—LeRoy T. Walker

Katherine Walker died on Easter Sunday, 1978. "It all happened in one month," recalled her husband. "She had a strange combination of diabetes and high-blood pressure that even Duke hospital couldn't get under control. I guess the only blessing is she didn't suffer in that month's time. If she did she kept it from us." Katherine had gone West to visit her daughter, Carolyn, and had stopped in Atlanta to visit her sister-in-law, Elsa Mae. The doctors at Duke ran tests just before she left town. Her physician called the Walker home and asked that she report to the hospital as soon as possible. "I went to Atlanta to get her and at the same time tried not to alarm her," LeRoy remembers. "On that last Saturday, I was at the hospital chatting with her. The next morning, Easter Sunday, I got the call. The lady said 'Dr. Walker I have bad news for you.'"

To this day, LeRoy Walker Jr. has a bit of a mental block about his mother's death. He still tries to erase the date. He, Judi, and the children had returned late from a trip to New Jersey where they spent Easter with Melodie's godparents. Arriving home about 1 a.m. following the long drive, they were surprised when the phone jangled ten minutes later. LeRoy, Jr. looked at his wife, Judi, and said to her that it was not a good sign. When he picked up the phone his father told him his mother had "passed away."

The beginning of Katherine Walker's demise was nearly imperceptible, but it was Judi who noticed first. Following a visit, Judi asked LeRoy, Jr. if he had seen anything different about his mother. He had not. Judi noted that Katherine could recall events thirty years ago but would forget what she had just been talking about minutes before and then repeat it. Judi suggested that they discuss her observations with LeRoy, Sr. He had, he said, regretfully detected a change in his wife. They got her in the hospital for an examination. Katherine was found to be in the clutches of severe diabetes that had already ravaged her kidneys. She was immediately put on insulin and a strict diet. Shortly, she began dialysis treatments. She put up such a good front for the family that LeRoy, Jr. would interpret her mood as "in good spirits" when he would come from Maryland on weekends to visit her. He was confused, however, when her dialysis treatments were increased. He demanded to see his mother's doctor and the encounter was not pleasant for either man. "He must have been having a bad day," said LeRoy, Jr., "or he may have been agitated with my insistence on seeing him, but he just looked at me and said 'She is never going to get better.' It was like somebody had hit me several times with a four-by-four. I was stunned. I went to the phone and called Judi. When she answered I told her what the doctor had said and we wept."

§

The beloved matriarch had fallen and the impact was devastating. As soon as LeRoy, Jr. arrived in Durham from Maryland, he demanded to be allowed to see his mother's body and had to be convinced that while the body was being prepared for the wake, it would not be appropriate to view it.

At the family home, LeRoy, Sr. was in the full grip of loss and grief as the children began to gather round him. The funeral was held at St. Phillips Church in Durham, the family's smaller church, St. Titus, could not hold the overflow crowd.

Katherine's legacy was her magnificent gift to her husband and children. Her unfailing devotion to them throughout her life had strengthened and sustained them, helping each to flourish and bloom in every way possible. She was a refuge in the storm, the ultimate mother, the supportive wife, the teacher-disciplinarian and the wellspring of the joy that permeated her home. It was to her husband that she bestowed the most unselfish gift of all, complete support and understanding of his goals and aspirations. Walker's work had kept him away from home a great percentage of the time. The training and discipline of the children fell to Katherine and she accepted the task without reservation. Her lively son learned early that even though Dad was often not on the premises, his impact was ever-present and flowed to him through his mother. The street that ran past the Walker's faculty house on the campus of NC College was paved past their front door but then became a dirt lane at the end of a long hill. The neighborhood boys on their bikes would gather momentum, come off the asphalt at top speed, continuing to race along the dirt road for another fifty yards. Once, in a reckless moment of jubilation, LeRoy, Jr. came down the hill steering the bike with his feet on the handlebars, his arms spread as if in flight. Katherine, who had watched this macho display of carelessness, emerged from the house, relieved her son of the bike and stored it for a week. When the boy protested, she shared with him her motherly mission. "When your father is away," she said. "I am responsible for you and your sister. Had you been hurt on the bike, your father would have asked me why I had allowed you to ride like that." Case closed.

"Her asset was that of an unbelievable mother," said LeRoy, Sr. "As things began to develop in my life and I could have taken her abroad, she did not want to do anything that would take her away from the children. The only time she went was Montreal and we were all there, the whole family. Added to the tragedy of her passing was that I had become a full professor, the kids were grown and out, and we could have had some time together." Shawn Walker was 10 at the time.

"It was upsetting when I went to see her before she died. I didn't realize how sick she was so I didn't get to say anything to her. Grandma was everything. I have not been to a funeral since."

Melodie recalled, "It hit the hardest the first Christmas. Grandma had given me a stuffed frog that I named 'Froggy' and she had told me if I kissed him a prince would come." Melodie was a pre-schooler when her grandmother died. Her parents had some concern about whether, in her child's mind, she had really understood what death was and the earthly finality of it. They told the child that her Grandmother had "gone up to heaven."

Sometime later when Melodie announced to her father that she wanted to "send Grandma a message," he quickly diverted the little girl to her mother because "Judi just knows how to handle things like that," recalled LeRoy, Jr. With characteristic sensitivity to the child's request, Judi asked Melodie what she thought would be a good way to accomplish sending the message. Melodie replied, "On a balloon."

Judi brought home a helium-filled balloon. Melodie scribbled a love note to her grandmother. Her brother, Shawn, also wrote out a message. The notes were tied to the string, and while tears were being choked back by the adults, the family stood in the yard and watched the little heaven-bound balloon until it disappeared, carrying the children's messages to their Grandma.

Continuing Without Katherine

For the first time in forty years, LeRoy Walker was without his beloved Katherine.

He increased his travel schedule and found that he dreaded returning to the home he had built for his wife and family, and that had been his safe refuge from the storms of life. It was now painfully empty. Katherine's cheerful voice was not there to welcome him from a long and tiresome trip, her clatter and chatter around the house had been silenced. The familiar sights and sounds of the children had long-since passed. LeRoy, Jr.'s bike was not parked in the yard and Carolyn's dance music was no longer a part of the cacophony of the sound of a family. LeRoy even considered selling the house on Red Oak Avenue. Just past 60, he found himself a widower.

As the years went by, family and friends began to speculate over whether he would seek out companionship or remarry. Although he was still vigorous and attractive to women, remarriage was not to be. "Katherine was the perfect wife for me," he said. "I was sure that I would never be that lucky twice in one lifetime."

No one knows precisely the extent of the impact of Katherine's death on LeRoy Walker. There were signs that it was deep and lasting.

Long-time friend Stan Wright said: "What kept him on the move so intensely was Katherine's death. She died in the prime of her life. LeRoy was depressed. He was grieving. He was alone, his son and daughter, grown and gone. "To get away from the grieving, he had to keep moving. A lot of what he has accomplished was in tribute to her."

CHAPTER SIX

THE EIGHTIES

1980 Boycott

In an interview before the 1996 Atlanta Games, former President Jimmy Carter was asked about the U.S. boycott of the 1980 Olympic Games in Moscow. He revealed that while he was reviled by many athletes and coaches for the action, he had the support and encouragement of some segments of the U.S. Olympic movement. Carter declared the boycott following the Soviet Army's crossing into Afghanistan. Sixty-one other free nations joined America in refusing to send teams to Moscow.

The impact on American athletes was devastating. In Durham, hurdler Charles Foster told the press he supported his President, but inside he was heartbroken. Only other Olympic athletes can truly appreciate the depth of that kind of despair. After years engaged in a bruising training regimen, the sweat, discipline and dedication to a lifestyle that others could never comprehend, and to suddenly have the opportunity to measure oneself against the best in the world evaporate and the dream of Olympic glory shattered is devastating. Most would never again be physically able, nor motivated, to reach the peak of Olympic competition again. Their time had passed. Among those athletes who felt they were being used for the country's foreign policy goals was Anita DeFrantz, a rowing bronze medalist in 1976 in Montreal. She vehemently opposed the boycott and sued the

USOC. "I didn't get to compete in 1980 and I believed that individual athletes should make their own decisions about whether they would compete in Moscow," she declared. DeFrantz was awarded the Olympic Order, the highest honor given by the IOC, "for her work on behalf of athletes' right to compete." Walker publicly supported the President and talked with Foster and his other athletes about it.

Walker and others were called to the White House for meetings that were designed to sell them on the boycott. He recalled the national security advisor "showing all these charts about how the Russian's moves were going to affect all of us in the U.S. My first confrontation with ABC's Sam Donaldson was (as I was) coming out of one of those meetings. He asked me one of his loaded questions about the boycott and about it being in the best interest of the U.S. I said, 'No!' He said, 'I don't understand.' I said that was the difference between sport and politics, and this was sport."

The Chancellorship

LeRoy has never looked at any student in any other way except that he or she is a child of God with some innate ability who, if pushed, can achieve.
—William C. Friday, President, Emeritus, UNC

The crown of LeRoy Walker's many achievements in academia was surely that of his tenure as chancellor of North Carolina Central University. The years of preparation, his varied experiences in the classroom and in the field of competition, the scars of battles well fought, and a keen sense of his and the university's place in the community all came together with such focus as to allow him to renew and refocus the goals of the institution and to reestablish its rightful place in the mainstream of the University of North Carolina system.

Dr. Albert N. Whiting was the first head of the institution to carry the title of chancellor. Whiting served with distinction from July 1, 1967 until June 30, 1983. When the school became a part of the University of North Carolina system in 1972, the title of President was replaced by that of Chancellor.

In the Fall of 1982, Walker returned from a successful and professionally satisfying fifteen months at the U.S. Military Academy at West Point. He was invited there to help the academy assimilate females into the rigors of the physical training requirements of the cadets. On an approved leave of absence from North Carolina Central University, Walker was there from May of 1981 to October of 1982. In his free time, he worked on a book for secondary-school coaches titled, *Track and Field for Boys and Girls.*

At West Point, Walker was in his element. He loved the discipline and high standards and was impressed with the cadets positive response to a crushing work load and their time management techniques. The academy needed his expertise to help revise the battery of physical tests so the females could perform the same maximum endurance standards as the males, but customized to their muscle groups and bone structure. The academy's faith in Walker's knowledge, training and experience was well-placed. He reviewed the fitness training standards for a field soldier and, from that, devised and recommended physical training and testing criteria for the women. He was sensitive to the attitudes of resistance facing the females and helped them every way he could to establish an acceptable posture in the formerly all male bastion of America's elite military training academy.

When Walker returned to Durham, the NCCU campus was suffering a full-blown case of anxiety over the selection of a new chancellor, following the retirement of Albert Whiting. Walker realized the depth of the turmoil when he attended an acrimonious faculty meeting at which divisions became even more pronounced over the names of candidates already submitted to the board of trustees.

UNC President William C. Friday had received pertinent information on two nominees for the post. He was beginning to feel, and resist, the strong push he was getting to quickly move forward with one of the two names he had been given. He had not satisfied himself that the names of those submitted to him constituted a sufficient search.

Friday had been the architect of the restructuring of the entire university system in 1971 and 1972, and had put up one of the most valiant battles ever waged in the history of academia to keep federal and state political control out of his campuses. The most tumultuous fight had involved the U.S. Department of Health, Education and Welfare over desegregation issues.

Now, Friday was deeply concerned about the direction of North Carolina Central University and was not about to be stampeded into a hasty decision. He recalled the campus had "an unstable administrative relationship at the time."

John Jordan, a Raleigh attorney and then chairman of the UNC Board of Governors, remembered the campus was "troubled." "There was dissension among the trustees and faculty. There was student unrest and racial problems. I remember going to that campus once when black students were trying to bar white students from working on the student newspaper. It was not uncommon to pick up a paper and read that trustee meetings at Central had turned into shouting matches."

On a Winter afternoon in 1983, Friday received a call from Central's Academic Dean Dr. Leonard Robinson requesting a meeting to which he would invite LeRoy Walker. Friday agreed and invited his longtime colleague, UNC Vice President Raymond Dawson, to attend the meeting. Friday recalled that for the next hour-and-a-half "We listened to a very clear analysis of the state of mind and the state of affairs on the campus at Central. "For about forty-five minutes LeRoy took the lead in outlining, in clear detail, what was wrong with the institution." Then with what Friday described as "an uncommon sense of devotion and concern," Walker outlined specific recommendations to address those issues. When the "impressive performance" was concluded, the men from Central said their farewells and left the room. Friday and Dawson sat quietly for a moment, looked at each other and said, practically in unison, "There's our chancellor!"

Without the approval of the Board of Governor, Friday had the authority to immediately appoint Walker as interim chancellor with no time limitation. He called John Jordan, of the UNC Board of Governors. Jordan said Friday was enthusiastic when relating his "remarkable experience" and finished a recap of the meeting by telling Jordan he wanted to appoint Walker as interim immediately. "Walker didn't go to Friday looking for a job," said Jordan, "but he was concerned about the school." Following that meeting, Friday phoned Walker and asked him to give thought to taking over the top job. Walker said he "took the comment as a compliment" and, as planned, headed out to the NAIA basketball tournament.

While Walker was gone, Friday quickly set the stage for his decision. By the time Walker returned from the tournament, the president was ready for an answer. The next day he called Walker to his office and officially offered him the job. Walker accepted and recalled "There was nothing in writing, we just shook hands." Friday said to Walker, "You need to turn it around. I know you believe in all those things you talked about during our previous meeting and you have my support. Now, go do it."

Friday was confident he would be on solid ground with the decision to install Walker. Faculty members as well as people in the community had already contacted his office supportive of Walker. But how would the academic community accept an untraditional selection for chancellor, even an interim chancellor, who came from the ranks of coaching and physical education? A "jock," as it were, taking the reins of a major university. It was a superb choice. Friday recounted: "What we had was a man who was widely known in the academic world, had a good relationship in the community, could pull people together, and everybody on campus trusted him." Walker's perspective was: "I had been there since Dr. James Shepard; I knew all the skeletons in the closet, so to speak."

When Walker took over on July 1, 1983, he was determined to shore up morale among the students, faculty and staff. He did this in a number of ways. He set a theme for his administration: "Excellence Without Excuse: A Shared Responsibility." He assured his faculty that he would live by that axiom and would demand it of them. More important, he measured them by it. Walker knew he had competent people who were, by his own description, "sitting on their hands." The new chancellor was familiar with the latest methodology of evaluation and he installed a tight system. No one was exempt. He also determined that the root of most of the morale problems among the faculty and staff was the personnel committee. "The committee was up in the 'Ivory Tower' deciding what everybody would get with regard to raises," he said. Walker dismantled the committee and called for a halt to the accepted practice of "across the board" raises. He knew that some people deserved raises, while others did not. He set up a system of pay raises based on merit.

Many were upset at these quick, dramatic measures, but Walker plunged ahead. With the elimination of the committee, he put the responsibility "back on the deans." He placed the merit moneys under the supervision of the deans. The system worked like this: Walker would evaluate the vice chancellors, they would evaluate the deans, the deans would evaluate the department heads, and they would evaluate the professors and teachers. The evaluations would be based on specific criteria designed to bring about a greater degree of proficiency in the classroom and a more energized commitment to the student.

In meetings with the faculty, Walker drove home his "no excuse" mandate. He exhorted his faculty to put aside the intimidation factor that he knew some of them harbored in the shadows of UNC-Chapel Hill, Duke, State and Wake Forest, and to concentrate on fully preparing Central students to compete. He said, "When industry comes to our campus to recruit they are going to put us in the same pot with those great universities."

Walker addressed the issue of tenure. He re-read the law of tenure with the faculty and pointed out that there was not one line in it about longevity. He warned that they should stop depending on the tenure law to keep them there. He said, "You don't have to worry about the adage 'publish or perish,' and please consider tenure as an avenue to free you up to be a better teacher."

Finding it necessary to terminate some people, he sent an undiluted message around the campus that he was serious about his mission. In the weeks before students returned for the Fall term, Walker refined his plans. He sought out and met with student leaders, the student government association president and the editors of the campus publications. He made a point to be visible and accessible to the students.

Two thousand people attended his first convocation in the Fall. Seniors were given a special invitation to appear in their caps and gowns in the impressive processional, with the faculty appearing in full academic regalia to engender an atmosphere of focus on scholarship. The new chancellor set a new tone. He challenged the faculty to be more demanding of their students, and the students to set aside any notion that society owed them anything. Then, this man who had spent more than half of his adult life on the receiving side of bigotry, urged his students to purge themselves of racial bias and religious intolerance. He assured them that the university would continue to celebrate its heritage as an historically black institution but only by "its performance in the mainstream of education."

Walker's speech was well-received. Among quotations in the campus newspaper were very positive student reactions, such as, "He presented me a challenge to strive for excellence." Walker reached out to the community for support and got it. On the solid belief that he would improve the University, some influential community leaders joined him in his quest. Industry CEOs with whom Walker had been consulting advised him to look at factors beyond simply the academic degree. They communicated their need for young people trained in life and communication skills, who could then be sent to customized seminars to train for the specific work required by their companies.

Walker was passionate about upgrading the quality of students entering his university as well as the curricula being offered those already enrolled. He was not at all comfortable with some of the enrollment standards that he inherited.

"We were just taking anybody," he said. "Our SAT (requirement) then was something like six or seven hundred." Central had installed a "catch-all" academic basin called the Academic Skills Center. It accommodated what Walker called "non-qualifiers," students who did not have the academic preparation nor the requirements to enter under the regular admission standards. The assumption was that within a semester, or at most a year, highly skilled teachers could move them to the level of the overall student body. "While on the surface it seemed like a good idea," said Walker, "I saw it as a distinct disadvantage." He had learned that some high school counselors were advising these borderline students that if they were unable to make it at Shaw University in Raleigh or at North Carolina A&T in Greensboro, then they "could always go to NC Central." The center was supported by a federal assistance program. Walker observed that once those students got into those "special" classrooms, the teachers, by Walker's description, "started teaching down to them. It affected the entire campus," he said, "They had some fine teachers, and all kinds of equipment, but this was not good for us." He eliminated the Academic Skills Center.

He took new scholarship money and targeted the opposite end of the scale—student prospects. It was called The Valedictorian Program. He sought out high schools of reputation to recruit their most accomplished students. "I knew that would change the attitudes of everybody on campus, including the professors," he said, "and in just two years we raised the SAT standard by 125 points!"

Another problem Walker saw as holding back the institution was student discipline, both in personal behavior and in college financial matters. A facet of the discipline problem was that of campus security. Chidley Hall, a men's dorm, got a significant amount of his attention. The safety of his students was a primary concern. When the school was founded it was on the outskirts of the city. Now it lies between two busy city thoroughfares. Off-campus visitors had a free passport to the campus simply by turning into the drive. At a meeting with the students, Walker reviewed his concerns and issued a new set of rules for visitation. Students and student visitors would only be able to enter one door of their dorms where credentials would be checked. He told them: "We are not going to have the public coming in and out of your buildings when we don't even know who they are." The student response was not unexpected by Walker. They told him there was no way they would agree to comply with such a rule. He replied that if they entered any door besides the one designated for the credentials check, they would be arrested. "I actually had some students arrested," he said. "Which, of course, was very unpopular." In keeping with his lifetime policy of dogged preparation for every eventuality, Walker had already talked with a local judge about what he wanted to accomplish and the judge agreed that if students had to be arrested, they would work out some public service and an official charge would not show up on their permanent records. "But I initially had to get the student's attention with a "two-by-four," he said. Walker's control of the student body and the university under his terms was not without difficulty. Nearly every student on campus, or those thinking about enrolling, were well aware that their new chancellor was a sports legend.

Walker's skill in dealing with youth on a personal level would be difficult to match. His commitment to the student is perhaps described best by his friend, Dr. William C. Friday, who said: "LeRoy has never looked at any student in any other way except that he or she was a child of God with some innate ability, who, if pushed, can achieve."

Walker worked hard to make it easier for students to get more scholarship money. Friday backed him with solid support. Walker said, "I wanted to help the 'C' student become a 'B' student and wanted to help the 'B' student to become an 'A' student."

A confrontation with the students arose over the issue of parking. The students parked their cars "all over the campus, often blocking access to the administration building." When he presented his more restrictive parking rules there was an uproar. Walker reminded the student body president that eighty percent of the students at Central were on some type of academic aid. Among the stipulations for academic aid was that those students were not to have a car on campus. Walker assured the student leader that he did not want to take away from any student, but that he would be tough in the application of the "no car" rule for students on aid if they decided to fight him on the new parking restrictions. The parking problem was solved.

Walker took perhaps the hardest line on the lax enforcement of policy regarding the student's financial responsibility to the university. "People were simply leaving and not paying," Walker recalled. "And the UNC system was charging me for that." The system was called "deferred payments" and Walker cut off these financial extensions. Five months before he put the new policy into effect Walker's office mailed the new rules for tuition payment to every student and every parent. The letters were mailed in early Summer "in plenty of time for the students and their families to process the new policy."

At the first attempt of administration enforcement of the new rules, the students organized a protest. With placards and chants, they occupied the administration building and blocked off access to the chancellor's office. Two-hundred-fifty students jammed into the building with the vow that they would not be moved until their grievances were addressed to their satisfaction. It was a direct challenge to Walker's authority and his handling of it was critical. Calling in a small group of student leaders, Walker drew the line. When the students claimed they had not been given time to respond to the new rules, Walker produced a copy of the letter sent to each of them and their parents several months before. Armed with facts and reason, Walker persuaded them that he took the responsibility for their welfare very seriously and that he needed their cooperation if at all possible, but if it were not forthcoming, he would look after the best interests of the University. The students hoped to get media attention with their protests but Walker had a long-established open relationship with the local reporters and they were not inclined to be manipulated on behalf of furthering students' demands if they were designed to simply bash the Chancellor. Some media contacted Walker about the uprising, but the students got little response. Faculty who were sympathetic with students' demands—and who tried to circumvent Walker's authority by going to UNC President Friday—found that he was totally supportive of his new Chancellor's decisions. They were sent back with the suggestion that they take up their grievances directly with Walker. Walker stanched the flow of those students skipping out on the University without paying: "Each time it happened, the $2,000 would come out of Central's allotment."

During the give-and-take stresses of change, Walker was held up to resistance and criticism by some, however, he never wavered from what he thought was best for his students and the welfare of the university. He had invested the better part of his professional life at that institution and now he was in a position to make the changes he thought necessary. When criticism arose about the high percentage of out-of-state students being admitted to Central, he pointed out that it was a UNC *system* problem rather than simply a problem at his own campus. He successfully argued that he needed to increase the enrollment, as well as improve the academic quality of incoming students. John Jordan said, "LeRoy began to move in his direct, forthright and honest approach—and you could just see the atmosphere on that campus improve." Jordan once expressed to Walker his philosophy regarding intercollegiate athletics; that he believed there were too many concessions made for athletes. "We are making professionals out of college athletes," he said. To Jordan's delight, Walker agreed. "Here is a guy," said Jordan, "former athlete, outstanding coach and yet he knew what was bothering me because it was bothering him, too."

While the search continued for a permanent chancellor, the sentiment for Walker began to grow. He had come to the chancellor's chair with the idea of staying about a year, but as UNC President Emeritus Bill Friday said, "He did not leave until the job was done." Before Walker retired from the position in 1986, the Board of Trustees would make his appointment permanent. Recalled Friday, "There was never any question about the selection from the Board of Governors, the Trustees, the people on the campus—you know, that's a rare quality today that a man can move through life and have that kind of untarnished reputation."

Duke's Al Buehler said that when UNC President Bill Friday named Walker chancellor, "LeRoy was put on the world scene with the same prestige as any other UNC chancellor. It was almost unheard of that a track coach and head of the physical education department could become the president of a university, but Friday realized how important LeRoy was and that he had all the credentials. He was a great administrator, great with people and he was academically prepared."

Walker summed up his four years as Chancellor: "Overall, it was so pleasant. Morale went up, academic standards went up, and enrollment went up. I enjoyed those times because I could see those positive changes every day." Friday said, "He simply turned it around."

§

When Walker received the prestigious North Caroliniana Society Award given those who "...have given long and distinguished service to the preservation, promotion and enhancement of North Carolina's historical, literary and cultural heritage," his name was added to an illustrious list that includes Sam Ervin, Paul Green and Charles Kuralt. Friday made the presentation and listed Walker's major achievement as that of Chancellor. "He created a new Board of Visitors to help guide the institution; he set about to give life and meaning to the development program and brought substantial moneys to the campus; he redirected the admissions' policies of the institution and spent a good deal of time straightening out financial aid to students and speeding up scholarship fund distributions. He added a General College Studies Program and a Bachelor of

Computer Science degree. A major new physical education complex was dedicated and this facility was at a later time named for him. He moved the school of Library Science to master's level education. But his greatest gift was that of a renewed self-confidence, an enormous sense of pride, and a determination to do all that was required to keep North Carolina Central University in the mainstream of higher education in North Carolina."

The chancellorship had significantly enhanced Walker's prestige, attracted national and international attention, and had accelerated his rise in the Olympic movement.

The Olympic Festival

A year before he stepped down from the University chancellorship, Walker was approached by a Raleigh man, Hill Carrow, who brought all of the exuberance of youth as he shared his dream of landing the Olympic Festival for North Carolina's Triangle area. The U.S. Olympic Festival was the brainchild of former USOC President Robert Kane. The first one was staged in Colorado Springs in 1978 and was called the National Sports Festival. The idea was to attract Olympic athletes to the best venues in America for Olympic-style competition, enhancing their visibility and popularity with millions of Americans who would most likely never be able to attend an Olympic Games.

The festivals became immensely popular, at their peak, attracting 3,000 athletes in thirty-seven sports, with thousands of spectators spiking the economies of the host cities. Carrow was convinced that the universities, colleges and private clubs in Raleigh, Durham, Chapel Hill, Cary, and Greensboro had the combined facilities to successfully stage an Olympic Festival.

The vaunted Research Triangle is truly the "goose that laid the golden egg" for thousands of people who live and work in that rarefied section of North Carolina, making good salaries and enjoying an atmosphere that is increasingly harder to find in America. It began as the vision of a half-dozen people who, four decades ago, eyed acres of undeveloped pine woods situated between

Raleigh, Durham and Chapel Hill, a half-hour's drive separating prestigious universities and colleges. Their dream of an attractive environment for research and development facilities resulted in a unique piece of America characterized by a low crime rate, an extremely low unemployment rate, high salaries, and water and air that, so far, are of semi-enviable purity. One hundred companies and corporations have headquarters or facilities a stone's throw from each other. Forty thousand people go to work in offices located in spectacular buildings in beautifully landscaped piney woods. Executives, deep into six-figure salaries, drive to work in Peugeots alongside well-paid technicians, scientists and administrative people. Whether scientist, technician, researcher or executive, every "park person" is filling some niche in a whirlwind of new concepts and products that citizens of America and the world will reap in the 21st century.

At the upper end of the scale, men and women, with powerful minds, arrive at and depart from Raleigh-Durham International Airport, often aboard corporate Lear jets. In offices surrounded by marble, glass and original art, the global atmosphere permeates. In private dining rooms, the business luncheon agendas focused on the visions of the world tomorrow and the profits to be harvested.

The State has capitalized on the marketing aspects of the success in the pine grove to the extent that North Carolina became the state into which more people were moving than any other. The Triangle is presented to the world as a place where the greatest resources of three wonderful communities have been pooled for the greater good, in a giving spirit of peace and unity. Only those who are forced to deal with the underside of the tri-municipal bellies of Raleigh-Durham-Chapel Hill know of the infighting, factionalization and downright jealousies that exist among the big three, especially those that divide Raleigh and Durham. While there are some municipal concerns where consensus-building and cooperation have been required, there are often significant territorial conflicts.

Into this volatile web wandered Hill Carrow, a young comer with Carolina Power and Light Company in Raleigh. The year was 1980.

Carrow and his buddies made a presentation to the U.S. Olympic Committee. "We were excited and didn't know any better," recalled Carrow. Their proposal was different. It was the first time a bid had been made for the event to be hosted by a multicity coalition. Carrow knew, however, that given the sports-charged atmosphere nourished over the decades by the University of North Carolina in Chapel Hill, North Carolina State University in Raleigh and Duke University in Durham, the event had the potential for success. Their bid for the 1983 Festival fell on deaf ears at the USOC. Raleigh's proposal was held at arm's length. The Festival went to Colorado Springs. Discouraged by what seemed to him a rebuff, Carrow headed back to Raleigh, his dreams temporarily dashed. He was made aware that his bid would be considered for 1987 and he was encouraged to try again. Carrow acted quickly, formed a nonprofit organization called North Carolina Amateur Sports, and began to seek more help. Carrow was well aware of the great success of LeRoy Walker as a coach, chancellor and now head of major committees in the USOC.

Walker agreed to help and, in 1985, he was asked to serve as Chairman of the Board for the Festival. His impact was immediate and positive. "LeRoy had tremendous political know-how," said Carrow, who had now been named the Festival executive director. For two-and-a-half years, the young group and the old sage worked together. Carrow described the mix as a "good blend." As they set about making the contacts, getting sponsors and gathering commitments from the Triangle cities, there were many "ups and downs." Carrow said that during the "head-buttings" it was Walker who lifted them back to the proper perspective and reassured them that their goals could be accomplished. His vast experience in forging coalitions among reluctant parties sustained and encouraged the younger ones. "LeRoy had been through a lot of that," said Carrow, "he was used to it. Besides, he has a tremendous network, is one of the most astute politicians I have ever seen, and never, I mean never, burns a bridge." The Festival selection committee of the USOC met in Orlando, Florida. "We were staying at the Hyatt

Hotel," recalled Carrow. "I was out in the hall passing out pamphlets and video tapes touting Raleigh's bid, and LeRoy was working his contacts on the inside." The vote was to be taken during the Saturday morning session of the USOC. Carrow studied the agenda carefully. He knew the selection vote was at the top of the list, which would allow just enough time for him to fly from Orlando to participate in his best friend's wedding that same day in Tennessee. To his horror, USOC President Bill Simon made a last-minute change in the agenda, moving the Festival selection vote to the end. Carrow was doomed to miss the voting. He left for the airport, yet still missed his plane. Alone and brooding, while waiting to board the next available flight, he was surrounded by Walker and other members of the Raleigh delegation who informed him that Raleigh had the bid.

Carrow, Walker and the Raleigh committee now had two-and-one -half years to pull it together. "LeRoy had a lot of know-how and great ideas," said Carrow. Walker was the visionary, the younger man, the implementer. They were committed to presenting a first-class event and staying within their budget.

To say that the Olympic Festival in Raleigh and the Triangle was a success is an understatement. Forty-five attendance records were broken and nearly a half-million people came to see the Games.

"And we were far and away the best ever financially," said Carrow. "We came out with a net profit of $1.5 million!" Walker and Carrow flew to a USOC meeting in Oklahoma City with a check for its portion of the profits. While the Committee had heard rumors of a large check, they were floored when Carrow and Walker unveiled a giant facsimile check for $750,000. Of the remaining money, $450,000 went to create a foundation for amateur sports and $300,000 went into North Carolina Amateur Sports to support the State games and to promote other amateur sporting events.

For Carrow, the years spent on the project were invaluable to him: "We made the area shine and it provided me a great opportunity to meet truly great people." In 1996, he was director of the Sara Lee Olympic Partnership. Sara Lee was a sponsor of the Centennial Olympic Games in Atlanta at what was called the partner level. That, in monetary terms, means a $40 million stake. The corporation also spent $21 million for licensee rights to sell official Olympic products and paraphernalia. In all, it was a $61 million bet that the corporation would make an impressive profit and promote its brands in a world venue. A company subsidiary outfitted all the U.S. athletes, coaches, staff and 60,000 volunteers with clothing for the Centennial Games. Carrow's assessment of Walker, following two-and-a-half years of intense work leading up to the Festival was this: "He was always professional, courteous and polished. His people skills are simply great. I admired his work ethic. He is a great role model—his physical build, the way he talks. He has a presence."

Proposition 48

And to all those power basketball coaches who keep wanting to lower the academic standards, I say they don't have the athlete's welfare at heart. I will argue that, and they will never change me.

—LeRoy T. Walker

After observing American basketball fans, a foreign visitor might question the notion that our favorite sport is baseball. The popularity of basketball at collegiate and professional levels has reached astounding proportions. Universities and colleges enjoy vast revenues from their winning basketball programs and television networks have found a pot of gold under the nets. A relatively easy and inexpensive event to produce, the telecasts provide ample "time-out" spaces for commercial sponsorship, with added "television time-outs" scattered throughout the game to further shake the money tree.

When Creed Black, who became president of the Knight Foundation, published a series of reports that exposed the rampant abuses in big-time collegiate basketball, there was an outcry for a thorough investigation. The Knight-Ridder publishing giant decided in 1989 that the John S. and James L. Knight Foundation would establish a major task force to study college athletics and make recommendations for reform. It was called The Knight Foundation Commission on Intercollegiate Athletics. The Foundations Board of Trustees selected two educators with national reputations and impeccable credentials to co-chair a select group of athletes, educators, coaches and journalists: William C. Friday, President Emeritus of the University of North Carolina and Father Theodore M. Hesburgh, President Emeritus of the University of Notre Dame.

Early on, Friday met with Father Hesburgh in Washington, D.C., to hammer out the blueprint. At that meeting, Friday strongly recommended that LeRoy Walker be asked to take a leadership role on the Commission and Hesburgh readily agreed.

In 1989, The National Collegiate Athletic Association met in Miami with a specific agenda to "do something about college athletics." A proposal for tougher academic admission standards for athletes and a system to monitor their course of study made it to the floor. Simultaneously, a proposal was offered that would exempt the TBIs, or traditionally black institutions, from the more stringent standards. Friday's description of the ensuing argument was that "divisions were clear and the bludgeoning was going on." Friday described the meeting in Miami as "dramatic, and it was LeRoy's voice, almost alone, that caused the enactment of Proposition 48, the first really substantive academic standard in athletics in modern times."

Walker got the Chair's attention at the Miami meeting, stood and made his forceful declaration, "I want it understood that I will never vote for any standard that treats one race as secondary to another." Walker made a moving speech to the entire delegation. A firestorm of criticism befell him following his impassioned and, in some quarters, unexpected stand for equal requirements for all. As black coaches from the powerful basketball schools came forward with their arguments, Walker never wavered. Friday recalled: "All through the nearly four years of deliberations of the Knight Foundation Commission, LeRoy was that voice. It turned the thing around and Proposition 48 passed and has been one of the best things to happen to intercollegiate sports."

Within Walker's unwavering support of Proposition 48 lies a part of the essence of the man himself. Having been on the receiving end of racism, inequality and unfairness throughout much of his personal and professional life, he simply found those practices contemptible, which forged a lifelong resolve to eradicate them at every level. First, Walker established his interpretation of affirmative action, how it was intended to work and how it can—and often is—used abusively. He wrote a paper titled, "Affirmative Opportunity vs. Affirmative Action."

"The legislation was to have provided equal opportunity," he said, "not to slot people into positions who were not qualified or not up to the standards of the other applicants; that's what causes the tensions and confrontations." Walker saw the legislation as a guide to any organization that truly wanted diversity in its ranks. An equally qualified minority or a female who might ordinarily be overlooked, would have a chance, but the key words for Walker were "equally qualified."

Walker found the idea of altering academic standards for minority athletes repugnant. At another meeting of coaches in New Orleans, Walker had been solicited by coaches to argue that all traditionally black institutions be exempt from Proposition 48. He surprised many delegates when he denounced their pleas for exemption. In his typical swiftness to the point, he said, "Let me rephrase what you are asking me to do. You want me to, in effect, tell every black child in the ninth grade that he or she is too dumb to make a 'C' and too dumb to make a 700 on the SAT. I can't do that."

Some coaches argued that Proposition 48 would cause them to lose access to top black athletes. Walker, again on point with stunning clarity, retorted that if a coach lost a potential black player because he could not meet the standards, it was highly doubtful that the coach would then go recruit a white player to take his place. "They would most likely recruit another black player so their argument doesn't hold water." Walker points to what he calls the classic example of how the initial attempt to provide "diversity" in recruiting in the college ranks was now having the effect of eliminating whites. "All you had to do was to watch the introductions of the starting players when Arkansas played UNC in the Final Four," he said. "They introduced five black players from Arkansas and four from Carolina. I use their own data to refute their arguments," he said, "Sixty five percent of all of the players in Division One are black."

There is irrefutable evidence that Proposition 48 was accomplishing that for which it was designed. "These days there is a much higher percentage of minority athletes graduating," said Walker, " so tell me why that is bad." Walker was outspoken about what he saw as flawed motivation in the coaching ranks. He claimed there were too many basketball coaches trying to get to the Final Four "on the backs of these athletes and if those athletes don't make it into the pros many of them will be selling crack because they can't see other options." Walker pointed out that he was not alone in his stand on affirmative action and on Proposition 48 but he concedes, "I get bashed because of the position I am in."

Bill Friday summed up Walker's contribution this way: "He was a forceful leader and helped draft the report of the Knight Commission that established clear academic requirements and reinforced university control over sports, repositioning the presidents and the chancellors as the authoritative voices in campus athletics. He stood up to criticism and took the heat. He has been a stabilizing influence and I think one of the pivotal people in that long series of deliberations and has done more than anyone on that Commission to settle down intercollegiate sports from the runaway mentality that it had."

The Treasurer

As treasurer, LeRoy was so far beyond the others in coaching and in administration. He taught them all.

—Herb Douglas, Olympian and friend

"No, No, No. The last thing I want to be is a bean counter." LeRoy Walker's initial response to the suggestion that he accept the nomination for treasurer of the U.S. Olympic Committee was not what Jim Morris wanted to hear. LeRoy had been caught off-guard.

"We were at a meeting in Phoenix in 1989. I was talking with USOC member George Steinbrenner at the time, when Jim Morris of the nominating committee tapped me on the shoulder and asked to speak to me," recalled Walker. His name had been placed in nomination for a USOC vice-presidency, but Morris and others wanted him to take over as treasurer, citing his experience as a university chancellor, the presidency of several national sports organizations and his accumulated outstanding service as chair of the USOC's grant-making committee.

The USOC, under the Amateur Sports Act, is charged with fielding America's Olympic Team, allocating money to the governing bodies of each Olympic sport and many grassroots development programs.

"It was my grant-making committee that decided on all the proposals that came to us from the National Governing Bodies of each Olympic sport. We installed an accountability procedure under which you had to prove that you could account for how you were going to use the money before you actually got it. I wanted to have criteria that could be applied in the beginning. I didn't want them spending all the grant money, then coming back and telling us it didn't work. We gave no partial funding for bad proposals. Therefore, the first year I had $3 million left over and with it got into some creative insurance programs. That became one of the most highly accepted pieces of committee work in the USOC. My serving on that committee sort of started my involvement in the officialdom of the USOC."

Morris wanted an immediate decision on the treasurer's post. Walker said he would think about it overnight. His trusted friend, Richard Hollander, an attorney and board member of USA Track and Field, simply said, "Take it!" He did.

Herb Douglas, now a retired business executive, shed insight from the perspective of an African-American achiever. "People actually came to me when they heard LeRoy had been elected treasurer and told me they didn't think he could do the job, and the treasurer who went out had his doubts. Many times people interpret a mild-mannered person as docile. But LeRoy is steel. As a young adult he was humble and reticent, but when backed into a corner he defended himself. "Another thing, we African-Americans who reach a certain level of position, paid or volunteer, can't (afford to) fail. When we handle money we are in the fishbowl. We have to be double-perfect." Douglas, who spent most of his professional life in corporate circles, and who, as early as 1968 became a vice president of a national company, added this candid perspective: "When we are successful we are accepted better in the white community than in the black. If we go too fast, blacks are suspicious and some will try to bring us down."

Walker's tenure as USOC treasurer and chair of the budget committee was marked with a number of creative innovations.

"I implemented the four-year plan. How could we decide where we wanted to be for the next Olympics without advance financial planning? When I first started this, I had to help people with the idea of developing a four-year plan. The executive director of one national governing body told me he didn't have time to do it. I told him that if he didn't give me a plan, he would not get an allocation. The thing I wanted to do most as treasurer was to increase the cash flow. When I came in we got $15.5 million to finance programs to begin the quadrennium. We had a $33 million line of credit. My goal was to have at least $50 million in the coffers to begin the next quadrennium. When I went out as treasurer we had $57.5 million. And, as we approached the Atlanta Games in 1996, we did not have to access our line of credit at all."

Herb Douglas summed up Walker's four years as USOC treasurer: "He was showing the world that African-Americans can run a corporation."

Around the time Walker was elected treasurer of the U.S. Olympic Committee, a young attorney in Atlanta named Billy Payne was about to reveal a daring dream. Neither man had ever heard of the other, yet their lives would collide in such a way that their names would forever be linked to the history of the Olympic movement.

❖

CHAPTER SEVEN

THE NINETIES

Atlanta Over Athens

The ancient Olympic Games go back three thousand years to Athens, Greece when youth gathered for Games and contests that included running, boxing and wrestling. The five-day event ended with a round of dancing, singing and elaborate banquets. It was from this practice that people recognized that the Games were conducive to better understanding among cultures, even among enemies, and a general nurturing of goodwill among nations. Instead of gold medals, the winning athletes were crowned with wreaths of olive branches, which they wore as proud symbols of their victories on the playing field. The Romans disbanded the Olympic Games. It was not until the late 1800s that an educator from France, Baron Pierre de Coubertin, decided to revive the Games as a way to promote better understanding among peoples of the world. It took more than half-a-decade before he could gain enough support from other nations to stage the first Modern Olympic Games in 1896 in Athens, at which 311 male athletes from thirteen countries participated.

One hundred years later in July 1996, 10,000 male and female athletes from 197 countries gathered in Atlanta, Georgia for the Centennial Games. Since 1896, the Olympics have been held every four years, except for the World War years of 1916, 1940 and 1944.

While every effort has been made, dating back to de Coubertin, to protect the Games from politics and nationalism, there have been notable exceptions to the ideals of the ancient Greeks. The Summer Games of 1972 are remembered for the blood bath in Munich.

The 1976 Games in Montreal, Canada were marred by a boycott by more than one-fourth of the nations of the world. The issues were apartheid in South Africa and the official representation of Communist China.

The United States joined sixty-one other nations in 1980 to boycott the Games in Moscow, USSR to protest the Soviet invasion of Afghanistan. In retaliation, the Soviet Union and most of the Eastern Bloc nations, refused to participate in the 1984 Games in Los Angeles, California.

The term "Olympiad," or the four-year Olympic period, was adopted from the ancient Greeks. The first Winter Games were staged in 1924 in Chamonix, France. The Olympic Games are granted to a city, not a country, by a site selection committee of the International Olympic Committee.

The history of the selection process is rich with intriguing stories of international politics and infighting among the representatives of the various countries. Needless to say, a city in the competition needs support from around the world if it ever hopes to gain the coveted honor as host.

The United States, with the most powerful contingent in the Olympic movement, is unable, without broad support from other countries, to tilt the table.

The United States Olympic Committee is responsible for taking applications from American cities seeking selection, applying the required criteria, and coming up with a single city to endorse and present to the IOC. As the one-hundredth year of the Olympic Games approached, no country was more aware of the historic significance of the century mark of the modern Games than Greece. By all reckoning, it was theorized by the Greeks and others, that the country where both the ancient and the modern Games were first held should surely be chosen as the Centennial site in 1996.

Atlanta's Billy Payne had other ideas.

Billy Payne

They were wonderfully committed people, mostly lawyers and housewives and they literally sat around the table with note pads.

–LeRoy T. Walker

The convergence of the paths of LeRoy Walker and Billy Payne resulted in significant, dramatic consequences. It is the classic story of the fusion of a young man's dream with an old man's experience. Each holding a part of the Olympic puzzle the other needed, their professional relationship was vital to Atlanta's quest for the Games. While the two were separated by decades in age and life experiences, they were very much akin in their drive to succeed, their work ethic and the depth of their tenacity.

To more fully appreciate the impact and complexities involved in the merging of personalities, a profile of the younger man is essential.

The Inforum in downtown Atlanta is one of those business structures that exudes an attitude. If you intend to make a deal inside, you had better be prepared. Not the tallest building in the heart of town but with enough glass and sufficient aura to convey that within its walls are powerful people doing important things. Inside, it gleams of marble, glass, huge curving staircases and glass-stainless-steel elevators. The Atlanta Committee for the Olympic Games offices occupied the fifth and sixth floors. Security at ACOG headquarters was a preview to that which would be put in place for the Games. A visitor to ACOG was put on a one-way track: the first stop a security check point, a metal detector gate and an X-ray belt through which every briefcase, piece of luggage, box, bag, and purse was viewed, the standard routine endured by travelers at airports. Once cleared, one was allowed to take the elevator to the sixth floor. Suite 6000 the penthouse office of ACOG's Chief Executive Officer

Billy Payne. The security in place at ACOG headquarters was a reaffirmation of the hostile climate of the times and particularly the realities of potential political terrorism.

Payne's office was probably no more ostentatious than that of any other corporate CEO in charge of a multibillion-dollar business, impressive in size, location and well-appointed in every detail.

Just behind Billy's desk and facing the room, a television monitor transmitted a live, closed-circuit wide-angle TV camera shot of Olympic stadium, several blocks from Billy's office. At any time of the day or night Payne could, at a glance, view the activity at the construction site of the centerpiece of the 1996 Centennial Olympic Games. This facility was viewed on television by an estimated three of every four people on the planet at sometime during the seventeen days of the Games. The TV picture of Olympic Stadium represented to Payne the physical manifestation of his dream of bringing the world to his beloved city for the commemorative Games of the modern Olympics.

Billy Payne is over six feet tall, of fit weight, with dark hair peppered with gray, a friendly, puggish face stamped with a perpetually boyish, though mostly serious expression. A man of impeccable manners, he exudes cordiality. His voice is a rich baritone with the unmistakable accent of a son of the South; not flat, but with the soft patina of a Southerner who has had the privileges of a good education, a solid grounding in the social graces and extensive travel in 100 countries. His voice carries an added element, hard to define, but a distinct, if not powerful characteristic of the sound that he makes. It is an earnest, evangelical tone that compels those within earshot to listen when he speaks. It is a sound found in the pulpits of not a few Southern churches, those that can boast a pulpit preacher of such power that, during alter call, people move from their seats and up the aisle.

"Let me show you something," he said, and quickly leads his guests to the terrace of his office, which is situated on an outside corner of the building. The view is an impressive panorama of the Atlanta skyline.

It is to the piece of real estate right next door that Payne directs attention. Immediately below Payne's office were twenty-one acres of city that had been razed and by February 1996, scraped clean to the bare earth. It became Payne's dream that this piece of ground in the middle of the city would become the Centennial Olympic Park, a meeting place where 100,000 people could rest, congregate, exchange Olympic pins and refresh themselves.

It had been a rundown area of warehouses and empty lots frequented by drug addicts and alcoholics. Payne looked down from his office in 1993 and visualized an immense park resplendent with trees, wide promenades and dramatic lighting that would become one of the city's loveliest spaces. It remains that today with the added legacy of being the place where a pipe bomb exploded during the Games, killing one and injuring many. At this writing the bomber is still at large.

Payne brought to bear all of his considerable persuasive powers to pull together the political and monetary support for the Olympic Games.

"I am not a visionary," Payne said. "What I brought to the table was a work ethic and the ability to bring focus to a task." Payne said he is a shy man but acknowledges that most people would have difficulty believing that. His work as a real estate attorney kept him behind the scenes and out of the public eye. His professional pursuits in Atlanta, while perhaps not insignificant, were virtually invisible except to his immediate circle of colleagues, clients and his family. Judged by the usual criteria, he was a success.

Billy was born in Athens, Georgia. His father, Porter, was a football star at the university and his son's idol. The boy spent much of the time during his father's rather short life trying to gain his unqualified praise and approval. Billy made excellent grades and distinguished himself in football at the University of Georgia, where he met and married a beautiful Georgian, Martha Beard from Moultrie.

Billy and Martha reared two children in the traditional parenting precepts, taking them to church on Sundays, turning out solid, caring citizens of whom they are justifiably proud. Throughout his life it appeared to the observer that Billy Payne had always given full measure in all his endeavors. The following candid revelation reveals a key to his fanatical drive, against all odds, to gain the bid and stage the 1996 Olympic Games in Atlanta. "I was always aware during my childhood, youth and even adulthood, that I was not performing at my optimum capacity. I knew that as an athlete, and I knew that was the case at work—while to the outside world I may have been pretty good, I always knew the truth. Periodically, I would experience a sort of out-of-body dream where I was doing something that was not physically possible to do. So I think what the Olympics represented was finally something that would give me that opportunity to be able to say that I had finally reached my potential. Consequently, I decided I would pursue this crazy idea at a sacrifice to myself, health-wise and otherwise."

The story of Billy Payne's success in securing the Olympic Games for Atlanta is how one person with an idea and the ability to communicate that idea passionately, can set into motion forces that may bring about monumental events. It all began on a Sunday afternoon in early February 1987. Payne had concluded leading a successful fund-raising effort to build a new sanctuary for his church, St. Luke's Presbyterian of Atlanta. On this Sunday, he heard praise and gratitude from the minister and congregation for his considerable and successful endeavor. Basking in the satisfaction of seeing the results of that church project, he began to think of other ideas of larger impact—much larger. That same day he shared with his wife his desire to be able to do something else that would make a difference before he died. Payne was not obsessed with death but surely aware of his own mortality, given his father's medical history as well as the reality of his own bypass surgery before the age of 35. After church, he startled his wife with his idea for Atlanta to host the

Olympic Games. If he could accomplish that, it would be his lasting gift to city, state and country. As loving wives do when they suspect their husband's schemes have outrun the realities of life, Martha smiled, thinking that the light of the next day would be the end of it. Billy, however, was consumed with this dream and over the years would sweep the world into it. From the moment he took the first step on this decade-long journey, his life would be changed forever. "In '87, I started this as if I had been born the day before," recalled Billy, "I had no knowledge of the Olympic Movement, had never heard of the International Olympic Committee, had no idea when the next Games were available and had never been to the Olympic Games."

Martha Payne insisted that her husband consult with his friend Peter Candler. "Peter is my friend and enormously conservative," recalled Payne. "I guess my wife thought he, hearing my story, would tell me I was crazy." Peter and Marcia Candler came to the Payne home where Billy presented the dream. When he finished, Candler enthusiastically endorsed the idea and Billy asked him to make a financial commitment. A short time later, Candler tapped on Payne's office window and placed a blank check against the glass.

Payne then took the following steps: He withdrew from his law firm, put up as collateral some property he owned and borrowed money to meet family obligations and to pay his expenses for the next three-and-one-half years as he set forth, without a salary, to persuade the Olympic world that he could offer the best place on earth for the Games of 1996. He traveled to wherever he thought he needed to go to garner support. City Hall, however, came first. Enter Andrew Young.

Payne had never met the mayor of his city. Young, a stalwart of the Civil Rights Movement in the 1960s, a friend and confidant of Martin Luther King Jr., a former state legislator, U.S. Congressman and U.S. Ambassador to the United Nations, had been elected Atlanta's mayor for two terms beginning in 1981. Without an appointment, Payne showed up at Young's office and when told that the mayor was busy with scheduled appointments, Payne said that he understood and would wait. That would mark the last time Payne would have the slightest difficulty gaining access to the mayor. When the two men finally sat together, the meeting was an electrified fusion of two strangers struck by the same lightning bolt of inspiration. "I didn't know Billy Payne," recalled Young, "and the first thing that ran through my mind was the City of Montreal, which in 1976 ran into debt by $700 million." Payne assured Young that he was not asking the city to finance the Olympics but, rather, it was to be a not-for-profit and privately financed business venture. While not committing the city, Young was excited by the proposal and pledged to Payne that he would do all in his power to help him. Young's enthusiasm was based on his true belief that somehow "Divine providence had a hand in guiding young Payne to seek this goal following his success on the church project. The Divine potential was there—that's how I think the Lord works and I thought this must be a message from heaven that we go after the Olympics; we had nothing to lose!"

Behind the scenes at City Hall and, unknown to Billy at the time, was a woman who had grave reservations. Shirley Franklin was the city's highest ranking staff officer. Bright, energetic and highly capable, Franklin had moved to Atlanta twenty years before and earned her way into the top echelons of city government and the politics that surround it. After meeting with Payne, Young stopped in the hall by Franklin's office, which was next to his, and said to her, "He has something here!" Franklin's reply was "You have to be kidding!" She then ticked off to the mayor all of the reasons why he and City Hall could not devote attention to what she thought to be an unrealistic adventure among dreamers. She reminded Young, now approaching the last two years of his final term, that he and the administration were already swamped by major projects and events. Even when she allowed herself to think that it might be a decent idea, Franklin did not believe it possible for Atlanta to secure the bid for the Games. When she concluded her list of reasons why the project should be abandoned, "Andy just looked at me with a straight face and said, 'Well, you go do all of those things and I'll help this fellow Payne get the Olympics!' And that," said Franklin, "was it! We never had another discussion about it because Andy was sold." Young's excitement, however, was partially pragmatic. He was impressed that Payne had quickly raised private seed money. Going over an IOC list of countries, Young surmised that, through his work as a Congressman and United Nations Ambassador, he knew people in practically every one of the nearly 200 countries sending teams to the Olympic Games. While that in itself would not assure anything, Young's relationships with leaders around the world would likely enhance the project. As mayor, Young began to make himself available to Payne and to the work at hand.

Payne threw himself into such a frenzied pace that it alarmed his wife and friends who were all too aware of his history of heart problems. With no regard for his health, he bore into the work day and night with such abandon that a twelve-hour day was considered short. He would often fly to meetings in Europe and be back in the office in twenty-four hours. For a trip to Australia, he might allow thirty-six hours, and often on his return would make a presentation or attend a meeting before he rested. Billy insisted that he was simply focused. Following a Sports Illustrated profile, he rejected one of the notions put forth by the writer. "I think that article touched on some fatalism in me which really does not exist," he said. "What is fair to say is that sometimes I have the capacity to focus on something that is important to me without regard to the consequences to myself." Later, when the project grew to overwhelming proportions, Billy was able to survive only by willing himself to focus on twenty-four hour increments. "I lived my life during that decade one day at a time," he said, "because I had no experience in this and had never even observed the process, I never really knew what would hit me from one day to the next."

While there were critics, there was little or no solid resistance to Payne's plans. "It was surprising, because Atlanta's civil rights history had gotten us accustomed to hard-core opposition to big ideas," he said. Payne believed that in the beginning, many people were so overwhelmed by the idea that they were tolerant of a nice, young man with what many believed to be an unattainable dream. Initially, critical questions raised by the press included: Who is this fellow and what makes him think he is he capable of handling such an enormous project? "A visionary would have been someone who knew the Olympic Movement, had observed it, dissected it and made the match," he said. "All I had was the idea and the willingness to work." His passion became so infectious that he snared some of the most talented people in the city and the country to help.

It was easy for him to recruit excited Atlantans of all ages, from housewives to business tycoons, all good-intentioned and highly motivated people. But those with Olympic experience were much more difficult to find. LeRoy Walker offered a rare combination of long-time Olympic experience and a vast reservoir of contacts in the national and International Olympic arenas. Payne said he had a "million people who could give me opinions based on knowledge they had acquired the day before, but in LeRoy I knew that when he talked about the Olympic movement, I needed to be listening. I can think of no one who would be the equivalent of LeRoy Walker in any sport or profession. In no other area of sport does that history of experience reside in a single person."

Payne also knew that Walker could accelerate the process. Walker was sought out by the Atlanta Committee to help it with a highly complicated process. The host city must first win the bid from the USOC to represent the U.S. at the international level.

Walker recalled his first meeting with the small committee in Atlanta when "They literally sat around a table with note pads. They were wonderfully committed people made up mostly of lawyers and housewives." Walker took them through, step-by-step, the factors involved in the first hurdle at the USOC level. Fourteen other U.S. cities also wanted the Games. Billy Payne recalled that he "probably disproportionately relied on LeRoy early on." There were so many questions about where to start, how and whom to approach and which of the constituencies involved were actually important to the process. Payne credited Walker with imparting to him a basic philosophy that he embraced and later mandated for his entire organization. He called it "a key to our success." Walker persuaded Payne that he should be concerned only about the people who would ultimately make the decisions. While all of the peripheral personalities surrounding the Olympic Movement would be heard and treated with respect, the major focus of the organization would be directed toward the ninety or so people who held the real power. Walker was good at paring down the list. "Our ability to dismiss the extraneous stuff became pretty remarkable," said Payne who recalled the day he walked into a meeting of his small staff, now called the "Original Nine" as if the idea had been his. "I admit that I have taken credit for it many times since then," he said. Payne believes that, more than any other overriding factor, it was that encapsulated, focused working philosophy that allowed Atlanta to move from a no-chance category to a position destined to win. "If I owed LeRoy a gift, it would be for that—he gave me the gift of his insight."

When Payne learned who made the decisions in the USOC, he went to their meetings wearing the name tag "Hi, I'm Billy." He pitched his city with a zeal so engaging that people began to ask each other, 'Who is this guy from Atlanta?'

"In April of 1988, the day the USOC voted for Atlanta, Walker was at home recovering from emergency surgery. His appendix had ballooned on a cross-country flight and he was rushed to surgery at Duke as soon as his plane landed at Raleigh-Durham. Later, however, Walker called Payne aside and asked for a moment with him and Andrew Young. "I remember LeRoy's exact words," said Payne. He said, "Remember that it is the journey and not the destination and that with all of this excitement and euphoria you have actually just begun. It will be a long journey full of emotional highs and lows. Whether or not you win the bid at the IOC level, ultimately these next two-and-a-half years are going to define you and your community forever. So, take your responsibility seriously and know that I am going to be your partner all the way." Payne remembered that. "I was shocked that a man could have this kind of vision and be able to say it so succinctly."

With the U.S. bid, Andy Young, now co-chairman of ACOG, and Billy Payne traveled hundreds of thousands of miles selling Atlanta's Southern hospitality to the Olympic leaders of the countries of the world. Young's contacts and knowledge of international politics from his days as ambassador to the UN were invaluable. Many observers believe that Young's impact led to the gaining of the crucial votes coming out of the continent of Africa. A key element of the presentation focused on the attitudes of the people of a Southern city, undeniably prosperous, which had a black majority of more than sixty-five percent, and the legacy of Martin Luther King and the American Civil Rights Movement. Young believed this new quest was being guided by a higher power. That belief, which had sustained him in many other battles, emboldened him with an unshakable fearlessness.

"I don't believe it was a coincidence that Billy Payne came up with the idea," said Young, "I just believe that coincidence is God's way of remaining anonymous. Therefore, I figured we had a mandate from God to go after the Olympics. I didn't tell anyone that, but after we presented our credentials to Seoul we invited some IOC members to Atlanta. One of them, the delegate from Nigeria, said to me, 'I don't know what the IOC wants, but I believe that God wants the Olympics to come to Atlanta.' So that was two votes of confidence!"

In September 1990, Payne, Young and a delegation from the Atlanta Committee flew to Tokyo where the announcement would be made of the host city for the 1996 Centennial Olympic Games. Walker, who was in Europe at the time, flew in to join them. When IOC President Juan Samaranch, in the accent of a man fluent in several languages, spoke the sound *Aht—Lahn—tah,*" there was an explosion of joy among those who had come to Tokyo, and on Peachtree Street in Atlanta tears flowed with the champagne. Payne's impossible dream landed in his lap.

The countdown to opening ceremonies began: only six years before the world came to visit. The enormous workload took on a new dimension. The Atlanta Olympic Committee became the Atlanta Committee for the Olympic Games.

Shirley Franklin, who initially thought the "dreamers" were "off the scope," became the senior policy advisor to ACOG's CEO Billy Payne. Her responsibilities included overseeing the meshing of ACOG and local government, community relations and the Equal Economic Opportunity Program Committee. Her department ensured that minorities and females participated as contractors and employees in the economic windfall of the Olympic Games.

Olympic host cities become islands of economic frenzy, very often left with a redefined landscape and character. Estimates of the overall economic windfall for Atlanta fell into the range of $5 billion to $6 billion.

ACOG made a firm commitment to the implementation and enforcement of affirmative action policies that would govern the handling of employment and contracts. Approximately one-third of the construction contracts were earmarked for minority businesses. Shirley Franklin believed that the mix of the three different personas of Payne, Young and Walker formed a potent trio of power. She saw in each of them a common tenacity for holding on during the stormy tides ahead. They were Southern men with strong ties to the City, each had been an athlete and each could produce a diverse list of accomplishments. And she added, regarding the dreamer: "...and then Billy Payne, who was completely oblivious to all of the problems and obstacles!" Payne reflected: "It was the best demonstration I have ever seen where a relatively ordinary person, who could only distinguish himself in the two areas—work ethic and focus—could have this experience, principally because his friends would not allow him to fail."

§

In 1992, LeRoy Walker was asked to accept the position of Senior Vice President for Sport for the ACOG. He would be paid an annual six-figure salary to oversee every aspect of ACOG's preparation for the Games from the sports perspective. He set up his office and began to gather up the people he needed to help him get the job done. Among the first to be hired was Charles Foster. Walker's tenure, however, would be short-lived.

Elected President of the USOC

On October 11, 1992, at its meeting in Miami Beach, Florida, the U.S. Olympic Committee did something it had never done since America founded an Olympic organization in 1900: It elected an African-American as its president.

While some have made the case that Walker was selected for reasons of racial diversity, the clearer case can be made that the 74-year-old was chosen because he was supremely qualified. Among his twenty-one predecessors, not one had approached the job with Walker's credentials.

The presidency of the USOC is a volunteer position and among the nations of the world it is the most powerful office in amateur sport, overseeing the largest national Olympic organization.

One of the prerequisites for serving is an ability to survive four years without a salary in a job that requires a full-time commitment. That alone narrows the list of candidates. Walker's personal financial picture was healthy enough that he stepped down from his six figure salary as ACOG's Senior VP for Sport to step into the prestigious top spot in the USOC. Walker's son, teasing his father about giving up that kind of salary to work free, added, "and Grandma always told me she didn't raise any fools."

The hours were long, the issues complex, press scrutiny intense and the travel schedule monstrous. The perks and the power, however, were enormously appealing. Flying around the U.S. and foreign countries with first-class accommodations, meeting power brokers, being feted and courted by sports organizations, corporations and television networks, and receiving invitations from the White House, all were heady fare, indeed.

When Walker was elected in 1992 there was little opposition. His interest in the post brought the nominating committee to attention. He was there when the USOC was dealing with a number of sensitive minority issues brought on by the phenomenal influx of African-American athletes into the U.S. Olympic Movement. Alpha V. Alexander, Ph.D. and director of health and sports advocacy for the YWCA of the USA was on the nominating committee when Walker's name came forward. "I actually had the honor of 'calling the question' to vote him into the nomination," she recalled. "I had really been in awe when I met him. He is my role model. I compare him with Roscoe Brown; they were the two major forces in physical education who were African-Americans. Dr. Walker was involved in the process through his work with the American Alliance of Health, Physical Education, Recreation and Dance, and in the development of AIW, the Association for Intercollegiate Athletics for Women. He made a major contribution to the birth and recognition of AIW and a governing process for women's athletics. The AIW eventually died when the NCAA took over women's athletics, but Walker's strong leadership regarding participation by women and minorities in the U.S. Olympic movement was a major contribution and his impact will be felt for years to come."

When his name was placed in nomination there was a discussion about his age and state of his health, but not about his credentials. Appearing before the committee, Walker brimmed with good health and, always prepared, brought with him the results of a recent medical examination that removed any doubt regarding his physical fitness to serve. His election was assured.

Walker now envisioned the dream position of his lifetime.

The USOC was given sole responsibility by the Amateur Sports Act for America's representation in the Summer and Winter Olympic Games and the Pan American Games. Its major function is to serve the athlete. With no government funding, the USOC marketing division generated the funding for the large and diverse Olympic program. USOC Broadcasting handles the highly lucrative network contracts. Corporate sponsorship has generated a windfall of moneys for the USOC. The USOC declares that financial support to athletes is at an all-time high and further that "The U. S. Olympic Movement is very healthy." Four hundred paid staffers, based at USOC headquarters in Colorado Springs, Colorado, served the organization. An executive committee was made up from the 100-member Board of Directors and the USOC officers.

Walker could look forward to the challenge of dealing with officers with whom he shared common high levels of intellect, motivation, aggressiveness and achievement, including George Steinbrenner, chairman of the American Shipbuilding Company in Tampa, Florida and more popularly known as the principal owner of the New York Yankees baseball team. He was in his second term as USOC Vice President; Dr. Ralph Hale, executive director of the American College of Obstetricians and Gynecologists in Washington, D.C., a ten-year veteran in service to the USOC who was in his first term as Vice President; Michael Lenard, member of the U.S. Olympic Team handball squad in 1984, and six-time national champion who was serving his second term as Vice President; Sandra Baldwin, top salesperson for Prudential Arizona Realty in Phoenix, and a ten-year member of the USOC Board who was serving her first term as Treasurer; Charles U. Foster, lumber broker with Bush-Foster, Inc. and former figure skater. The USOC's executive director is the chief administrative officer and is salaried. Dick Schultz took over the post in 1995.

§

1992 commenced a four-year period during which Walker faced challenges that would bring to bear all of his experience, skill and character.

Immediately, Walker set up his office. He chose to remain in Durham, in an office complex on the edge of the Research Triangle park, a few minutes from his home and, most importantly, a ten-minute drive from Raleigh-Durham International Airport. His operating budget provided for an assistant. He chose a young man, Tony Britt.

Tony Britt

I realized that he was so superior in his intellect. He sees far more than those around him. I had to adjust to that.

−Tony Britt

Tony Britt's business card read: Executive Assistant to the President, United States Olympic Committee. Another of his cards read Special Projects Manager. Britt said, "The only reason I had that job was to serve him in any way that I could." Simultaneously, Britt served as assistant and super-secretary-confidante-bodyguard-driver-and PR guru for the president. He arranged air travel and ground transportation, handled correspondence, screened telephone calls and managed a schedule of titanic proportion for one of the world's busiest men.

The USOC President's office at 2525 Meridian Parkway, Suite 230, in Durham, North Carolina, consisted of two rooms, simple but spacious. Britt's outer office was his exclusive domain; a neat, no-clutter tribute to his efficiency, decorated tastefully with Olympic flags, pictures, awards and framed Olympiad posters.

Two small clean-lined couches for visitors were arranged around a glass coffee table laden with neatly arranged sports publications, mostly dealing with the work of the USOC, the Olympic Movement and the Atlanta Centennial Games. When a visitor pushed open the door from the hallway, it swung just past Britt's desk where he spent most of his time behind a giant computer. There was only one way to the inner office of the President and Britt was either the "entree or obstacle." Between phone calls, faxes and office appointments, Britt estimated nearly "100 opportunities a day to represent him." Britt had not attained his position by happenstance, luck or nepotism. Rather, as a 13-year-old sitting in Wallace Wade Stadium at Duke University in 1974, he was "enthralled" watching his first international track meet. Among the vivid memories he carried away that day was that of a naked man chased by security people across the field in full view of the crowd. (This was near the end of American youth's silly period of "streaking," or running naked through some grand event, the larger the crowd the better.) Britt also took home the names of Coaches LeRoy Walker of North Carolina Central and Al Buehler of Duke, who had put on this history-making sports spectacle.

Several years later, still in his teens, the boy landed a part-time job as prep sports writer for the Durham Morning Herald. It was there he began to learn more about the coach at the black school across town. "While I was learning who this legend was," said Britt, "I was on one side of town, he was on the other." After receiving a degree in speech communications and journalism from the University of North Carolina at Chapel Hill in 1985, and an MBA at UNC, he was accepted for an internship in public relations at the U.S. Olympic Training Center in Colorado Springs, Colorado.

"That is when the Olympic bug bit me," he recalled. The young man never removed his learning cap and the Colorado Springs experience would bode well for what was to follow. In 1987, Britt served with North Carolina Amateur Sports, the organization that brought the Olympic Festival to the triangle cities of Raleigh-Durham-Chapel Hill that year. The board chairman for that organization was LeRoy Walker. "We got to know each other indirectly there, and I was always looking for some way to stick my face in front of his," said Britt. "I made a point to make a favorable impression on him and, of course, I liked the association with a hero." This was a part of Britt's quest to become known to the man he admired and to become a member of his staff, whether paid, part-time or as a volunteer. When Walker was elected to the presidency of the U.S. Olympic Committee, Britt was even more determined to land a job close to him. Britt plotted an aggressive plan to get Walker's attention. Eventually, his ploy worked. In 1993, Britt enrolled in the Sports Management Institute at UNC Chapel Hill. In June, LeRoy Walker was invited to make a presentation to the class. Tony saw this as his chance to reach for the brass ring.

Britt made sure he was at the door of the classroom to greet Walker, then positioned himself directly in front of Walker, so that "at least two-thirds of the time" when Walker looked up, he could not avoid contact with the big guy with the beard. When the speech was over and other students rushed up to speak with Walker, Tony repositioned himself at the door. When the coach approached, Tony spoke. "Good to see you again, Dr. Walker." Walker did a double take and simply said, "Tony, tell me, what you are doing these days?" Tony recalled thinking, "That was the door I was looking for." He replied, "Dr. Walker, let me walk you to your car." As they walked, Tony made his case. Walker said, "Stay in touch, I may have something for you." Britt recalled. "I did backflips back into my classroom!"

Six months later, after Britt finished his MBA work, he wrote to Walker reminding him of their conversation and re-emphasizing his interest. The day after he mailed the letter, Walker called and asked him to come to his office on January 6, 1994. At that initial meeting, Walker explained to Tony, in general terms, how he saw his role as president of the USOC and ended by asking Britt if he could make a commitment to him for the next two-and-a-half years. Britt said he could and would do so for a longer period if necessary. Walker asked if he had any questions. Britt replied, "Only one: What will my role be?"

Walker leaned back in his chair and said, "I want you to be my clone." Britt remembered thinking how professionally flattering those words were and did not know exactly what Walker meant in terms of the job, but he jumped up and said, "I'll do it; I'm yours!"

Driving home from that meeting, Britt heard on the radio of the clubbing attack on U.S. figure skater Nancy Kerrigan. That episode, and Kerrigan's injury, would dominate the news of the Winter Olympic Games in Lillehammer, Norway.

Walker was thrust into the center of decision-making that would become, for better or worse, a part of his legacy. The fallout would also change forever how the U.S. Olympic Movement would view its responsibility for protecting its athletes. There were elaborate protections in place from terrorism, politics and sponsor influence. Now loomed the complicated issue of how to protect athletes from violence within.

When Walker returned from the Games in Lillehammer, Britt learned that his title would be Assistant to The President. He was elated. On Monday, March 14, 1994, Britt reported for work. Walker was in Montevideo, Uruguay and had left a note for his new assistant. That ever-so-brief note was a telling comment on Walker's analytical mind. It read: "Lay of land in the office: Relocate furniture any way you want. There are paintings on the floor, hang those; reduce paper files to computer access, mail, inventory." Britt recalled the realization that he was in the environment he had been looking for: sport, business, and organization. Walker gave him a lot of latitude: "There was a lot of creativity required and it was ideal for me," Britt said. He loved watching the process at the executive level and enjoyed the excitement of the international arena. And he enjoyed meeting the famous people involved.

"The first time you talk with George Steinbrenner on the phone can be intimidating," said Britt. "In executive committee meetings he is loud and forceful, but I was surprised to see that what he brings to the table has incredible logic and common sense. I could immediately see the influence of his business background and, while I did not see him as a rude person, I did view him as someone who has gotten his way." Britt liked and admired Steinbrenner.

Britt's greatest and constant challenge was to get inside the mind of his mentor. Walker was, in many ways, a complex man. As with most independent thinkers, there was an assumption that surely those who need to will know how to tap into it. Instead, even those closest to him were sometimes frustrated. "There are things that frustrate the hell out of me," said Britt, "but then I realize that he is so superior in his intellect and I am looking at things through a small mind. Dr. Walker can anticipate what the issues are without a second thought. He was a visionary who was respected around the world and it was my responsibility to adjust to him. He saw far more than those around him." What Britt admired most about Walker was that, "He has compassion, patience, the ability to listen and understand, knows diplomacy at the international level, but the greatest of these is his compassion for others. If you watch him stop to talk with a child you will see him make the connection."

Barcelona, 1992

When the people who knew about the flap saw them with the flag draped over their shoulders, they were disgusted. They knew it was not a gesture of patriotism. Only the Nike guys draped the flags.

—LeRoy T. Walker

The term "dream team," in reference to an official U.S. Olympic Team, rankled LeRoy Walker. That name prevailed throughout the Games in Barcelona, Spain, and was the media's identity for America's basketball squad. Walker cringed every time he heard it used or saw it in print. The 1992 Games would set Walker, the Olympic purist, on a course destined for a philosophical clash with the power of the National Basketball Association superstars and their agents. "The Chef-de-Mission, or Chief of Mission, was involved in every sport, in charge of it all," said Walker. "In that capacity, I did not stay in town with the staff but I lived in the Village because most of the problems you deal with are going to be there."

The Barcelona Games would force the U.S. to redefine the word "amateur."

The story of the "dream team" began when an NBA player watched the U.S. team lose to another country and became angry that his country, which invented the game, was losing court prestige in international competition. He urged the USOC to use the pros and put the best team America could field on the floor for the next Games.

"The international federations are the organizations that decide whether or not professionals can play," said Walker. "The National Governing Body, USA Basketball, abstained in the voting to allow the pros to play, but the foreign countries, assuming they could be competitive, voted for it."

On the roster were NBA superstars Michael Jordan, Magic Johnson, Larry Bird, Charles Barkley, Clyde Drexler, Patrick Ewing, Chris Mullen, David Robinson, John Stockton, Karl Malone and Scottie Pippen. Representing the collegiate ranks was Duke star Christian Laettner. The Olympic Team would be coached by Chuck Daley who had by then already produced two NBA championship teams. He was assisted by Duke's Mike Krzyzewski.

"The USOC has a strict Code of Conduct that is required to be signed by our athletes," said Walker. "We sent them to the professional players and they did not send them back. They were playing in their qualifying procedural tournament in Portland, Oregon. Time was running out, so I gave up my Fourth of July holiday and flew to Portland to talk with them. I wanted them to understand that I, as Chef-de-Mission, had been misquoted, that I had nothing against the pros, but was against how they were selected. They were selected in a smoke-filled room. I also wanted them to know that they had to sign the Code of Conduct and turn it in. They had agreed to my visit, and knew I was coming to talk with them and their coaches.

"However, when I got there, all of them had gone to Drexler's for a cookout and the Coaches Krzyzewski and Daley, primarily Daley, decided that all of this was an athlete's problem. They sent their junior lawyer to talk to me and I told him he couldn't help me very much, that I had flown all the way from Atlanta to talk to the players and coaches and if I couldn't, I would get on the next plane back. I did tell him I would answer any questions he might have of me while I was waiting for my plane. Very soon I contacted the officials of the NBA who told me the Code of Conduct agreements were in the mail. However, the athletes handed us the forms when they were coming through the line to pick up their credentials in Barcelona. They were signed, but four of them had altered the forms at the section that stipulated they must wear the official USA uniform to the awards podium." Walker was angry and continued his battle.

The official uniform to be worn by the U.S. team at the awards ceremony had been designed and furnished by Reebok, a corporation that had signed on as a major sponsor for the right to see its logo flashed around the world from the peristyle or podium. According to Walker, "Reebok had given millions of dollars to the USOC for that privilege."

The conflict arose because some of the stars were under commercial contracts to Nike. Walker was fighting to honor the USOC's agreement with Reebok, going so far as to threaten to keep the players out of the finals who didn't conform. That produced a half-hearted response from the NBA players' representative, which led Walker to believe that the Nike players would wear the official U.S. awards presentation uniform.

When the Nike players appeared on the peristyle, however, they draped American flags over their shoulders, covering the Reebok logo. Walker recalled, "When the people who knew about the flap saw it, they were disgusted and they knew it was not a gesture of patriotism." Walker had been beaten, but all involved knew they had been in a fight.

"My stance in Barcelona helped later in Atlanta because the sponsors knew I would try to protect them. I didn't think I was being an idealist." Some of the athletes, in interviews with the press, said Walker was "behind the times." "On behalf of the pros," said Walker, "after all the monkey business, when they're on the floor they do play basketball. It was a real show. Some people were very critical of us. They thought it was overkill. It was like killing a gnat with a sledge hammer. It was an NBA marketing device. You didn't have to have that level of play to win the gold medal. For instance, I could take twelve players whose names are not known out of the ranks of those teams playing pro ball and easily win the medal."

Walker truly believes in the unique opportunities the Games offer the youth of the world for cultural exchange and he holds tenaciously to that ideal, which was the initial and stated goal in the establishment of the Modern Olympic Games in Athens 100 years ago. He believes that the true "Olympic experience" may be gained only by the athletes living together in an international village. When the basketball team refused to live in the village, Walker urged them at least to visit.

"But when they came down to the village, they came with an entourage and great fanfare, complete with fifteen media people behind them with cameras. Despite their complaints about being mobbed, their arrival was always announced, the PA system blaring out 'the dream team is here.' Of course, that meant that everybody was going to come out to see them. It was an NBA marketing device. It was just a show, the Olympic version of the Harlem Globetrotters."

Walker believes he has adjusted to the financial realities of the times. "I don't mind the marketplace concept. The 1932 Games in Los Angeles cost $450,000. In Atlanta, the tab (was) $1.7 billion to run the games. We could only recoup $450 million of that on ticket sales. The difference had to come from sponsors, marketing and TV rights. I don't have a problem with that. I do have a problem with dehumanization. You don't need to lose the spirit of the Games just because it takes more money to run them."

Walker fears the maverick shenanigans of some of the millionaire pros will infect the U.S. Olympic movement, that some athletes will basically do what they please and trash whatever rules they don't like. The behavior of some players in the NBA represents to him a trend that leads to a loss of control.

"You see, this stuff is catching. I get sick to my stomach when I see behavior that does not set a good example for impressionable youth. It is also the general managers—they protect the players. I know a lot of those coaches and they might try to do something about bad behavior, but the general managers and owners just tell the coaches they are paying millions a year for the guy, that he has a no-cut contract, and does what he pleases. The coach has to play him.

"I don't object to the pros being included. I accept the Federation's decision, but the selection system is so unfair to so many others. The general managers want their marquee players on the team so they can help them merchandise the NBA. That's what it is, you know.

"We are going to get sued all over the place. I talked with some professionals out in Indianapolis and they already resent the fact that they didn't stand a chance of getting on the team in Atlanta. So, what I am saying is I resent the disenfranchisement of so many others. My ethnic persuasion and background do not permit me to permit you to disenfranchise anybody."

As he was leaving Barcelona, Walker made a solemn promise to himself and to the world: "Believe me, we will not have another Barcelona in Atlanta....believe me."

Organizational Structure

It is necessary to understand the basic structure of the International Olympics' flow chart in order to understand where and how the USOC fits into it. To outsiders, the lines of jurisdiction are often complicated and layers of authority, even within the family, are often subject to debate and controversy.

At a substantial risk of oversimplification, a word graph of concentric circles may help convey the structure. At the center is the International Olympic Committee, created in 1894 and headquartered in Lausanne, Switzerland, under which all other circ les are subordinated. It is charged with the control and development of the Modern Olympic Games.

At the center of the power is a Spaniard, Juan Antonio Samaranch, who has served as president since 1980. There have been only seven presidents; the only American, Avery Brundage, served for twenty years, beginning in 1952.

The IOC is a small and elite group. In 1996, there were three Americans: Anita DeFrantz, president of the Amateur Athletic Foundation of Los Angeles and a rowing medalist in 1976, was named to the IOC in 1986; James D. Easton, president of the International Archery Federation was selected in 1994; and George Killian of USA Basketball was seated in 1996.

The IOC selects the host cities for the Games. Its members are jetted to the greatest cities of the world and are pampered and coddled by committees clamoring to have their cities chosen. They enjoy the best accommodations and cuisine the world has to offer. They are well aware of the power they wield. There have even been recent allegations of unusual individual demands made by some members in exchange for their votes.

Moving from the center, within the next ring of authority are the International Sports Federations and the National Governing Bodies, which govern every Olympic sport, from archery to wrestling, regarding eligibility, rules and championships. The National Olympic Committees charged by the IOC with advancing the Olympic Movement around the world.

The United States Olympic Committee is one of 197 National Olympic Committees that presented teams in Atlanta. The USOC, headquartered in Colorado Springs, Colorado has been described by Samaranch as the "flagship" of the committees. As the largest committee, it presents the most athletes and wins the most medals. In summary, the USOC puts the American Olympic Team in the field as mandated by the Amateur Act of 1978. There are thousands of people involved in the process.

§

From the moment he stepped into the office of the USOC presidency in October 1992 until October 1996, Walker faced one of the most controversial and exciting periods in the history of the organization. There was no let-up following Barcelona. The Summer Games were coming to Atlanta, a city now well into a monstrous sports venue construction timetable.

Walker dealt with an array of momentous decisions as the head of the National Olympic Committee of the next host country. Ahead of him were known and unknown events of dramatic consequence: Lillehammer and the Kerrigan-Harding saga, the Salt Lake City bid, the Centennial Games and the controversial election of his successor.

Walker was at the center of the whirlwind and he loved it. In his mid-seventies, he worked seven days a week, logging hundreds of thousands of air miles and astounding people half his age with his energy.

Walker's presidency came on the heels of a sensitive period in the USOC's long history brought on by events surrounding the presidency of Robert H. Helmick, a highly regarded attorney from Des Moines, Iowa, who had worked his way into the ranks of the USOC and was elected President following the sudden death of John Kelly in 1985. Several years later, Helmick was in trouble following allegations of conflict of interest. The story became a lightning rod for the media. The revelations were negative and the USOC, sensitive to the maintenance of a pristine image, suffered a serious setback. Helmick stepped down in September 1991.

Chosen as interim president was William J. Hybl, the head of El Pomar Foundation in Colorado, one of the nation's largest and richest philanthropic organizations. Hybl was credited with beginning the healing of the USOC's deteriorating image. With Walker's election in 1992, Hybl moved away from center stage, but remained in the wings. His personal goal had not yet been fulfilled.

While Walker's general health was excellent, deterioration of the ligaments and cartilage in his knees had now reached a serious state, resulting in a painful limp and, in the last few years, an alarming bowing of his legs to the extent that he lost almost two inches of height. Because Walker prided himself as a strong-limbed former star athlete, the condition greatly distressed him. His friend Herb Douglas recalled that Walker never shirked his duties and on at least one occasion conducted a national meeting from a wheelchair.

His educational background gave him a thorough understanding of his problem, the corrective surgery that was necessary, and the prescribed physical therapy that would follow. The surgical procedure called for the installation of stainless steel plates and screws. Duke's renowned orthopedic surgeon, Frank Bassett, performed the operation. Bassett's preference was to repair one knee, have it heal, then repair the other. Walker wanted both surgeries done at once. He prevailed.

Walker scheduled the operation to allow for recovery in time for the upcoming Lillehammer Winter Games in February 1994, the first opportunity he had to represent America in the Olympic Games as President of the USOC.

His recovery proceeded excellently. Dr. Walker's basic good health, along with his determination and grit, facilitated the healing benefits of physical therapy. Following the surgery, his height increased by two inches and his legs were straight once again.

Awaiting Walker in the frozen north country was fire on the ice.

Kerrigan-Harding

Everybody around me was saying she was guilty. I said she may be, but she hasn't been declared guilty in court yet.

—LeRoy T. Walker, Lillehammer, Norway, February 1994

From the moment a thug took a metal club and attempted to disable U.S. figure skater Nancy Kerrigan at Cobo Arena in Detroit on January 6, 1994, the Olympic Winter Games in Lillehammer, Norway were destined to become the Nancy Kerrigan-Tonya Harding saga.

The incident occurred during the U.S. Figure Skating Championships in Detroit. No Olympic story since the massacre of the Israeli athletes in Munich, Germany in 1972 had so captivated the news media and the public. The story embodied every element of a "made-for-TV" drama.

Nancy Kerrigan, from Massachusetts, tall and elegant, with flowing black hair, was the embodiment of a princess on ice. She enjoyed a close-knit and supportive family. There had already been touching television coverage of her visually impaired mother, her face almost touching the television set, attempting to catch an image of her daughter flashing around the rink.

Tonya Harding, from Oregon and just over five-feet tall, was a gifted athlete who had scrapped her way to the top tier of American figure skating through both talent and tenacity. She was the only U.S. woman skater whose freestyle repertoire included the triple axel.

What the young women held in common was the demanding commitment each had made to Olympic achievement. They had dedicated their young lives to the pursuit of Olympic Gold, and the dream of financial rewards and fame beyond that.

After the attack and under doctor's orders, Nancy Kerrigan could not skate in the U.S. finals in Detroit. The finals were to determine who filled the two positions on the U.S. Olympic women's figure skating team.

Two days after the attack, Tonya Harding skated to first place. Nancy Kerrigan, with a swollen and bruised knee, sat out. The International Committee of the U.S. Figure Skating Association, however, allowed her to fill the second spot on the U.S. Olympic Team in Lillehammer. Opening ceremonies were set for February 12, with the skaters' technical or "short" program scheduled to begin February 23.

§

Four men were arrested in connection with the attack: Shawn Eckardt; Derrick Smith; Shane Stant; and Jeff Gillooly, Harding's divorced husband (despite the divorce, the couple had reconciled).

Shawn Eckardt not only admitted his participation in the plot, but implicated Tonya, saying that she had known about it from the beginning. Later, Gillooly implicated her as well. Tonya Harding underwent hours of questioning by authorities in Portland. She denied any prior knowledge of the attack. She admitted, however, that she had neglected to report what she learned after the incident. Failing to report knowledge gained after-the-fact was not a crime in Oregon, nor in many other states. She said she was sorry.

The question became whether Tonya Harding would be allowed to skate in Lillehammer.

The U.S. Figure Skating Association indicated it would remove Harding from the Olympic lineup if it could be proved that she was involved in the attack. On January 17, LeRoy Walker said he hoped to hear from the U.S. Figure Skating Association about Tonya's "status." The USFSA is the national governing body which, together with the International Skating Union, oversees the sport and determines eligibility, rules and championships.

At his home in Durham, Walker was recovering from the surgery performed in November on both his knees. He was house-bound, but gaining strength and planning his trip to Norway. While the surgery and therapy had gone well, a rigorous trip to a frigid climate was not advised. Following the Kerrigan attack, IOC President Juan Samaranch phoned Walker for a progress report on his recovery, indicating that he needed him in Lillehammer.

On February 5, a panel of the U.S. Figure Skating Association found "reasonable grounds" to hold a disciplinary hearing involving the Harding controversy—and made it clear that the final decision on whether or not she would skate would come from the USOC. The hearing was set for February 15 in Norway.

On February 9, Harding dropped a bombshell by filing a $20 million lawsuit against the USOC, contending that the USOC's scheduled hearing denied her due process, the right to call witnesses, the right to cross-examine, and that the organization's conduct was "arbitrary, capricious and contrary to law and "fact." Two days later, Walker arrived in Norway.

As he often did when the media were circling, Walker worked behind the scenes. "I learned as Chancellor when to talk to the media and when not to talk," he said. "I thought it was important for me to be talking with the judge in Portland. I was not out front talking about it all the time.

I went down to meet those two kids, was nice to them, of course, but I never even mentioned the controversy. I would not accept the fact that their coaches wanted them to have different practice times. I said, 'No, these are team members. What are you going to do if they pull the numbers out of the hat and find that one has to skate right behind the other? On the ice, they are focused, so go on and have them practice together.'"

The big decision had finally landed in Walker's lap. "The judge told me that we would have bigger problems if we took (Harding) off the ice. Some were saying I made the decision to let her skate because she threatened a $20 million lawsuit. The judge had already told me that she couldn't get twenty dollars because she had nothing to sue about. We had not made any decision that affected her welfare, and she could make no claims that we had prevented her from making the millions of dollars in endorsements if she could win the gold."

Walker made his decision and the deal was cut.

Harding would drop her lawsuit and be allowed to skate. The USOC made sure it was understood that while Harding could skate, the incident was still of great concern and was "an assault on the basic ideals of the Olympic Movement."

When the settlement was announced the Games had already begun in Lillehammer and on the ice rink the stage was set for high drama. The media clamored for the lead each day in the Nancy-Tonya story, which would virtually dominate the Olympics.

CBS sent Connie Chung to stake out Harding at practice or anywhere else there might be an attempt to talk with her. CBS producers were counting on the hype to make competition night one of the most viewed television programs in history. They would not be disappointed.

In the finale, Kerrigan skated well. Harding was not at top form; she even had trouble with the shoelaces of one of her skates.

While most of the world's television viewers had been prepped by the media hype to concentrate on Nancy and Tonya, a winsome teenager from the Ukraine, Oksana Baiul turned in a breathtaking performance and walked away with the gold. Kerrigan was second for the silver and Harding was not in the running.

On reflection, Walker says, "People viewed it as a tough decision, but it wasn't so tough if you looked at the issue. Remember that when the decision was made Tonya Harding had not been charged with anything."

"We learned a lot from it", said Walker, "we developed a new code of conduct that has been accepted by the National Governing Bodies. Growing out of that we put together the code of conduct that we had for the Centennial games in Atlanta."

Tony Britt's assessment was that time was running out and his boss faced "the hottest issue in Olympic history. The USOC caught a lot of heat on how it was handled. Instead of fighting her figure skating NGB she came right at the USOC demanding due process— and the U.S. Constitution is greater than the Amateur Sports Act."

Many athletes and USOC members were upset by the incident and the outcome.

However the Lillehammer decision will be weighed historically, Walker's name will forever be associated with it.

§

Some not-so-insignificant footnotes:

Walker recalls that Hillary Rodham Clinton, as official U.S. representative to the games "...was a hit in Lillehammer. She was cheerleader for our hockey team and later left a reception in order to attend the award ceremony for skier Tommy Moe."

The stainless steel that had been surgically implanted in Walker's knees reacted to the frigid weather in Norway, causing pain so severe that he called his physician in the U.S. and asked if he had any suggestions. The doctor replied "Yes, come home." Walker left Lillehammer earlier than he had originally planned.

Interest in figure skating shot through the roof. In vastly increasing numbers, children are making reservations at ice rinks all over America and signing up for instruction. Television networks are scheduling many more skating competitions and exhibitions. Top professional figure skaters are now given a level of star treatment rivaling that of rock stars and have enjoyed stunning increases in salaries and fees.

Oksana Baiul, who became an international star, later faced personal problems adjusting to fame at such a young age.

Tonya Harding was barred from officially sanctioned skating events.

Nancy Kerrigan married her agent and became a professional skating star.

The Old Lions of the CIAA

Some of our boys from the north went into a restaurant and it caused such a fracas we all nearly got put in jail. LeRoy interceded but we barely escaped being locked up.

—Coach Clarence "Bighouse" Gaines...recalling old times

They are grandfathers now, most graying or balding or both. Their voices warm, laughter hearty, and their greetings to each other made loving by the years of familiarity. The gathering of the old "lions" of the Central Intercollegiate Athletic Association Tournament in February 1995 in Winston-Salem, North Carolina marked the fifty-year milestone of the organization that was originally formed to provide a governing body and a venue for competition for "colored" institutions.

Today the CIAA Tournament features an exciting series of basketball games beginning mid-week, but also serves as a homecoming for the predominantly black institutions, mostly in North Carolina and Virginia.

The fiftieth anniversary version, in addition to the usual festivities, parties and fashion shows, would feature a unique Hall of Fame Banquet on Saturday, February 25, 1995.

With LeRoy Walker presiding as master of ceremonies, every member of the famous North Carolina Central Basketball Team of 1946 was inducted into the League's prestigious Hall of Fame. The revered John McLendon had coached the team; Walker had been his assistant. The team had traveled from their homes across the U.S. with their wives, children and grandchildren to receive the award and retell the stories of their athletic triumphs.

As the old men of the squad began to gather at the M.C. Benton Convention and Civic Center in downtown Winston-Salem, they were accorded the adulations of yesteryear. Flashbulbs exploded as family, friends and the press moved in to record the reunion. Each knew stories about the others, told with relish and high humor.

When the room calmed some, Walker walked to the microphone at the elevated head table, gave a word of welcome and introduced the special guests. The first speaker that Walker introduced was Jonathan Matthews, manager of Reebok's U.S. Sports Marketing for basketball, cleated footwear and men's fitness merchandise. Matthews brought greetings and congratulations to those present, along with a reaffirmation of his company's commitment to the CIAA.

The North Carolina College Team being honored in Winston-Salem, along with its beloved coach John McLendon, produced one of the great stories in sports history:

Ranked in fifth place among the teams to compete at the first CIAA Tournament held in Turner Arena in Washington, D.C., the NC College Eagles were given little chance for victory. The squad surprised its own fans by fighting its way into the finals with a display of skill, stamina and courage that earned it the nickname "The Mighty Mites."

Going against the powerful Virginia Union Panthers, the Eagles made the most of their small wings and stout hearts. The score was tied ten times and the lead changed fourteen times. It was only after three overtime periods that the exhausted team and its delirious fans celebrated a 64 to 56 victory and the tournament championship.

Reporter Lem Graves wrote: "The 2,000 fans who saw the championship game went away as thoroughly exhausted as the players, but, whether they were Union or North Carolina College partisans, they agreed they had witnessed their greatest sports thrill."

One by one former coach John McLendon introduced his former team with an affectionate remembrance of each man.

They were Frank "Frog" Galbreath; Richard "Mice" Miller, Marland "Buck" Buckner, Robert "Skull" Herring, Aubrey "Stinky" Stanley, "C" Galbreath, Thornton "Fat Bread" Williams, Rupert "Rupe" Johnson, and W.T. "Tommy" Moten. Awards were presented posthumously to Frank "Blue" Harvey and Elmer "Daddy Mac" McDougald.

It was a special moment in the history of the CIAA Hall of Fame.

Among those looking on from the audience was the legendary coach Clarence "Big House" Gaines, former head basketball coach and athletic director at Winston-Salem State University.

At the time, his record of "most wins of any living basketball coach" was still intact, but Gaines was first to remind everyone that UNC's Dean Smith was approaching his mark.

Gaines' earliest recollection of LeRoy Walker was fifty years earlier, when Walker came to the campus of NC College as assistant football coach. The two men had a lot in common. As assistant coaches, they wore many hats. Gaines recalled that he was "assistant coach for everything. You only had two people." LeRoy jokingly introduced himself to Clarence as "driver of car No. 2."

Gaines and Walker saw each other often since they coached for colleges that were in athletic competition. They would later find themselves on the campus of Columbia University studying for master's degrees.

Gaines was impressed with Walker's organizational skills. "He was a natural leader, even in the beginning." Years later, Walker organized a trip to the Penn Relays in Philadelphia for the athletes from the black colleges in North Carolina. The schools shared the expenses for a chartered bus that would start at Charlotte's Johnson C. Smith, take on passengers at Winston Salem State and Greensboro's A&T, then go on to the NC College campus in Durham before proceeding to Philadelphia.

Gaines recalled the year they nearly missed the relays. "We stopped for gas not too far out of Durham. It was a time of strict segregation. Some of the boys from the North went into the restaurant and were, of course, refused service. It caused such a fracas that we all nearly got put in jail. LeRoy interceded but we barely escaped being locked up."

When Gaines and Walker were at Columbia University doing postgraduate work, Walker organized study sessions.

Gaines attributed a great deal of his success to his friend. He likened it to drafting the lead car in a race. "LeRoy was a team player but the lead car. It was a matter of getting in his draft and you could make more progress than you normally would," said Gaines. "The guys respected him and when he opened his mouth, he said something." Added Gaines, "He helped me develop a professional attitude. Whatever progress I have made over these seventy-some years is because I had role models, and LeRoy Walker was one of them."

§

More than a year before the Atlanta Games began, Walker and others spotted trouble areas, certainly to be expected in the creation of a work so massive as to boggle the imagination. There was a budget of $1.5 billion with which to stage the Games. A large percentage of the money was planned for construction of venues.

In early Spring of 1995, Walker received a thirteen-page progress report from ACOG on the strengths and weaknesses of the project.

Among the problems to be remedied was a slight pitch in the field hockey venue that affected the play of the ball.

"I had gone to the football field at Morris Brown" (a small, historically black, inner-city college in Atlanta), "where we were going to build another stadium for field hockey," recalled Walker. "The field had an east-west orientation. When I commented that they must face a glare there all the time, they laughed and said they used the eye-blackening cream. I laughed and replied that they already had enough of that. When we turned the planned orientation of the field, we ran into another problem. The field now went over the MARTA train tunnel, and MARTA has a rule that you can't put anything over that rail line. We had to get special dispensation to do it.

They had a warmup track misplaced such that athletes would have to cross another event getting from warmup to the starting lines. They made a lot of mistakes early, but early enough to be correctable," Walker said. There are two lines when you start to do something, a vertical cost line and a horizontal time line. The farther you extend the time line, the higher the cost line rises. But those errors were caught early," Walker noted.

I had never seen anybody more dedicated than Billy Payne.

Two areas of greater concern for Walker were transportation and compilation of games results for the media. He believed there were weaknesses in both systems.

Selecting A New Executive Director

The decision process on the selection of our new Executive Director became very bitter and confrontational. Groups came in there with hidden agendas that were not-so-hidden. They wanted to delay the process. They were most upset that I had beaten them to the punch...

—LeRoy T. Walker

The Presidency of the U.S. Olympic Committee involves many tough decisions. Those are often easier to deal with than are the strong personalities who make up the governing structure. Events leading up to the 1995 selection of the Executive Director of the USOC were divisive and perhaps a harbinger of a new level of power politics within the USOC, which would play out two years later when Walker's successor was elected.

When Harvey Schiller resigned in October 1994 to become President of Turner Sports, the USOC turned to its Deputy Secretary General, John Krimsky, who was pressed into service as interim Executive Director. Krimsky is the organization's money man. Skilled and aggressive in high finance, he had been in the USOC for nearly a decade. His forays into the coffers of corporate America are legend. The pockets of the organization jingle because of Krimsky.

Candidates for the permanent position included some of the most highly motivated people in the country, among them Richard D. Schultz, former head of the NCAA, former Director of Athletics at the University of Virginia and a member of the USOC executive committee since 1990.

Walker was delighted that Schultz had applied for the job.

"I had been knowing Dick for years, he was arms lengths above anybody else and he wanted the USOC to move forward," said Walker. Schultz had served as Executive Director of the National Collegiate Athletic Association from 1987 to 1994.

His sterling record came with a footnote. There had been allegations of compliance violations during the time he had been director of athletics at the University of Virginia. While he was exonerated of any wrong-doing by the NCAA hearing committee, Walker believed that many people misunderstood the nature of the allegations.

USOC bylaw requires that every standing committee must include a twenty percent representation of athletes. Among them, according to Walker, "was one who just hated the NCAA. He is still upset about some NCAA decisions and wanted to relate all of his grievances toward Dick Schultz."

Members of the National Governing Board Council were planning to protest the USOC selection process and make the case that the person selected should come from the ranks of their Council. They would make their move at a meeting scheduled in Boston with the ultimate goal of delaying the selection process.

By now the initial 150 applicants had been reduced to three through the process of secret balloting.

"Steinbrenner (who was on the selection committee) and I weren't pushing Schultz," said Walker, "we just needed the best person and we had prioritized the criteria. I wanted this to be very objectively done. Dick Schultz kept coming up on top."

Walker refuses to list the names of the others seeking the post because some had requested anonymity. Walker got wind of the planned uprising over the selection process as he was preparing to depart for a meeting in Budapest, Hungary.

He immediately called an emergency meeting of the Executive Board, scheduled it in Boston the night before the NGB Council was to meet there. "The Council (learning of Walker's move) then tried to cancel their meeting but they were already in Boston. I had been at this long enough to know that I could not come to the table unprepared."

When the athlete faction challenged the search committee, they made "diligence" the focus of their protest.

Walker was livid.

He asked how they could presume to challenge the extensive work of a committee on which they had not served. He further told them this reminded him "of those educators in the 1960s who were permitting 18- and 19-year-olds to tell them how to run their colleges and universities and spent millions of dollars putting in subjects being demanded by some special group or other, and today most of those courses have been abandoned." He added, "Those educators may have been dumb, but we are not going to be."

Walker's preparation for his emergency meeting was airtight.

He first reviewed the extent of the background work of the search committee on each of the finalists which included an FBI background check. He showed those at the meeting how every legal avenue available to the committee had been used to ensure that the diligence criterion had been more than met.

Walker had put together a file that included official records of Schultz's exoneration in the NCAA-University of Virginia hearing.

The tone of the meeting was petulant but Walker held firmly to the position that every possible question of diligence had been addressed. The Atlanta Games were approaching. He was determined that there would be no delay of a decision on the executive director's post. "I am not going through this again," he told them.

His forceful stand began to embolden the members of the search committee who now joined in, voicing their own opposition to any delay.

Even in the face of all that, a motion was made to delay. Before it could be seconded, Walker jumped in with a re-statement that there should be no delay and quickly called on someone else. The un-seconded motion died.

"When you have dealt with cantankerous professors at the university level, and some of the people I have had to deal with in some of my national organizations", said Walker, "it becomes hard for a young buck to beat you down. They had tried to ambush me but I beat them to the punch. I just went up to Boston the night before their meeting and took care of it."

Floor fights were not to Walker's liking and ran against the fiber of his style. The incident had left some people with the feeling of having been battered, including Walker. While he maintains a good relationship with the press, is accessible, candid, and does not hide behind the "no comment" line, Walker was determined to have the selection process conducted in privacy for the Executive Director's position.

There had been some press criticism of the $350,000 to $375,000 salary range for the job but, in truth, some of the people sought by USOC were already drawing a salary of twice that amount.

He had gone to great lengths to keep the selection process out of the press, including keeping the meeting place of the finalists a secret. He had the candidates enter the designated hotel through a secluded door, they were escorted to a holding room until they were to appear before the committee. The meeting did not appear on the hotel's daily directory in the lobby.

Walker was upset to pick up a *New York Times* to read the list of candidates as well as inside information on the meeting.

In a closed meeting with the Committee, Walker admonished them, saying, "*The Times* could not have gotten some of that inside information had it not come from this search committee. You may not have told (the reporter) directly, but one of you told a best friend whom you thought you could trust to keep a secret and they told someone else. I wish I could pinpoint the individual but I can't."

Walker decided to put another issue on the table. A friend of his had overheard a conversation among some in the organization raising questions about whether Walker had the vitality to bring leadership to the organization.

"I finally told them at the Boston meeting that some of them must have thought I had fallen off the chicken truck yesterday. I reminded them I had already been the president of three national organizations. I never raised my voice but simply said, "I have tried to lead this organization by consensus, but that doesn't work. Your stated belief in confidentiality doesn't work. By the time the door slams on one of our meetings, some of you are calling the media. Too many of you like to have your names in print. From now on, I will listen to your opinions. Then, having done that, the decisions will be made by me."

Olympic Congress 1995

No one knows how hard my grandfather works, no one.

—Wanda Wade

Enthusiasm and expectations were soaring for the success of the fifth annual United States Olympic Congress. The meeting was scheduled from October 4 through October 7, in Atlanta. The 1996 Olympic Games were now nine months away.

As LeRoy Walker and the delegates to the Congress arrived for the last big conclave before the Atlanta Games, reporter Joe Drape of the Atlanta Journal-Constitution dropped a bombshell, a sixteen-page special report titled, "On The Wrong Track." His scathing indictment of the USOC had a running theme: the meager portion, as he saw it, of USOC's budget that went directly for developing young athletes.

The subtitle for the piece was, "The Program Congress Created to Develop U.S. Olympic Athletes Is Failing." The article appeared, headlines blazing, as a special insert in the Sunday edition.

According to Drape's calculations, for the four years beginning in 1992, the USOC had put less than one percent of its $414 million budget into "grassroots" programs for future Olympians, but it had poured millions into the training and development of the superstar athletes.

The reporter concluded that not only was this an elitist approach, which catered to the cream of the nation's athletes, but it was a violation of the mandate of the Amateur Sports Act of 1978.

Prepared to deal with a week of volatile issues, some of which he knew held dangerous implications, Walker now suddenly was faced with a news story that that might reflect negatively on his organization, and which was quickly seized upon by the national and international press.

When Walker and the new USOC Executive Director, Dick Schultz, arrived in Atlanta they were forced to deal with the distraction of immediately addressing the issue. Walker responded that the USOC was "making strong efforts in those areas." He pointed out that the financial support given the National Governing Bodies was substantial, and that those moneys were used by the NGBs to recruit young athletes and to help them attain their goals, thus creating a feeder system for America's Olympic program. "The truth is," Walker said, "we put $35 million into grassroots programs."

While clearly troubled by the fallout from the Drape article, Walker needed to get on with the most important Olympic Congress to date. Walker works on two levels: in public and behind the scenes. The pressures on him at the USOC Olympic Congress in Atlanta were enormous. At the public receptions and banquets, he entered the rooms a smiling, warm, dignified and approachable father figure. He usually takes about three steps into a room before being surrounded by friends, well-wishers and a host of other people trying to get his attention.

The first Olympic Congress was held in Colorado Springs, Colorado in 1991. Each Congress features a series of meetings and seminars on a wide range of topics. Among the workshops held in Atlanta were these: "Grievance and Arbitration," "Synergy," "Business," "Finance," and "Taxes."

In addition, the basement level of the Atlanta Hilton featured a display of old-fashioned American free enterprise. including 119 booths, where people hawked everything from Olympic baseball caps to communications systems..

Opening ceremonies of the Congress on Thursday, October 5, were held in the Hilton's Grand Ballroom. They were designed to impress the delegates and the reporters.

Following the presentation of the colors and the national anthem by the noted Atlanta Boys Choir, the festivities began with a parade of banners representing each Olympiad over the past century. The banners were carried by a galaxy of past and present U.S. Olympic stars. The feelings flowed as, one by one, some of the greatest athletes in the world streamed down the long aisles to the front of the room.

One Olympian, in particular, generated an emotional high point. When his name was called, 91-year-old gold medalist Harrison S. Glancey, a member of the 1924 and 1928 U.S. Olympic swimming teams, made his entrance. He held a cane in his left hand, while waving to the crowd with his right. The announcer noted that Glancey was a teammate of Johnny Weissmuller, who had played Tarzan in the movies. As the old man took his seat, he saluted his late teammate Weissmuller with a weak but enthusiastic Tarzan yell. The sustained applause grew louder as the crowd came to its feet. America's oldest living gold medal Olympian stopped the show!

In a tender gesture, LeRoy Walker walked to the old gentleman's seat and, offering his hand, invited him to stand and face the crowd. At first, Glancey seemed confused by the commotion. Then he realized he was the recipient of the rush of emotion that had swept the room. Steadying himself with his cane, Glancey blew kisses to the cheering crowd. Once more, he basked in the ringing applause Americans reserve for their Olympic champions.

Behind the Scenes

Walker spent much of his time trying to reach a consensus on sensitive issues before they came to the floor in the general session. As Walker describes it, "I have tried to operate in a mode of getting agreement before it gets on the floor where it becomes so emotional. I will lock them in a room if necessary. You just don't want chaos or lost friendships. I have seen that in floor fights. I also don't want crucial issues passed by this body by just one vote."

In the smaller committee meetings, Walker was a persuasive diplomat, highly skilled at selling his ideas to those who cast the votes and set the policies on matters of importance to the USOC. Walker's preparation was such that he was seldom blindsided by any officer or delegate. Many have tried, most have failed.

The use of drugs by athletes in competition had become permanent baggage for the USOC and the Olympic Movement around the world. Walker was an adamant supporter of out-of-competition, as well as in-competition, drug testing. The sticking point, however, was in attempting to establish the procedures and protocol for testing. When and how samples were collected was the subject of the debate.

Walker had been horrified earlier when he was telephoned by an athlete in New York who described to him what she had been subjected to.

There was a knock on her apartment door at 10 p.m., and she was met with a demand for a urine sample. "There are some things you just need to forbid in this testing process," he said.

He kept reminding those around him that, unlike in many countries, Americans have the right to due process. Having served in the top echelons of the USOC, he was aware of the lawsuits that can come with improperly administered or hastily conceived policies that could violate constitutional rights.

Although one of his highest priorities was to come out of the Atlanta meeting with a protocol for drug-testing, he abandoned the idea of presenting it on the floor when his committee came apart over some of the complicated issues. "They just couldn't get it together before Saturday's Board meeting, so we lost it," he said. "But it was later accomplished."

A key accomplishment, and one close to Walker's heart, was the establishment of a task force on women and minorities, in order to nurture diversity within the ranks of leadership of the USOC.

"This issue has not as much to do with ethnicity and gender as it does with being able to tap the great talent pool that is out there," he said. Following leadership seminars for women and minorities in the Spring of 1996, a list of candidates was provided for consideration by the next President of the USOC.

Walker also was pleased by the efforts made to "bridge the gap that has existed for two decades between the USOC and the NCAA."

Walker appointed USOC members George Steinbrenner and Cedric Dempsey to co-chair a group to work on that issue, which resulted in "a much better working relationship." Walker and Dick Schultz advocated closing ranks with the National Collegiate Athletic Association to provide a broader training and developmental approach for the Olympic Movement in the United States. Both men realized that the two organizations needed to be under the same umbrella rather than following disparate goals. In a departure from previous emphasis on centralized training sites, Schultz promised there would be more attention paid to the "...900 great training facilities at the NCAA schools all over the U.S.A."

Walker pushed hard for a Code of Conduct for Olympic athletes following a string of disappointing incidents he observed as a coach and an officer.

He had witnessed disgusting displays of arrogance by some American athletes, including the abuse of coaches, inappropriate behavior during medal presentations, refusal to wear the official team awards uniform, even allegations that a skater was linked to a plot that harmed a competitor. All of that, to Walker's thinking, demanded the establishment of rules of conduct that would be signed by the athletes long before the 1996 Atlanta Games began.

The keynote address at the Congress was presented by Bud Greenspan, the official filmmaker for the 1996 Olympics. Greenspan, a powerful storyteller, has won many Emmys for his Olympic documentaries, and has been honored by admittance to the prestigious Olympic Order by the International Olympic Committee for his contribution to the International Olympic Movement. Following a warm introduction by Walker, Greenspan held the audience in rapt attention for more than an hour of powerful commentary and film clips.

The other centerpiece speaker of the week was Billy Payne, the irrepressible young President and CEO of ACOG. Payne obviously relished this opportunity to share his excitement with the press and the cream of the U.S. Olympic Movement. He was at once gracious for the support of many people in the room who helped him realize his dream and was proud to report to them that Atlanta would be ready to welcome the world in the Summer of 1996.

He stressed that there were "two things that we can't control at the time of the Games: the weather, and the political climate in the world at that time."

§

Ten days after Walker and Schultz left the Atlanta meeting, still chafing from the Drape report in the *Atlanta Journal-Constitution*, they found themselves under fire at a Senate subcommittee hearing on Wednesday, October 19, in Washington. The hearing had been scheduled for some time but it was now colliding with echoes from the Drape report and the perception would be that it had been called in response to the story.

Chaired by Republican Senator Ted Stevens of Alaska, who authored the Amateur Sports Act of 1978, the meeting bristled with acrimony. Tom McMillen, co-chairman of the President's Council on Physical Fitness and Sports and former NBA star, blasted the USOC for what he described as an elitist philosophy that focuses on the Olympic stars, to the detriment of supporting programs that develop the physical talents of children, teenagers and disadvantaged youth.

But it was Senator John McCain, Republican from Arizona, who raised the heat that came close to a scorching personal attack.

"They have displayed arrogance," he said. "They think they can come in here and throw some pearls of wisdom at us and go their own way."

McCain got even more furious when both Walker and Schultz refused to reveal to him the salary Schultz was being paid. Walker pointed out that the USOC had no obligation to do that until IRS forms were filed.

Following the fiery opening volley directed at the USOC, Walker and Schultz stood their ground and, through corroborations in budget presentations, made their case that the USOC was on course in its grassroots support of aspiring young athletes. Walker said that "The response to all of those allegations was very positive."

While the events of the first half of October 1995 were stressful for him, Walker has weathered many storms, like the willow tree that bends in the wind but never breaks.

He works seven days a week with rare exception. Wanda Wade has said, "No one knows how hard my grandfather works." Few people have inside knowledge of his work and travel schedules. Most would be shocked to see what a man in his seventies will routinely take on. A ten-day schedule from September 1995 is instructive and not atypical. At each location Walker was either presiding over a professional meeting, conferring with Olympic officials, making a speech or receiving or presenting an award. The following is taken directly from a Tony Britt printout of one two-week period:

Fri., Sept. 15	*Fly Raleigh to Atlanta*
Sat,, Sept. 16	*Meeting with Juan Samaranch President, International Olympic Committee.*
Sun., Sept. 17	*IOC Congress on Sport Science. Fly Atlanta to Raleigh*
Mon., Sept. 18	*NCAS Golf Tourney*
Tues., Sept. 19	*Speech—Elon College Boys and Girls Club*
Wed., Sept. 20	*Office appointments*
Thur., Sept. 21	*Fly RDU to D.C.—Rainbow Coalition Award*
Fri., Sept. 22	*Fly D.C. to Winnipeg, Canada*
Sat., Sept. 23	*Winnipeg to Salt Lake City, UT*
Sun., Sept. 24	*NAIA Graduate Award*
Mon., Sept. 25	*Fly Salt Lake City to Lausanne, Switzerland*
Tues., Sept. 26	*Arrive Lausanne*
Wed., Sept. 27	*IOC Olympic Solidarity Commission*
Thur., Sept. 28	*Lausanne to RDU*

He maintains his strength and vigor with daily workouts, good diet and shunning the use of tobacco or alcohol. A final, important factor is his ability to put aside his pressures and get a good night's sleep. He goes to bed early and is able to sleep on airplanes. His late wife Katherine once observed that he was "almost asleep before he could pull up the covers."

Olympic Year

January 1996 marked the beginning of the year of the Centennial Olympic Games. The months would fly quickly and there were daily, sometimes hourly challenges to be dealt with by the USOC President. Walker was well-suited to the pressure and seemed to enjoy it immensely. He had trained himself over a lifetime to expect the unexpected. The problems and issues to be faced came to him in a steady stream.

Barely into the year Walker was embroiled in trying to mediate a brouhaha involving the cycling team of Australia. According to Walker, "It was quickly becoming an international incident."

Australia suddenly demanded that its cycling team be booked for practice at the velodrome of the U.S. Olympic Training Center in Colorado Springs, Colorado a few weeks before the Atlanta Games, and at precisely the same time the facility had been set aside for the U.S. team to practice.

The Australians pressed the point that they wanted high altitude training just before the games, and if they couldn't get the facility then surely the host country was trying to get the advantage.

Walker offered to find excellent training facilities in other high-altitude practice sites such as Mexico. He even offered them the velodrome at Stone Mountain, Georgia where the actual competition would take place. The Australians wouldn't budge and took their case to the press, while behind the scenes Walker was on the phone constantly until he had worked out a solution and a practice schedule satisfactory to all that provided for Australia to come to Colorado Springs.

The issues were endless.

A swimmer who tested positive made the claim that someone else had spiked a beverage she had consumed and that she was innocent. In Judo trials, an American athlete had broken his neck.

Meanwhile, Walker was in great demand for public appearances, speeches and social events related to the approaching games. Every civic club was in a frenzy to have him speak.

At the same time Walker and Al Buehler were working on a pre-Olympic track meet they would stage at Duke's Wallace Wade Stadium just before the Games in Atlanta.

His energy never failed him and, except for a painful spur that developed in a shoulder joint that would require surgery and a brief recovery period, Walker kept up a breathless pace throughout, one that would have been impressive for a 30-year-old, much less for a man in his mid-seventies.

The Torch Run

First Lady Hillary Rodham Clinton and daughter Chelsea flew to Olympia, Greece for the impressive ceremony surrounding the lighting of the Olympic flame from the rays of the sun, from which a relay torch would be lighted each day during the longest torch relay in history.

The flame would be handed off to thousands of people, after its arrival in the U.S. on April 27, 1996, in a spirited jaunt that would snake across America from west to east ending in Centennial Olympic Stadium in Atlanta on July 19, 1996.

Millions of Americans turned out to see the torch pass through their cities, small towns and villages across the land, and countless thousands had signed up for the honor of carrying the flame for short distances during this historic and sometimes hysteric event. There are numerous accounts of people standing for hours to catch a glimpse of the first Olympic flame to cross the continent since Los Angeles hosted the games in 1984.

The USOC boasted the torch would "come within a two-hour drive of 90 percent of the U.S.A.'s population."

The improbable task of coordinating 10,000 eager torchbearers in forty-two states fell to Jeff Cravens. He required that participants promise to run the torch at any time of the day or night they were assigned. Sometimes, that meant driving to another town for a middle-of-the-night appearance.

On its southern route to Atlanta, the torch passed through Raleigh, North Carolina's capital city. The next day, Sunday June 23, it headed for the campus of North Carolina Central University for one of the most dramatic moments in LeRoy Walker's life.

While not listed among "torch relay highlights" in an article published by the USOC, the significance of the event was not wasted on the throng of people gathered on that bright Sunday morning. LeRoy Walker had brought the Centennial Olympic flame to the campus where a half-century before he had begun teaching and training track athletes—even when there was no track they could run on.

The torch came down NC Highway 55, a byway that had become the most significant in Walker's life. The highway ran past his neighborhood and the home on Red Oak Avenue where he and Katherine reared their children; past the office complex of his USOC headquarters. It was a street he had traveled every day since 1945 to reach the campus of North Carolina Central University. It was here, forty years ago, that he and gold medalist Lee Calhoun had returned in triumph from the Games in Melbourne, Australia. Here he had coached many athletes to championship titles in national and international competition, bringing honors and recognition to the institution that he eventually would serve as Chancellor. Now he returned as USOC President to bring the Olympic flame, on its journey from Greece, to his beloved campus and to share the occasion with some of his most cherished people.

The highway forms the eastern boundary of the campus. The person selected by Walker to hand him the flame on the highway was his former champion athlete Charles W. Foster. From there 78-year-old Walker, clad in white jogging shorts and support stockings to cover his surgically scarred knees, ran onto the campus toward the speakers' platform and into a cheering mass of spectators. About thirty yards from the platform and the cauldron he was to light, he slowed, passing the torch off to people who held special places in his heart.

He arranged to honor each of them by having them carry the torch for a few steps before returning it to him at the cauldron, a symbol of how they had helped him realize this triumphant day in his life. Among them were his friend and collaborator from Duke, Al Buehler, and a small middle-aged woman, not known to most of the people watching. She was Lee Calhoun's widow, Gwen.

Walker then climbed the steps, held high the torch, then touched it to the cauldron. The ceremony took place in the shadow of the physical education building named in his honor. Standing at the microphone as he faced the crowd, the words flowed from his heart, loving words of appreciation to those who had helped him arrive at this moment.

"I see, as I stand here today, many upon whose shoulders I have stood over the decades in this place, making this day possible. Whatever I may have accomplished, you are the ones who made it possible. I am most grateful."

As the torch left Central and headed across town, Walker made sure that it was Al Buehler who would have the thrill of receiving the flame before the throngs of people gathered near Duke's impressive Gothic chapel. Once again the two old friends shared a day to remember forever.

NBC—The Money Machine

Americans have always loved their Olympians and since the advent of television have developed a voracious appetite for the Games.

Among the audience-builders was Jim McKay, an articulate television journalist who educated hordes of would be Olympic junkies from 1960 to 1988. Long before there were superstar, multimillion dollar anchor contracts, this dedicated professional shared his sophisticated knowledge, like an overseeing father, protective of the young people on the field of competition below.

McKay elevated the level of the presentation of Olympic contests for a vast and diverse television audience, winning ten Emmys along the way.

Another who continues to perpetuate the spirit of the Games was the award-winning documentary producer Bud Greenspan, who shares, through his cameras, the intimate stories of the individual athlete, the heartwarming and the heart-wrenching. His work earned him the Olympic Order, conferred by the International Olympic Committee.

Any televised event that can hold a lot of people before their sets for long periods of time becomes a lucrative commercial vehicle. Bidding by the networks for the TV rights was approaching financial obscenity. The National Broadcasting Company won with a record high bid of $456 million for the rights to televise the Summer Games. For the next two Olympic Games, NBC put a package on the table of $1.2 billion: $705 million for the Summer Games in Sydney, Australia in the year 2000, and $545 million for the Winter Games in Salt Lake City in 2002.

A billion-dollar bid for television rights is not out of the question for the near future. Here is a measure of the acceleration of fees for rights to the Summer Games: in 1988 in Seoul, Korea NBC paid $300 million; in 1992, $401 million for the Barcelona Games; and $456 million for Atlanta. In 2008, city unknown, NBC will pay $894 million for the Summer Games alone. Under the current system, the USOC receives a ten percent share of U.S. network fees.

The Olympic Order

The Olympic Order is the highest honor bestowed by the International Olympic Committee and of all the honors that Walker had earned, this one, perhaps above all others, held a special place in his heart. Transcending the boundaries of the United States, the award represented and documented his work in the history of the International Olympic Movement.

IOC President Juan Samaranch of Spain told Walker that he wanted to make the presentation a few days preceding the Atlanta Games. It would be an opportunity, he said, for Walker to have his family and friends around him for the occasion. The date and time had been set for over a year: Monday, June 15, at 9 a.m. in the main ballroom of the Marriott Marquis in Atlanta.

In excited anticipation of the big event, LeRoy, Jr., his wife Judi, and their son, Shawn, left by car from Durham, North Carolina in mid-afternoon on the 14th. They would make the seven hour drive to Atlanta, get a night's rest and be prepared for the ceremony the next morning. That same day their daughter, Melodie, who lived in Washington, D.C. arrived in Atlanta by plane about the time her parents left Durham.

A number of Walker's dearest friends were planning to be with him. Among them was Ollan Cassell, executive director of USA Track and Field, who flew in from Indianapolis. It was a happy time for Walker and a chance to have members of the family together for a proud occasion.

When Walker entered the hotel late Sunday afternoon after picking up Melodie at the airport, he learned that the IOC hierarchy had moved the ceremony. Walker was "as mad as I have ever seen him," said a friend, Gail Jones.

"They can have it," he fumed, "I'm not going to accept it."

Jones and others were able to convince Walker that he must go along with the change. The press was there, the stage was set. He swallowed his disappointment and was gracious in his acceptance.

Meanwhile, LeRoy, Jr. and his family were three hours out of Durham when they received a call on their mobile phone that the ceremony was about to take place in Atlanta. They were shocked to hear the news and contemplated turning back. Melodie was the only family member to witness the impressive ceremony.

There was little or no explanation for IOC's changing of the award schedule except from Dick Cecil, a long-time observer of the workings and autonomy of the IOC, who simply said "the IOC has its own clock and there's nothing you can do about it. " Cecil, an old friend of Walker's had been hastily called at his office in Atlanta thirty minutes before the ceremony and had rushed across town just in time.

Walker did his best to conceal one of his greatest disappointments. While it was true that his award ceremony was exclusive and had received maximum press coverage at the IOC's opening session, he was hurting for his family.

§

The stage setting for the 105th International Olympic Committee Session in Atlanta took the large ballroom at the Marriott Marquis.

Large white columns formed the backdrop for the high-rise platform that held the speaker's podium and head table at an impressive elevation from that of the main floor.

The committee's executive board from around the world made up the head table. The speakers images were reproduced on a large television screen. Lining one wall at the rear of the room were booths of translators. Much like the system of communication in place at the United Nations, one had only to pick up earphones and dial in the proceedings being translated in several languages.

Papa

Papa is a motivating factor, but I don't want to be overshadowed by being the grandson of Dr. LeRoy Walker.

—Shawn Walker

The grandchildren came to Atlanta to be with their awesome Papa in his hour of triumph. Twenty-seven-year-old Shawn Walker laughed heartily and his eyes glistened with joy and admiration as he listened to his grandfather's ad lib quips with an audience that included the hierarchy of the American Red Cross and other dignitaries in the auditorium of an Atlanta hotel a few days before the Olympic Games began.

He had watched Papa many times addressing audiences at important gatherings, and as he had grown older his appreciation for the considerable speaking skills of his grandfather had grown accordingly.

Shawn admits, "I'm not a crowd person; it still takes me time to get used to crowds."

The impact of Papa on his grandchildren has been significant. While he never exerted pressure on them, his giant shadow grew increasingly more difficult to dodge.

"I thought of sports as something I had to do to try to keep up with "Papa," said Shawn. "In junior high school I went out for track and field and in high school played football and wrestled. I have always been inspired by him—he has shown me excellence."

Shawn had considered NC Central for college, "but I knew I would be known as his grandson and that with all the changes he had to make at the school to make it better he had probably made some enemies. So it was not comfortable for me." Instead, Shawn chose the University of Maryland at Eastern Shore.

At this writing he was separated from his wife and said, "We will be divorced." His 6-year-old son Desmond lives with his mother in Baltimore, Maryland.

When Shawn came to Durham in 1993 to start his own business, for the first time he experienced the full impact of his grandfather's fame. "I was star-struck," remembers Shawn, "it was awesome, a strange feeling, and the pressure was great. We know who Papa is....we are still learning who Dr. Walker is."

Shawn's sister, Melodie, three years his junior and youngest of the grandchildren, also felt the pressure: "When I was 6 or 7, I was enrolled in a school of gymnastics and Papa was invited to come over and see our class perform a routine. When I looked up and saw him I started crying and refused to go out. When he came back to talk to me I told him I knew that he worked with Olympic athletes and that I was not as good as they were."

"He told me that he did not expect me to be an Olympic athlete and said I would not have to perform if I didn't want to, but it would be nice if I would join my class and do it. I did."

"I tried everything in athletics but settled on riding. Riding is my love."

"I am proud of him for all that he has accomplished, but I just wish people could know him as I know him. I will never forget how nervous I was when I had to introduce him at a convocation at Elon College when I was a student. The college had invited him to speak and asked me to do the introduction."

"I shared with the audience the story of the picture of the three grandchildren at the Olympics in Montreal that appeared in the newspaper. The photo showed us all slouched in our chairs and distracted while Papa was giving a speech. The caption went on the say something about how unimpressed we were by what was happening. But to us, Papa is just Papa! That's the story I told and that's how I introduced him that day at Elon...just Papa."

Many of Melodie's most pleasant childhood memories are of the Summer trips with their grandparents.

"We went everywhere, Disneyland, DisneyWorld, Sea World, Carowinds, Six Flags...we went everywhere."

Melodie was graduated from Elon College near Burlington, North Carolina in 1994. With a degree in psychology she works for a national professional organization for women business owners. She plans graduate work in education and hopes to someday open a learning center, a dream that has its roots in childhood experiences: "I had a learning disability that was discovered when I was in kindergarten. I got great family support. Later on, when I was older and having trouble in a history class, was blanking everything out, my mother, Judi, devised this game that helped me learn the material. My mother could always figure out how to do things. I wound up making the highest grade in the class."

"Later, when I was working as a student teacher's aide in college in some of the local schools, I could see all these children who did not have the family support I did. That's why I would like to open a learning center."

Among the three children, it is Wanda Wade who is, by her mother's assessment, considered the most like her grandfather, and comes closest to matching his competitive drive.

"She is much more like her grandfather than she is (like) me," said her mother, Carolyn Hopp, "in her intestinal fortitude. She is strong-willed and just goes about what she needs to do. She is probably the only true athlete in the family, starting out in track and field—she is a multi-lettered athlete...track, soccer, softball and basketball. She and her grandfather have always had one of those kindred-spirit type relationships. You just sort of step aside from it and let them work at it."

Wanda now teaches in Orlando, Florida in a new system of educating youngsters called "Celebration."

Each child loves Papa dearly and each has had to figure out a way to deal with his notoriety.

❖

CHAPTER EIGHT

THE GAMES

In many respects, these were LeRoy Walker's games. He was our secret weapon.

—Andrew Young

For the duration of the Games, Walker had set up the USOC office at the Marriott Marquis and moved his personal staff from Durham, along with several volunteers. In addition to Tony Britt, there were Ruth Noonan, an office administrator who was serving as a hostess, Jillian Austin, who handled protocol and coordinated the gifts Walker presented to individuals and delegations on behalf of the USOC; and Britt's wife, Lori, who served as receptionist or wherever she was needed. Gail Jones of ACOG served as Walker's official escort and took care of his scheduling.

The lobby of the hotel was a microcosm of the world, a colorful palette of cultures, languages, and dress. It seemed there were people from all 197 nations represented in the Games. As he moved about, LeRoy Walker was one of the most recognized figures in this international setting.

Over two million visitors were now in the city and security was pervasive. Many inner-city streets were barricaded. Visitors to the Marriott Marquis were met out on the street by uniformed soldiers before being allowed to continue toward the entrance. There, a thorough airport-type security check was performed. They then were restricted to the lobby unless they had a special pass to the elevators to reach other parts of the hotel.

Beginning with opening ceremonies, long lines snaked outside as ticket holders lined up to walk through metal detectors and have their bags X-rayed. Every pocketbook was searched; every camera and film canister inspected.

For the most part, the crowds maintained remarkable decorum during the inconveniences of security checks, a credit to the pleasant demeanor of the security force and the volunteers. With smiles, friendly chatter, and a sense of humor, they were magnificent. It may be safely said that in the 100 years of the Games it would be difficult to match the gentleness and sincerity of the Atlanta volunteer force. They were truly proud to be a part of the Games. They came from all walks of life, from teenagers to 94-year-old Charles Fram, who said, "Me and Billy Payne, we are having a good time!" The night before opening ceremonies they were treated, as special guests, to the dress rehearsal and spent the next day excitedly telling the media about the spectacular show.

The huge crowds initially strained the transportation system beyond its capacity. The city's trains and buses were jammed. The MARTA rail system that had made rehearsal runs the week before, was now approaching grid-lock. Thousands of passengers were stranded on boarding platforms. MARTA police began standing at the foot of the escalators moving people from the trains to the streets, forcing gaps in the solid lines. There were reports of passenger panic and angry shoving. After the first two days, and many frantic meetings of ACOG's transportation team and MARTA officials, there was marked improvement. Far more public relations damage was done when some reporters were not getting to events on time. In one case, several of them commandeered a bus and ordered the driver to take them to their assignments.

With the Games underway Walker's calendar was filled from early morning until midnight. His administrative duties took him to daily meetings. He attended all operational meetings between ACOG and the IOC. He was well aware of and sensitive to his social duties, and made himself available for dinners, parties, and receptions, at which he would be the honored guest of the delegations of other countries or of major sponsors. It was not uncommon for him to attend a luncheon every day and two of these events per evening.

Walker attended every competition he could squeeze into his schedule. Most of the time, members of his family were with him. Cush, Judi, Shawn and Melodie were there during the first days of competition; Bruce and Carolyn Hopp and Wanda Wade were with him during the last days of the Games.

The Bombing

At 1:30 a.m., on Saturday, July 27, the unthinkable happened. A planted pipe bomb exploded in the popular Centennial Olympic Park, Billy Payne's pride and joy which he referred to as "the people's park." At the time, it was crowded with people, mostly young, who were enjoying the music and party atmosphere. One woman, Alice Hawthorne, from Albany, Georgia, was killed, and 100 people were injured, some seriously.

Walker was awakened. The news sickened him.

"I was suddenly reminded of Munich and the friends I had lost in the violence there." Walker and Dick Schultz, along with USOC security people, contacted American athletes. As a part of the security system, each athlete had been issued a pager. Within a short time, everyone had been contacted by phone, pager or a knock on the door, save the one who was out and checked in later.

Following the bombing, the park was closed for several days. Police frantically searched for a suspect, while the television footage of bloodied people lying on the ground in Atlanta ricocheted around the world. The Atlanta Journal Constitution, citing law enforcement authorities as its source, reported that a security guard was being questioned as a suspect. He was never arrested and when his name was withdrawn as a suspect, his attorneys filed lawsuits against the newspaper and a TV network.

The reopening of the park had become more emotional and symbolic than its opening. Andrew Young recalled: "It was an awe-inspiring occasion. When I got out of the car at the far end of the park, the first thing I saw was a group of Japanese students singing. The fearlessness with which the people continued to pursue these Olympic Games without letting violence intimidate them or turn them around was a beautiful experience, essentially a religious experience."

Long ago, when IOC President Juan Samaranch began to proclaim to the host city at each Olympic Games that they were the "greatest ever," it became a much-anticipated phrase and a precedent from which he could not escape. When the Games ended in Atlanta, 42,000 exhausted volunteers caught their collective breath at the closing ceremonies when Samaranch withheld the phrase that had become his ultimate blessing. The volunteers who had put forth their best effort felt slighted.

Reflected Walker: "I knew from our press conference prior to the closing that he wasn't going to make that 'greatest ever' statement. The IOC looks at these Games a lot differently than the ordinary person, wondering about the glitches we had, the problems with transportation, and the results system. Samaranch did much better at our meeting following the closing ceremonies and paid great tribute to the fact that Atlanta had brought the Games to a new level."

There were, to be sure, criticisms of the Atlanta effort involving some serious problems with transportation, and the difficulties in tabulating game results quickly enough for the media. However, many Southerners, particularly Atlantans, believe that the media, from regions other than the South, were predisposed to deny Atlanta an objective assessment.

In October 1995, during the Olympic Congress, ACOG offered the media a preview tour of some of the major venues in and around Atlanta, many in the final stages of completion. Following the stop at the Georgia Dome and Olympic Stadium, as the buses headed toward the unfinished venues at Stone Mountain, a level of derision rose beyond the normal din of reporters on a bus.

A dilapidated farm was described as "their governor's mansion" by an especially loud reporter whose comment was followed by gales of laughter and guffaws. When the bus driver made a wrong turn and drove a few hundred yards to turn around, there was immediate speculation that when two million people come, "it will all be a disaster."

On the return trip to Atlanta, a number of reporters asked the driver to let them off near their hotels, ignoring the pleas of the press tour guide and passing up a lunch at the just completed state-of-the-art aquatics center at Georgia Tech. They had, they said, "seen enough." Many Southerners, traditionally wary of the media, believed that many journalists come into their region with skewed preconceptions or plain ignorance.

Perhaps making something of a case for that was the cover of The New Yorker by artist William Joyce, July, 22, 1996 issue, coinciding with the opening of the Games in Atlanta. The rendering was that of a cheering crowd facing a rotund farmer, complete with bib overalls and straw hat, and chewing a straw. Holding high the Olympic torch in his left hand, a pig under his right arm, the farmer was preparing to light the Olympic cauldron, which resembles an old-fashioned wash-pot, as chickens peck around the base of it. Around the farmer's shoulder was a sash on which is printed one word "Howdy." While the magazine may have presented the cover in all good humor, to some Southerners it was more of what they have grown to expect.

In the opening ceremonies, more was made of a very short segment featuring pick-up trucks than the far more lengthy segments by the excellent Atlanta symphony, an exquisite massed choir, and a brilliantly choreographed light and shadow depiction of Olympic athletes in action.

The next day critiques by reporters of some of the elite publications were not complimentary. One even charged that Billy

Payne had duped the IOC into believing that the Summer temperatures in Atlanta were more moderate than hot. Payne had given the average Summer daytime highs. Any enterprising reporter, however, could easily have obtained records of Atlanta's mid-Summer high temperatures. Instead, some claimed to have been "tricked."

In retrospect, it is tragic that the bombing in Atlanta had a chilling effect on the assessment of the Games. However, attendance records were shattered and on the field by the athletes were magnificent. Women's events pulled record attendance, and interest worldwide.

It was Andrew Young who finally placed Walker's impact into perspective, when he said, "In many respects these were LeRoy Walker's Games, the fulfillment of a lifetime career in sports. He was our secret weapon in the battle against fourteen other American cities to get the bid to represent our country. Nobody knew he was from Atlanta. He planted the seed that if anyone could bring the Games back to the United States, it would be Atlanta. He understood my connections with the world through the United Nations and immediately saw that as different from the contribution that could be made in Minneapolis or San Diego or some of the other cities hoping to get the bid."

The morning following the closing ceremonies on August 4, Walker attended a farewell breakfast at which he was asked to speak. His words was gracious in thanking Samaranch and the IOC for choosing Atlanta for the Games.

Then to the ACOG and USOC staff people he said, "Some will always think of the bombing, but if you look at the real meaning here, the four things that were provided a rating scale by USA Today were the things that were most important: the athletes, the volunteers, the essence of the games, and the spectators. Surely the media had some problems early on, and wrote about it prolifically too....but they were not the things that were affecting the other constituencies. Surely the results systems were important. But whether you got the results out quickly or not, you can't overlook Donovan Bailey's world record or Michael Johnson's world record. Surely there were glitches. In all of the Games I have attended I have never seen one that was perfect. But these are problems you have to look at in order to make the Games better."

§

It was the Atlanta volunteers who were most wounded by the media criticism. Their hurt is understandable. For seventeen days and nights, following months of preparation, they had represented the face of America and it was a beautiful face.

Walker said: "My heart goes out to those people in Atlanta who were so affected by some of the press coverage."

When he left Atlanta, Walker had a little more than two months left in his term.

His tenure would be lively to the very end.

Tumultuous Election

It always distressed me to see infighting break up friendships.

—LeRoy T. Walker

The election of Walker's successor would finally reach a level of acrimony never before witnessed since the founding of the USOC. The candidates for Walker's seat were strong contenders, each having ample justification for putting themselves forward. Among the leading candidates were Sandra Baldwin, a successful Realtor in Phoenix and Treasurer of the USOC; Michael Lenard, a USOC Vice President, ten-year veteran of the executive committee and former Olympic athlete; and Bill Hybl, Colorado business executive and head of the powerful El Pomar Foundation.

Several opposing factions surfaced and set off the controversy, which gripped the election, beginning with complaints about how the nominating committee was selected.

Walker's assessment was that the "allegations were not really substantial." However, to avoid any perception that he was not giving the complaint proper attention he turned it over to Harry Groves, Chairman of the USOC Ethics Committee.

"The nominating committee was being challenged and there was lots of bashing," said Walker.

Hybl was chosen by the nominating committee as its candidate for the presidency and Walker flew to the USOC's meeting in Indianapolis to preside over the election.

"I did not openly support either candidate and I was upset because they were trying to go around the process and I didn't think it was right," he said.

When the votes were counted, Hybl had defeated Lenard by the slimmest margin possible.

The hair-breadth election and the accompanying turmoil, both private and public, had left the organization in a state of divisiveness and lingering bitterness and Walker knew it.

"I told Hybl his biggest challenge would be to put the organization back together," said Walker.

He was personally hurt that his quadrennium as president had ended in such tumult and negative press. At the final meeting he warned the membership:

"I move in a number of circles and I can tell you with certainty that the welfare of our organization is being questioned, and in the minds of many is at risk."

Walker Steps Down

Walker's four years had been monumental.

His fight in Barcelona to make the U.S. professional super-stars who participate in the Olympic games a more integral part of the Olympic family will be remembered, and his involvement in the Kerrigan-Harding decision in Lillehammer is a part of Olympic history.

Among the accomplishments of his presidency that are most satisfying to him are:

"The establishment of a four-year plan and a six-year budget; the redirecting of athletes support programs so they get more services; my task-force for women and minorities; and the progress we made toward unifying the USOC and the NCAA."

Farewell
Indianapolis...October 1996

The time had come to face them for farewell. Newer faces were scattered among those he had known for many years. There were those he loved among those with whom he had clashed. This was his parting shot and a final chance to reach out, as he had done throughout his life, to unify divided factions.

"This has been a labor of love over three decades of service and relationships, which have made me keenly aware of the value of time, the obligation of duty, the dignity of simplicity, the worth of character, the power of kindness, the virtue of patience, the joy of originating, and the influence of example."

Walker listed the issues that concerned him most.

He made a plea for "greater trust among the family."

He exhorted them to put aside their personal agendas and to work for the good of the organization, reminded them that "It was the worst of times when the media advanced headlines castigating the USOC for internal strife."

Then he spoke of the best of times, "when I followed the American flag into the stadium at Albertville, Barcelona, Lillehammer and Atlanta to witness the stellar performances of our athletes."

In closing remarks Walker said:

"I am indeed fortunate to have had the opportunity to develop friendships which will last forever. I can state boldly that whatever I may have achieved in discharging my tasks as your president is because I stood on your shoulders to see out into the horizon to chart my course and for that privilege, I will be forever indebted to this body."

When he finished there was a motion by Anita DeFrantz and a unanimous vote by the Board. Walker was named President Emeritus of the United States Olympic Committee, a first in the history of the organization.

❖

CONCLUSION

The hero is known for achievements, the celebrity for well-knownness. The hero reveals the possibilities of human nature, the celebrity reveals the possibilities of the press and the media. Celebrities are people who make the news, but heroes are people who make history.

Time makes heroes but dissolves celebrities.

—Daniel Boorstin, historian

In assessing the impact of the life of LeRoy Walker, it is difficult to enumerate those areas that best paint his legacy. While the Centennial Olympic Games in Atlanta were the culmination of the dream of Billy Payne, the realization of that dream was marked by Walker almost from the beginning.

Andrew Young noted: "This was the fulfillment of a life-long career in sports for Dr. Walker. With all of our difficulties, I think that: we never had such good weather. We never had so many people coming together and behaving so well, and even in the face of the tragic violence of the bombing, there was a rising up of the human spirit, particularly in the places where there has been trouble. It was encouraging for me to see Iran and Iraq marching in together, to see Croatia and Yugoslavia and Bosnia, all of them in the Games, and to see differing nations of Africa, particularly South Africa, coming in with a multiracial delegation. I am convinced that everything has worked out.

Young continued: " LeRoy Walker and Martin Luther King are much more alike than either would imagine. Both were good athletes, (although) nobody thinks of Martin as a good athlete. Both went to Booker T. Washington High School and grew up facing the same kind of segregated South, but they both went on to achieve a level of excellence and competence through education. It was not typical that kids from their neighborhoods would get doctorate degrees, yet both did.

"Both were committed to the long haul in social change. The difference is that Martin's life stopped at 39, but LeRoy has been blessed to carry on in good health and even better spirits for many more years. His mind is just as young and vibrant today as it was when he was a student at Booker T. Washington High!"

§

To say that Walker was responsible for the successes of the athletes he coached would be to diminish their own determination and drive. To say that he did not contribute significantly to their success would be a graver injustice.

He took countless bright, young people, most often from the lowest rungs of America's economic ladder, and gave them a will to win, a specific and customized plan by which they could reach their goal, and the confidence to execute under adverse circumstances.

They saw in him an exemplary level of character and integrity, committed to excellence without excuse. They observed in him a real man, in action, with a disdain for shortcuts. He demonstrated an unfailing work ethic, and a devotion to them that never faltered.

He was the embodiment of old-fashioned parenting and a teacher who earned respect, exuding confidence without arrogance.

Walker's athletes became distinguished men in numerous professions. Among those whose lives were touched by him were the late Lee Calhoun, who earned his master's degree, coached at Yale and Western Illinois University.

Charles W. Foster did post-graduate studies at UNC, was recruited by the U.S. Information Service to train and teach African nations, became assistant track coach at UNC and in 1992, became manager of sports planning for the Atlanta Committee for the Olympic Games.

Julius Sang became a top official of Kenyan Juvenile System, and his teammate and fellow countryman, Robert Ouko, moved to the top tier of the Kenyan Olympic Committee.

Educator James Courtney was named Principal of the Year in Connecticut, and Andrew McCray earned a Ph.D.

Edwin Moses, an investment counselor in a major firm, became president of the Jesse Owens Foundation.

Walker takes the most pride in "the human legacy and you see they are passing it on to other young people."

The last chapters of Walker's life have yet to be written. His stated goal is "to continue to try to be of service to youth."

Walker's passion to help athletes is evident in the establishment of an International Human Performance Center at East Carolina University in Greenville, North Carolina. Walker was instrumental in the multipurpose facility that tests athletes, assists people working on degrees, and provides data for sports medicine.

The crown jewel of his efforts in the next few years will be his work as president of the Special Olympics World Games to be staged in North Carolina.

Walker's professional footprints across the continents became a pathway to cultural understanding and tolerance. Young people in America and around the world have experienced a rare individual, and one who refused to allow racial barriers to stand in the way of achievement. Through the difficult times he heard the echoes of his mother's teaching: "Don't let this environment determine what you can do."

Much of Walker's work was accomplished away from the public spotlight.

Andrew Young observed that, "Circumstances and the times create great men and people somehow think of these great men as accidents, sort of springing full-blown out of the head of Zeus, but they are all a part of a process. The world ends up knowing Martin Luther King and Nelson Mandela, but there are probably 100 other people who have labored virtually in anonymity....but who have been just as effective in their fields and in terms of peace-making around the world, who never get any attention."

"LeRoy Walker is one of those."

❖

REFERENCES

BOOKS AND ARTICLES

Anderson, Jean Bradley. *Durham County*. Durham, NC: Duke University Press, 1990.

The Eagle (Yearbook of NCCU); editions 1955, 1961, 1966, 1976.

Hughes, Langston, Milton Meltzer, Ossie Davis, et al. *Black Magic: A Pictorial History of the African-American in the Performing Arts* NY: DaCapo Press, 1990.

Lewis, David, ed. *The Portable Harlem Renaissance Reader*. NY: Viking, 1994.

Link, William A. *William Friday : Power, Purpose, and American Higher Education*. Chapel Hill: University of North Carolina Press, 1995.

New York Times, September 1972 issues.

Newsweek, September 1972 issues.

The Roaring Twenties, 1920-1930. (This Fabulous Century). NY:Time-Life Books, 1982.

Simon, George T., comp. *The Big Bands*. NY: Macmillan, 1967.

Sulzberger, C. L. *World War II*. NY: American Heritage, 1970.

USOC. *Athens to Atlanta*.

USOC. *USOC Fact Book*.

Watson, Steven. *The Harlem Renaissance*. NY: Pantheon Books, 1995.

Interviews with LeRoy Walker in 1995: Feb 15, 21, 25; March 2, 24, 27; April 20, 25; May 8, 17, 19; June 8, 19, 28; July 7; August 22; Sept. 19; Oct. 30; Nov. 8, 21; Dec. 18.

Other interviews in 1995: Carolyn Hopp, Feb. 21; Coach Cal Irvin, Feb. 22; ACC Commissioner Gene Corrigan, Feb. 24; Olympian Charles Foster, Feb. 24; DeLores Todd, Feb. 24; Coach Clarence "Bighouse" Gaines, Feb. 25; Coach Al Buehler, March 26; UNC President Emeritus William C. Friday, April 19; Lawrence Scales, Aug. 21; LeRoy T. Walker, Jr., Sept. 6; Dick Schultz, Executive

Director USOC, Oct. 3; Bruce Hopp, Oct. 6; Tom Halleran, Oct. 7; Alpha Alexander, Oct. 7; Charles T. Brooks Oct. 9; Leola Caison, Oct. 9; Tony Britt, Oct. 11; John Jordan, Oct. 18; Wanda Wade, Oct. 19; LeRoy Walker, Jr. , Oct. 24; Tony Britt, Oct. 24, Nov. 15, and Nov. 20; Alex Rivera, Dec. 18.

Interviews with LTW in 1996: Jan. 16; Feb. 8, 13; March 28; April 15 and 29; May 3, 15; June 15; July 1, 2, 7, 8, 10, 15, 16; Aug. 5; Sept. 3 and 5; Oct. 8; Nov. 4-14 and 25; Dec 10.

Other interviews in 1996: Alex Rivera, Jan. 25; Anita DeFrantz, IOC, Feb. 13; B.T. Mcmillon, NCCU Feb 15; Billy Payne, ACOG, Feb. 20; Andrew Young, Gail Jones and Shirley Franklin, ACOG Feb. 20; Bill Campbell, Atlanta Mayor, Feb 21; Al Buehler, April 1 and 29; Tony Britt, May 8; Al Buehler, May 29; Hill Carrow, May of 1996; Coach Stan Wright, June 17; Dick Cecil, June, 17; Dr. Evie Dennis, June 16; Larry Ellis, June 17; Dave Maggard, June 17; Ollan Cassell, June 17; Ted Wheeler, June 17; Shawn Walker July 17; Melodie Walker, July 17; Ambassador Andrew Young , Aug 6; Olympian Herb Douglas, Sept 19.

Interviews with LTW in 1997: Feb.13; March 14; June 27.

❖

Achievements

Positions & Selected Board Affiliations

United States Olympic Committee, President Emeritus (served 1992-96) and Board of Directors since 1976; NC Central University, Chancellor Emeritus (served 1983-86) and School of Law Board of Visitors; Board of Directors, Association of National Olympic Committees, Executive Board & Vice President for the Americas; Atlanta Committee for the Olympic Games Executive Committee and Board of Directors; Benedict College Board of Trustees; Duke Children's Classic Honorary Co-Chairman; Duke University Fuqua School of Business, Board of Visitors; Georgia Technical Institute Advisory Board; National Football League Education Committee; Pan American Sports Organization Executive Committee; Special Olympics 1999 World Summer Games Board of Directors; Special Olympics International Board of Directors; USA Track & Field Executive Committee as Past President & Board of Directors; U.S. Olympic Foundation Board of Trustees.

Career Highlights

President: 1999 Special Olympics World Summer Games;

President: United States Olympic Committee, 1992-96;

President: The Athletics Congress, 1984-88;

President: National Association of Intercollegiate Athletics, 1980-81;

President: American Alliance of Health, Physical Education, Recreation & Dance, 1977-78;

President: Central Intercollegiate Athletic Association, 1960-64;

Senior Vice President for Sport: Atlanta Committee for the Olympic Games, 1992;

Chef de Mission: 1992 U.S. Olympic Team at Barcelona;

Treasurer & Chair of Budget Committee: U.S. Olympic Committee, 1989-92;

United States Delegate: International Amateur Athletics Federation, 1976-87;

Chairman: United States Olympic Festival 1987 (served 1985-87);

Amateur Athletic Union Track & Field Committee, 1973-76;

College Commissioners Association, 1971-74.

North Carolina Central University

Chancellor: 1983-86;

Vice Chancellor for University Relations: 1974-83;

Head Track & Field Coach: 1945-83 (111 All-Americans, forty National Champions, twelve U.S. Olympians, eight National & World records and at least one NCCU athlete in seven Olympics);

Chairman: Department of Physical Education & Recreation, 1945-73.

§

Head Coach, Athletics Director and Professor: Benedict College, 1941-42; Head Coach, Dean and Professor: Bishop College, 1942-43; Coach and Professor: Prairie View State College, 1943-45.

§

National Track & Field Coaching Coordinator: AAU & The Athletics Congress, 1973-80;

U.S. Olympic Track & Field Head Coach: Montreal, 1976;

Coach: Israel & Ethiopa, Rome Olympics 1960;

Consultant: Jamaica, Mexico City, 1968; Trinidad & Tobago, Tokyo, 1964; Kenya, Munich, 1972;

Commissioner: Mid-Eastern Athletic Conference, 1971-74;

Member: Knight Foundation Commission on Intercollegiate Athletics, 1991-96; Duke University Medical Center Advisory Board, 1980-90; President Eisenhower's College Advisory Committee for Operation, Physical Fitness USA;

Director of Programming, Planning & Training for the African Continent, Peace Corps, 1966-68;

Consultant, Coach & Visiting Professor: United States Military Academy, 1981-82;

Other Coaching & Consulting Missions: USA/People's Republic of China Athletics, 1975; All-China Physical Education & Sports Committee, 1980-83; U.S. Track & Field Team in France, Italy,

Germany, the USSR & West Africa, 1970-76; United States
Department of State Cultural Exchange Program (1959 in
Ethiopia, Israel, Lebanon & Syria; 1960 in Ethiopia & Israel; 1962
in Haiti & Jamaica).

Books

Track & Field for Boys & Girls, The Athletic Institute, 1983.

Championship Techniques in Track & Field, Parker Publishing Co., 1969.

Physical Education for the Exceptional Student, William C. Brown Co.,
1963.

A Manual in Adapted/Advanced Physical Education, Piedmont, 1961.

Education

Benedict College (Columbia, SC), B.A., Magna Cum Laude, 1940

Columbia University, M.S., 1941, Health Sciences & Physical Education

New York University, Ph.D., 1957, Exercise Physiology & Biomechanics

Honorary Doctorates (16)

Benedict College, 1977; Defiance College, 1981; U.S. Sports Academy,
1983; Eastern Kentucky University, 1985; North Carolina Central
University, 1986; Morehouse College, 1987; Tuskegee Institute, 1993;
Wake Forest University, 1993; Duke University, 1994; Queens College,
1995; UNC-Greensboro, 1995; Springfield College, 1996; Princeton
University, 1996; UNC-Pembroke, 1996; UNC-Wilmington, 1996; East
Carolina University, 1997; University of North Carolina, Chapel Hill, 1998.

Selected Honors & Awards

1996   The Olympic Order (International Olympic Committee's highest
honor)

Golden Gavel Award (Toastmasters International's highest honor)

100 Black Men of America Distinguished Leader Award

1995   *The Sporting News* "Most Powerful People in Sports," 40th (also
'94: 46th; '93: 61st; '92: 59th)

National Jaycees, Chamber of Commerce Healthy American
Fitness Leaders Award

National Association of Intercollegiate Athletics Distinguished
Graduate Award

North Caroliniana Society Award

Youthlinks of Indiana/Pathfinder Award

1994 International Olympic Committee 100th Anniversary Centenary Medal

1993 National Ethnic Coalition of Organizations Foundation Ellis Island Medal of Honor Award

James J. Corbett Award (National Association of Collegiate Director of Athletics' highest honor)

Charlotte World Affairs Council World Citizen Award

1992 The Pigskin Club of Washington, D.C. Award (for outstanding contribution to sport)

1991 President's Council on Physical Fitness & Sports Silver Anniversary Award

1990 Robert Giegengack Award (USA Track & Field's highest honor)

1989 University of North Carolina Board of Governors' University Award

1985 AAHPERD's C.D. Henry Award

1982 Gulick Award (AABPERD's highest honor)

1977 *Encyclopedia Britannica* Achievement in Life Award

1976 O. Max Gardner Award (University of North Carolina System's highest honor)

1974 North Carolina Governor's Ambassador of Good Will Award

1972 National Track & Field Coaches Association Coach of the Year Award

NAIA National Coach of the Year Award

NAIA District 26 Track Coach of the Year Award (also 1970 & 1971)

Southern Christian Leadership Conference Martin L. King Jr. Drum Major for Justice Award

1964 North Carolina Central University Hamilton Watch Award (for outstanding teacher)

Halls of Fame (17)

Benedict College, 1982; Black College Alumni; Central Intercollegiate Athletic Association, 1967; Central Intercollegiate Athletic Association Officials; Georgia Sports, 1988; Helms Foundation Sports, 1971; Mid-Eastern Athletic Conference; National Association of Intercollegiate

Athletics; National Association of Sport & Physical Education, 1977; North Carolina Central University, 1984; North Carolina Sports, 1976; South Carolina Sports, 1977; South Carolina Black Sports, 1994; The Athletic Congress, 1983; U.S. Olympic Committee, 1987; U.S. Track Coaches Association, 1995.